THINKING
OUTSIDE THE
GIRL BOX

"Writing between hope and despair, and with tremendous grace, this extraordinary pair of mother-daughter researchers reveals the limits that young Appalachian women face in breaking free of the strictures of gender and the injury of being working class in America."

> —**Ruth Behar,** Professor, University of Michigan, and author of
> *Traveling Heavy: A Memoir in between Journeys*

"I read the entire thing in two days! It is incredible! It is like a love story! I laughed, I cried, I was angry, I grieved . . . simply incredible!"

> —**Shelley Gaines,** founder, Girls' Resiliency Program of Lincoln
> County, West Virginia

"*Thinking Outside the Girl Box* reads as a delicious, compelling, collaborative ethnography that escorts readers into the delicate, rugged human terrain of life in Appalachia, where girls contend with dreams, relationships, possibilities, disappointments, the delights and struggles of rural life in a stretch of disinvested America. The book is written with a spirit of sweet invitation into a love story indeed; a mother-daughter adventure; an intimate essay on girls' desire for lives of meaning and creativity; a sad obituary on a program that carried the girls on the wings of possibility. We meet young women, adult mentors, Shelley and Ric who carve the space and hold the girls, and we bear witness to the possibility and fragility of programs devised to support youth in a nation that has banished them to the margins in times of swelling inequality gaps.

This book is beautifully accessible to undergraduates or graduates; if you are trying to teach students to appreciate 'difference' and imagine 'Others,' you don't need a passport. Come to West Virginia and meet young women in our own country, sisters in the mountains, with few opportunities, enormous capacity, and rich desires. Spatig and Amerikaner are gifted storytellers. Together with the young women and their mentors, they have crafted a sweet jewel, opening the box of ethnography, challenging the girdle of evaluation, asking us to peer inside the intimacy of growing up girl in rural America."

—**Michelle Fine,** Distinguished Professor, The Graduate Center, CUNY

"The aim of this book is to tell the story of rural, Appalachian girls in a youth development program—their lives presented through their own words, and the words of the authors, Spatig and Amerikaner, highlighting the girls' challenges, struggles, fears, likes, and dislikes. . . . Situating these girls' voices in a framework of 'collaborative ethnography' amidst a preferred research focus in the U.S. on quantitative, standardized, accountability models is refreshing, timely, accurate, and serves to highlight what we need to know most about girls and schooling."

—**Brett Elizabeth Blake,** Professor, School of Education, Curriculum and Instruction, St. John's University (New York), and author of *She Say, He Say: Urban Girls Write Their Lives*

"This book grows out of a ten-year community-based research project and exemplifies the possibilities of what can happen when outsiders tell stories about Appalachia. Beginning as a program evaluation of a youth resiliency program, it morphed into a collaborative ethnographic study of much reflection and fun, too much data, too little money, many mothers and daughters, and too many necessary losses. Honest about the tensions, it is designed to move beyond the walls of the university as it tells stories about the positive legacies of a program that helped adolescent girls in small-town West Virginia live bigger lives. What results are complex tales of living poor and girlhood, girl-driven interventions, the violence of low expectations and the weight of gender norms. It is a life history of an organization told through strong characters about lessons learned, loving and leaving, poetry and song, and questions of power, voice, and language. I recommend it to those interested in Appalachian studies, girlhood studies, community-based activism, and collaborative ethnography as well as general readers interested in a darn good story."

—**Patti Lather,** Professor, The Ohio State University, and author of *Getting Lost: Feminist Efforts toward a Double(d) Science*

"Written with great tenderness and insight, this book portrays West Virginia through the eyes of those who seldom appear in the literature about Appalachia: rural girls. The stories of their struggles and transformations are revelatory—instructive and beautiful in equal measure. I love this book!"

—**Barbara Ellen Smith**, Professor, Department of Sociology, Virginia Tech, and coeditor of *Transforming Places: Lessons from Appalachia*

"Far too often theories become abstract and convoluted—losing connection to reality in the pursuit of ever higher levels of elaboration. Theorists cite other theorists to prove their erudition. This book, however, is a story that advances theory. Spatig and Amerikaner take life experience that they have felt—love, disappointment, and suffering—and conceptualize that knowledge into critical theory. This book is not just about Appalachian girls. This book is about how we study and think about life around us. This book is about how scholars should expose social inequality and oppression and then write about it."

—**Lynda Ann Ewen**, founder, Center for the Study of Ethnicity and Gender in Appalachia at Marshall University

"This is an extraordinary collaborative ethnography, one that authentically involves research participants in multiple stages of the research and writing processes. But it is also much more than this. It is, as Spatig and Amerikaner suggest, a love story that both warms and breaks the heart. *Thinking Outside the Girl Box* documents the amazing successes, and then the unsettling demise, of the Girls' Resiliency Program, a community-based youth development program in one of the poorest counties in one of the poorest states in the country. Make no mistake, though, this isn't another account about victims of rural poverty. The adult leaders and young women who are both subjects and research partners in this study do struggle against enormous odds; yet their remarkable and resilient commitment to model positive relationships and to make a difference to each other and within their communities inspires hope for what is possible when we decide to work together for change. Anyone with an interest in youth programs, Appalachia, rural poverty, or gender studies—and, of course, collaborative ethnography—should read this book."

—**Luke Eric Lassiter**, author of *The Chicago Guide to Collaborative Ethnography*

"Thinking Outside the Girl Box will change the way you look at words like resiliency, development, democracy, girls. Spatig and Amerikaner remind their readers that a real feminist analysis begins with love and that its methodology is necessarily one of loving collaboration. In a period in which multinational agency after multinational agency is 'discovering' that girls exist, the story of the Girls' Resiliency Program, from efflorescence to almost complete demise, is a necessary one, and I, for one, can't image anyone better to tell that story than Linda Spatig and Layne Amerikaner."

—**Daniel Moshenberg,** Director, Women's Studies Program, George Washington University, and coeditor of *Searching for South Africa: The New Calculus of Dignity*

THINKING
OUTSIDE THE
GIRL BOX

OHIO UNIVERSITY PRESS

Series in Race, Ethnicity, and Gender in Appalachia

Series editors: Marie Tedesco and Chris Green

Memphis Tennessee Garrison: The Remarkable Story of a Black Appalachian Woman, edited by Ancella R. Bickley and Lynda Ann Ewen

The Tangled Roots of Feminism, Environmentalism, and Appalachian Literature, by Elizabeth S. D. Engelhardt

Red, White, Black, and Blue: A Dual Memoir of Race and Class in Appalachia, by William R. Drennen Jr. and Kojo (William T.) Jones Jr., edited by Dolores M. Johnson

Beyond Hill and Hollow: Original Readings in Appalachian Women's Studies, edited by Elizabeth S. D. Engelhardt

Loving Mountains, Loving Men, by Jeff Mann

Power in the Blood: A Family Narrative, by Linda Tate

Out of the Mountains: Appalachian Stories, by Meredith Sue Willis

Negotiating a Perilous Empowerment: Appalachian Women's Literacies, by Erica Abrams Locklear

Standing Our Ground: Women, Environmental Justice, and the Fight to End Mountaintop Removal, by Joyce M. Barry

Shake Terribly the Earth: Stories from an Appalachian Family, by Sarah Beth Childers

Thinking Outside the Girl Box: Teaming Up with Resilient Youth in Appalachia, by Linda Spatig and Layne Amerikaner

THINKING OUTSIDE THE GIRL BOX

Teaming Up with Resilient Youth in Appalachia

Linda Spatig

Layne Amerikaner

ILLUSTRATIONS BY
LAYNE AMERIKANER

OHIO UNIVERSITY PRESS • ATHENS

Ohio University Press, Athens, Ohio 45701
ohioswallow.com
© 2014 by Ohio University Press
All rights reserved

Printed in the United States of America

ISBN (hardcover) 978-0-8214-2059-1
ISBN (paperback) 978-0-8214-2060-7
ISBN (electronic) 978-0-8214-4467-2

23 22 21 20 19 18 17 16 15 14   5 4 3 2 1

Library of Congress Cataloging-in-Publication Data available upon request.

SHELLEY GAINES, FOUNDER OF THE GIRLS'
RESILIENCY PROGRAM: The kids that we were
working with were really carrying around a
lot of labels that people gave them and . . . it
just got perpetuated within the family, or from
the community. . . . Everybody has had these
girls in these little tiny boxes that were very
disempowering.

INTERVIEWER: How would you like to impact the
girls' lives?

SHELLEY GAINES: I guess I hope . . . that the box
they have drawn, that all women have to fit
in, is at least a thousand times bigger than
when they started.

Contents

Preface

The Nutshell. Or, The What, When,
How, Where, Who, and Why

LINDA SPATIG

This book is a true story about a group of girls in rural West
Virginia and a group of adults who devoted years of their lives to working with them. Though people in universities might call it a study about
"community-based youth development," I call it a love story. It's a story
about a program for girls in a poor area of West Virginia where opportunities are scarce, a program bound and determined to challenge the
small, disempowering "boxes" girls and women are expected to stay in.
Based on the fourteen years I spent studying it, this book traces the life
of a program, the Lincoln County Girls' Resiliency Program (GRP), but
it focuses on people. Although my research with it didn't start until 1999,
the program began in 1996 and closed its doors for the last time in 2007.
Like many love stories, the GRP saga has its share of intense passions,
commitment struggles, emotionally tumultuous high and low points—as
well as a heartbreaking ending and an uneasy, delicate period of trying to
understand it all and recover afterward.

I could describe what we did with two words—collaborative
ethnography—but I realize that research terminology is familiar to only a
small number of people who work in colleges or universities. To everyone

else I would say that I, as well as many graduate students, worked along-side adults and young people in Lincoln County, West Virginia, to describe and understand a remarkable program and what it meant to those most closely involved with it. To do that, we participated in countless program events and activities and conducted more than a hundred interviews with individuals and groups. We ended up with mountains of data—observation notes, interview transcripts, program brochures, photographs, and girls' poems, artwork, and songs. Every so often, we organized and analyzed the data we had collected and wrote reports for program staff and board members, did presentations at conferences, or wrote journal articles about doing collaborative ethnography with youth.

How and why I, and other participants, were involved in the project is part of the story, from the first page to the last. In fact, to a large extent that *is* the story. The experience has been transformative for each of us in different ways. For me, the project involved learning to listen hard—to adolescent girls, to program staff and board members, to my graduate students, to my daughter and coauthor, Layne Amerikaner, who writes beautifully but has little research experience, and to my own sometimes uncertain voice. I learned to keep a light spirit and to love the process, even when editing chapters for what felt like the billionth time. And I learned to let go (at least a little) of long-held notions of "proper" academic research and writing and of a long-time-in-the-making authoritative parental role with my capable, confident, now fully adult daughter.

I mainly did this project, culminating in the book you are holding, to *learn* something from the research with the Girls' Resiliency Program and to share what I learned with other people. The program founder, Shelley Gaines,★ whom I frequently call "the woman with the vision," wanted me to do research with the program so she could learn about what the program meant to the girls it was serving. (She also wanted the girls themselves to learn how to do research.) She and I had questions such as, "What can this program teach us about youth development, especially with girls in small-town, Appalachian communities?" As you might expect with research that goes on for over a decade, the study produced more than a few insights on everything from immediate, everyday issues in the lives of teenage girls in

★All names are real unless marked as pseudonyms.

a rural community to definitions of youth development generally. What we learned, our research findings, come directly from our firsthand study of the Girls' Resiliency Program, but they are unquestionably applicable to other programs, especially those that are community-based, in rural locales, or serving girls. The research methods used in this project do not allow me to say that what was found to be true for this program is predictive of outcomes for other programs. I *can* say, though, that through sustained, deep study of one program, we gained a wealth of information and insights that have implications for people and programs elsewhere.

I want to draw attention to two overarching themes that capture what we (Shelley, other participants, and I) learned from our study of the program. One is about the meaning of community: how we *think* about community and how we *do* community, if you will. The other is about how researchers and policymakers evaluate community-based programs, how we define program success and effectiveness in an age of increasing emphasis on evidence-based best practice.

What did we learn? First, we learned that youth development work comes down to people. It sounds simple, but in all the discussions of "community," it is easy to gloss over the obvious but central fact that community comes down to particular people in a particular place trying to do particular things together. In other words, community programs are both enabled and constrained by actual people who—through their ideas and actions, individually and together—"define and limit the possibilities of each others' lives" as Wendell Berry, renowned Appalachian writer and activist, put it in a description of community (1969, 61). What happened with the Girls' Resiliency Program, from remarkable successes to heartbreaking disappointments, was directly related to the ideas and actions of specific individuals you will meet and come to know chapter by chapter.

And the program wasn't created in a vacuum. Developing the Girls' Resiliency Program in a materially poor rural county in West Virginia, people drew on available resources, the quantity and quality of which changed dramatically over time. The program began in the nineties during a period of economic stability and a climate of at least moderate support for social reforms and ended in the mid-2000s during the beginning of a serious economic downturn and a move toward conservative politics less inclined to support spending on social programs. Without a doubt, it was a diverse group of deeply committed, youth-oriented people who created the Girls' Resiliency Program, who defined and limited what was possible. But the way the story unfolded was profoundly affected by contextual factors, especially in terms of financial and human resources. If we neglected to pay attention to *both* individual choices and larger contexts, it would be easy to oversimplify. Ultimately, we attribute program successes and shortcomings to complex interactions between individuals' actions and ideas and the contexts within which they were acting.

The second overarching insight of the book concerns how program success or effectiveness should be determined. This study of the Girls' Resiliency Program revealed that effectiveness goes beyond questions of sustainability and replicability. As you know already, the program doesn't make it, and I don't know that it could be replicated. However, I view it as an effective program. In addition to specific findings illustrating its effectiveness, I argue that it was a model program in the sense that it demonstrates what can be learned from understanding successes achieved and mistakes made by hard-working, knowledgeable, caring people implementing an innovative program in tough circumstances. As John Dewey said many years ago, writing about his University of Chicago Laboratory School, the idea of a model program is not to have others "literally imitate what we do. A working model is not something to be copied; it is to afford a demonstration of the feasibility of the principle, and of the methods which make it feasible" ([1899] 2007, 110). The Girls' Resiliency Program demonstrates the good that is possible when women and men come together, even in an economically distressed community, to support young people by challenging them to recognize and build their strengths, to speak and be heard, and to engage critically with the world. In doing so, the GRP dealt a major blow to the "girl box" and thus is worthy of being called a model program.

This understanding of success is also applicable to other community programs that may or may not survive or be replicable. They still may be important as rich sources of knowledge about what is possible with certain kinds of programming in certain contexts. The kind of knowledge gained about the GRP was possible because my research teams used ethnography, a qualitative—rather than quantitative—method of research. Rather than conducting experiments or sending out surveys, qualitative researchers spend time in communities observing and talking with people, thus gaining invaluable information about *how* programs work, especially from the point of view of people directly involved in them. Qualitative methods shine a light on the day-to-day realities of groups such as the Girls' Resiliency Program—giving others access to the "complexity and messiness of practice-in-context" (Lather 2004a, 768) for real people involved in real programs.

Unfortunately, what I am seeing these days is a strong push for program evaluation that uses surveys, questionnaires, or other tests to measure and quantify program outcomes. These methods can provide useful information but rely on narrowly defined ideas about "successful" outcomes. And increasingly, this is what funders are looking for. Qualitative program evaluation methods are often overlooked or disparaged. Some program directors are not even aware of the existence of qualitative program evaluation, and those who *are* aware—especially those working in financially strapped nonprofits—often feel pressed to opt for one method or the other. If they choose only qualitative research for their program evaluation, they may find themselves in a tough spot for funding. If they choose only quantitative program evaluation, they forfeit a chance to get valuable information about how their programs are working and what they mean to participants—information that could help them make the programs better.

The bottom line is that I credit our method, collaborative ethnography, for enabling us to learn so much about, and from, the GRP—a remarkable program, despite its demise. And as is often true with love, even when relationships don't work out as we had hoped, with hindsight and reflection they can teach us a great deal.

THANK-YOUS

People in Lincoln County were the heart and soul of this whole project. I am speaking here of main characters in the book, such as Ric MacDowell and Shelley Gaines, but also of others who are not featured but were important to the project. Longtime board member Nona Conley, assistant director Jessica Lehman, program director Greg Wilson, *Mountain Stage* musician Ron Sowell, and West Virginia poet Colleen Anderson all spent countless hours working with the girls. I thank them, first and foremost, for the way they live their lives. They make this a better world for us all. I also thank them for inviting an outsider (me) into the project to begin with. They allowed me extensive access to the program and to their own ideas and feelings, trusting me with sensitive personal information and insights.

Lincoln County High School principal Dana Snyder and other school personnel made us feel at home at the school even for unscheduled or last-minute visits. They helped us locate girls we were there to see—not always an easy task in a large school on lunch break—and found places for us to meet. I am deeply grateful for the friendly, helpful, and generous teachers, secretaries, counselors, and principal who assisted us.

Finally, I thank the girls, for the way they lived *their* lives—their willingness to be part of a program that expected them to see themselves as in and of a community they could contribute to. I also thank them for their work on the research. In addition to Teresa, Cassi, Irene, Virginia, and Ashley, each featured in chapters of the book, many other girls gave their time and trust over the course of the project. We especially thank Sara, Marycait, and Jennifer who worked closely with my doctoral student LeAnne Olson during her dissertation research.

Speaking of LeAnne, I could not have done this research without the capable, conscientious young women in my graduate classes. In addition to LeAnne Olson and Betty Sias, featured in chapter 6, others who contributed to the research include Lara Dial, Jennifer Estep, Courtney Grimes, Laura Haynes, Jaime Kuhn, Heaven Rangel, Kathy Seelinger, Anne Swedberg, and Jennifer Zinn. Also, undergraduate students Ary Amerikaner (who happens to be my other daughter) and Megan Thomas assisted with fieldwork.

Another important thank-you goes to the Drinko Academy at Marshall University. A Drinko Fellowship provided funding for the two years when we did the post-project reflection and book writing. I especially appreciate the efforts of Drinko Academy director Alan Gould and, of course, the Drinkos, Libby and John, who developed the endowment that funds the academy.

I am grateful to colleagues Lynda Ann Ewen and Mary Thomas for introducing me to Appalachian studies and inviting me to be involved in an initiative to increase research on gender and ethnicity in Appalachia. I also thank Lynda Ann for insightful feedback on an early version of the book prospectus. Eric Lassiter is another colleague to whom I am deeply grateful. When I met Eric, my research with the Girls' Resiliency Program was well under way, but he introduced me to new ideas about collaborative ethnography that influenced the remainder of my work with the project. Finally, I will be forever grateful to my friend and former colleague Eddy Pendarvis, to whom I turn in my most insecure moments for writing guidance and encouragement.

In addition to my enormous gratitude to Layne, I am grateful to my partner, Marty, and our other daughter, Ary. When she did fieldwork with the project as a college undergrad while relatively close in age to girls in the program, her own reflections on their experiences helped me hear what the girls were saying in new ways. I could never adequately thank Marty Amerikaner, my in-house reviewer and supporter in chief. He has read every single thing I ever wrote about this project—reports, conference presentations, journal article drafts, and each chapter of this book. His responses have been thorough, insightful, and kind-hearted. He never belonged to a research team for this project, but it almost seems like he's been on every one of them.

Layne, too, has some thank-yous:

First I'd better thank my mom, Linda Spatig. It's not every day that your mom asks you to write a book with her. What started for me as a summer project in between a job and graduate school unfolded into more than three years of researching, writing, editing, and editing again. I feel honored to have played a role in telling the story of the remarkable girls, women, and men of this program. My dad, Marty Amerikaner, and sister, Ary Amerikaner, were also extremely supportive and helpful. I know that no one saw as many chapter drafts or title ideas—and you cannot fathom the number of title ideas we considered—as the two of them. But they persevered.

My closest friend, Lacey Johnson, spent countless hours across the table from me in libraries, coffee shops, and our apartments as I did my portion of the writing for this book. Her encouragement—as well as blunt, and occasionally scathing, critique—was invaluable. She also donated the photograph and design art featured on the front cover. A big thanks to Aurora Photography for allowing us to use the cover image free of charge.

My partner, Joe Levin, and roommate, Jess Halperin, cooked me a lot of food during this process and were unceasingly supportive. I am so thankful that my friend Hannah Moulton-Belec took the time to read the manuscript in its entirety and to provide valuable feedback. Other people who shared their support and enthusiasm were Julia Blencowe, Jason Crighton, Eranda Jayawickreme, Chris MacPherson, Sauleh Siddiqui, Keely Swan, and Rachel Wilson.

I am also grateful to the professors, staff, and fellow students in both my women's studies graduate program at George Washington University (especially Todd Ramlow, Rachel Riedner, and the Graduate Feminists) and in my undergraduate studies at Franklin & Marshall College (especially Doug Anthony, Simon Hawkins, and Judy Pehrson) for shaping my understandings of gender, social justice, and research. Special thanks to Toodie Ray, Laura Bentley, and Marcy Dubroff for teaching me how to write.

We are both grateful to Molly Barker, founder of the organization Girls on the Run and originator of the phrase "the girl box," for giving us permission to use the phrase throughout the book. Thanks also to University of Nebraska Press for permission to use material previously published in their journal *Collaborative Anthropologies.* We gratefully acknowledge Ric MacDowell again—this time for the photographs of program artifacts such as CD covers, poetry book cover, and organizational timeline. Thanks to Ron Sowell who gave permission for us to use lyrics from CDs that the girls recorded with him and who helped with arrangements to link the CDs to our book website.

AN IMPORTANT FINAL NOTE TO READERS

We, Linda and Layne, are donating our share of book proceeds to the Appalachian Women's Leadership Project (AWLP), a 501(c)3 nonprofit that sponsored the Girls' Resiliency Program featured in this book. Although the AWLP does not have staff at this time, the organization's board of directors, headed by Nona Conley, continues to seek and use funds to support programming for girls, and in some cases for boys, in the local community. The group's mission statement reads: "We work to develop the leadership and skills of youth in our community as a strategy for improving the future of Lincoln County." For additional information about the AWLP, or to make a contribution—which would be most welcome and put to good use—contact Ric MacDowell at ricmacdowell@gmail.com.

But for now, it's time to dig out your stonewashed jeans and scrunchies. We're heading back to the nineties where this story begins.

Introduction

When I Fell in Love with Shelley Gaines

Every good love story has to start with a time and place—you know, to set the scene—and this one is no different.

It's the spring of 1999. I am sitting in my university office, surrounded by menacingly tall stacks of student papers and scribbled field notes from ongoing research projects. A large wooden sculpture sits perched on my desk, spelling out a message that my husband and daughters think I desperately need to be reminded of each day: "RELAX." As one of the few qualitative research experts in the area and a lifelong "yes" addict, I am severely overcommitted. My next meeting is with a Shelley Gaines, and my plan is to have a brief chat and then regretfully decline to work with her—*"Your project sounds fascinating. If only I had the time!"*

Enter Shelley: baby on one hip, bright smile on her face. Radiating enormous energy and optimism, she tells me about the Girls' Resiliency Program (GRP), in Lincoln County, West Virginia, a community nonprofit aimed at helping girls identify strengths, become active decision makers, and advocate for social change. Shelley describes how it began with fewer than ten girls in one school and quickly grew to include almost one hundred girls in three schools. Being in the program, she explains, means monthly after-school discussions about everything from day-to-day happenings with friends to the roles and rights of girls and women. It means regular out-of-school activities, such as volunteer projects, art workshops, and social outings. She talks about the poor, rural county with little in the way of facilities or programs for youth and about the hard lives of the girls served. As she speaks passionately about this grassroots, "girl-driven" program focused on developing leadership in Appalachian youth, I feel my own enthusiasm growing. *Oh boy, I'm in trouble.*

But this was an unfair battle to begin with; given my personal and professional interest in gender equity, Appalachia, and community development, I never had a fighting chance. Shelley's intense commitment to the girls in Lincoln County was palpable. By the time she left my office that day, I had agreed to conduct evaluation research for the program. What I didn't realize then was how long the research would go on and how much it—and I—would change along the way. Although the research questions multiplied over the course of the project, at the outset they were fairly broad and simple. I wanted to understand what the program meant to the girls, how it played out in their lives, what aspects of it they valued and why, and what they were concerned about.

I think about long-term ethnography as a long-term relationship. I have a commitment to stick with it, to represent people fairly, to seek and present accurate information, and to learn lessons that can be used in other relationships. In the case of this study, I committed myself not only to my research students and to the teen girls in the program but also to the staff and board members, whose fierce devotion to rural youth is extraordinary. And to the woman whose passion I fell in love with that first afternoon, Shelley Gaines—the woman with the vision.

Every good love story also needs strong characters. In fact, it may need those above all else. Hence, the telling of this story is people-centered. Each chapter uses an individual and her or his experiences as a springboard for telling a piece of the organization's history, as well as for discussing key issues that arose in our research. Although my research teams did not collect the life histories of individual girls, the book in its entirety might be understood as a life history of an organization.

You'll notice the first-person singular writing. My daughter, Layne Amerikaner, who joined the project in 2010, cowrote the book. She and I had to decide what voice to use, what our presence should be in the writing. We agree with Corinne Glesne that first person singular is fitting for qualitative work, especially given that I was the lead researcher for the project. "The presence of 'I,'" writes Glesne, "says that yours is not a disembodied account that presumes to be objective" (2011, 236). The decision to narrate it in *my*, rather than *our*, voice is fully explored in the methods chapter.

I'll be frank up front: this story does not have an unequivocally happy ending. In the late '90s and early 2000s, the Girls' Resiliency Program flourished. Its accomplishments were significant, at times astonishing: the girls recorded their own CDs, published poetry, conducted action research, opened a coffeehouse, performed an original play, and held political rallies in West Virginia's capital. The organization won national awards, and funding flowed in. By 2005, however, the program was struggling to survive. At the same time that programming responsibilities grew, grant funds became harder to obtain. Frustrated and burned out, Shelley Gaines, the founder, resigned, and other staff followed. The program began to shrink, serving fewer youth in fewer schools with fewer staff. Today, summer 2013, the organization is nonexistent.

Those of us still involved (my role as "university researcher" doesn't keep me from counting myself as someone "involved") are left with the common end-of-love-story refrain: *What happened?* What made it work so effectively when it did, and what caused the decline? Is it possible to get back to the healthy, thriving organization of the 1990s? What does all this mean for the girls' lives? What can this story contribute to knowledge of youth development? Of adolescent girls? Of rural Appalachia? This book is an exploration of those questions, as well as an exploration of the research methods—what we in my field call "collaborative ethnography"—themselves. In each case, lessons learned—our research results, if you will—are woven into the story as it unfolds chapter by chapter.

Chapter 1 is where I lay out the setting of the story, Lincoln County, West Virginia, by way of introducing Ric MacDowell, who has lived and worked with youth in the area for more than forty years. Using Ric's experiences as a starting point, the chapter explores the poverty of the county and of West Virginia generally, much of which was created by the exploitation of local resources and people by large, out-of-state companies. I learned, as have others before, that local context matters in youth development work. More specifically, I learned about (1) the physical and social challenges of rurality for programs with youth whose homes are geographically remote, whether in Appalachia or elsewhere; (2) the importance of long-term relationships between youth and caring adults—even with individuals initially viewed as "outsiders" in close-knit communities; (3) the bitterness of poverty as experienced day to day by adolescent girls; and (4) the girls' critique of, and resistance to, stereotypes of the region and, more specifically, the assumption that West Virginia girls are incapable. Finally, chapter 1 reveals the girls' ambivalence about their home county, which they love but plan to leave someday.

Featuring Shelley Gaines, the founder and long-time director of the resiliency program, chapter 2 lays the foundation for the rest of the story. It describes the organization's early successful years and presents our research findings about resiliency and positive youth development—from the vantage points of adults who worked with the program, girls who participated in the program, and members of the community where the program was located. As has been true for other positive youth development programs, the idea that youth are capable, rather than in need of repair, was a core belief for adults who founded the program. Still, this belief was complicated by concerns that emphasizing group activities to build leadership might have unintentionally let some individual youth with pressing needs fall through the cracks. For girls, many of whom joined initially for the fun activities, the resiliency program meant being with caring adults and friends who could be trusted in safe, girls-only spaces where they could think in new ways about storms they had weathered. In the community, the program raised a few eyebrows. The fact that it was only for girls and that it explicitly challenged sexism was threatening for some. Reactions were hostile at times, including accusations of lesbianism, which is discussed from the perspective of a lesbian member of the group.

Chapter 3 features the transformation of Teresa, who joined the program at age twelve and stayed until its collapse. Drawing on Teresa's story, I explore the issue of "voice," tracing her journey from being virtually silent in the first year of the study to confidently vocal a few years later. Her transformation was related to two kinds of program experiences: arts activities (poetry, songwriting, photography, pottery) and community action research. Teresa's story illustrates the benefits that can come from investing substantial human and fiscal resources in activities that invite girls to acknowledge, express, and act on their views and experiences. In relaxed but structured activities led by professional artists, girls named and portrayed personal life events (sometimes quite painful ones) and were met with respect, encouragement, and suggestions. Original poetry and song lyrics are included in the chapter. The summer research internship was another activity in which Teresa and other girls were expected to speak and be heard—in this case in their community. The structured, paid research internships, including a university research workshop, were transformative. As interns, their jobs were to identify community problems and design research to learn more about and alleviate the problems.

In chapter 4 we meet Cassi. Whereas Teresa was one of the first girls in the program, Cassi and her friends were among the last. Cassi's experiences provide an opportunity to explore two other key aspects of the program: its focus on healthy relationships and its challenging nature. The focus on healthy relationships was explicit and pervasive in the program. On a day-to-day basis, adult staff members modeled positive relationships and coached girls as they sharpened their own relationship skills—the ability, in one staff member's words, "to trust," "to be open," "to be loved, to care about another person." The coaching was a blend of nurturance and challenge. Adult staff listened, but also talked back, to girls—raising questions, offering ideas, and at times directly challenging their thinking. The program challenged girls in other ways, too, by requiring them to try, in the words of one girl, "a thousand new things." Many new things, whether a trust fall in a ropes course, white-water rafting, or Chinese food, made the girls feel "scared to death." Girls who accomplished difficult tasks in the context of supportive relationships came away with expanded senses of their own capabilities. Cassi credits her relationship with a GRP staff member for her ability to overcome a long-standing fear of art, to successfully create pottery, and eventually to become, in her words, the "extraordinary and confident person" that she is today. Girls were especially pleased when their accomplishments made positive and noticeable community contributions, such as the coffeehouse they opened and the house they built for Habitat for Humanity. Program staff found it harder, though, to engage the girls in social activism. The chapter examines this issue, taking a close look at the group's involvement in anti–school consolidation activities.

Outspoken Irene and quiet Virginia, both of whom were girls in the program for five years and then became GRP staff members, come into the story in chapter 5. Their experiences illustrate the successes and struggles that can occur when participants become program deliverers. Moving girls into staff positions strengthened girls' ownership of the program. But it did not decrease staff turnover, a major challenge for the organization, and it may have diminished, rather than strengthened, staff effectiveness. Two related factors are key to understanding why some transitions from participant to staff were smoother than others, and in understanding the lack of success of this ambitious endeavor generally: timing and training. Transitions were more successful when girls took a longer, slower path to becoming staff members working directly with other girls. Beyond increasing girls' ownership of the program and enhancing staff stability and effectiveness, Shelley had hoped to strengthen the local community by "nurturing what's here," or making it possible for capable people to stay and work in Lincoln County. This happened to some extent, but it may have been at the expense of the organization. The decision to groom girls for staff positions and to preferentially hire local individuals—even when they had lesser qualifications than outside applicants—contributed to the group's downfall.

Graduate student researchers LeAnne Olson and Betty Sias are introduced in chapter 6. With the youth resiliency programming—the focus of their doctoral dissertations—unraveling, they gradually became de facto program staff. The chapter explores reasons for the program's collapse, the nature of the researcher/staff hybrid roles that Betty and especially LeAnne played as a result of the collapse, and overarching lessons learned from the study. In analyzing the program's collapse, three factors not already addressed in prior chapters are pinpointed: (1) overreliance on a single individual, namely Shelley Gaines; (2) declining funds for nonprofit work generally and specifically for projects featuring social justice activism for girls; and (3) untimely and underresourced program expansions. The chapter also explores how LeAnne and Betty negotiated—uneasily at times—a researcher/staff role that evolved with the program's decline. For the girls, the blurry line between researcher and staff was mainly an opportunity to develop trusting relationships with other caring women. For their part, the graduate students were rewarded with unusually deep, full understandings of the girls (and in Betty's case, the boys) and their lives.

Finally, the chapter discusses the GRP as an effective positive youth development program and presents four more general lessons learned from the study: (1) programs with atypical missions or strategies may suffer from a lack of role models and training about how to solve problems they encounter; (2) seeking balance, rather than a complete shift in one direction, is a more sustainable way to resolve organizational tensions (for example, between hiring short-term versus long-term staff or hiring insiders versus outsiders); (3) although there are no guarantees of success for new programs, major benefits—for individuals and for communities—can result from making commitments to them anyway, even programs that are not sustained in the way that was originally intended; and (4) there is value for organizations in being willing to change and grow in response to new information and circumstances. Beyond these four lessons, I—along with others who participated in the project—learned what girls' lives are like in this particular space and time, unquestionably important new knowledge.

The program ended, but the girls' lives went on. In chapter 7, featuring Ashley, I trace the experiences of five girls who were high school juniors when the program ended. Coauthored with LeAnne and based on her dissertation study, the chapter follows the five former GRP girls through their senior year of high school and into the first two years of college (or other postsecondary circumstances). From the study, I learned about barriers, as well as about factors that were helpful, in making the transition to college. The key issues were money, math, moms, mentors, and "me" (referring to each girl's own agency). In addition to money problems for four of them, all five girls faced obstacles related to mathematics. The girls' relationships with their mothers were helpful in many ways, but there were also family-related barriers. Finally, their association with LeAnne and their own agency were factors in their transitions from high school to college.

Chapter 8, featuring Layne and me, is about research methods. It traces the twists and turns of the process as it evolved over the years of the study. I began the research viewing myself as a qualitative program evaluator and ended up in the role of a "collaborative ethnographer," teaming up with adult community members and high school students. For Layne, who joined the project more recently, it was a transition from being an undergraduate anthropology student raised here in Appalachia to an author writing about "others" with different experiences of the region. The process of writing the book together transformed our mother-daughter relationship, opening new connections between us. In addition to our personal research journeys, the chapter highlights tensions related to doing community-based collaborative research with youth. The first tension relates to power, voice, and language, raising questions about whose voices are heard, what words are spoken and written, and how those decisions are made. A second and related tension concerns the balance of participation in the research. Who does how much of which tasks (e.g., data generation, analysis, presenting, writing)? We examine the feasibility—even the desirability—of the research work being evenly distributed when there are unequal resources for participants and in a rural context where transportation is a real obstacle to youth participation. We conclude that the collaborative methods were a strength of the study. They produced knowledge that is truer, closer to the experiences of the perceptions and experiences of the people involved, than it would have been had we used traditional ethnographic methods. The collaborative nature of the research let us explore differences in our understandings—for example, about what positive youth development *is,* anyway—that were important to constructing a full, relevant analysis of the project overall.

But this isn't just the story of an organization's trajectory; it's also a story about girls. I want to make sure that their voices are heard. These girls have things to say. At times they are heartbreaking; other times they are funny, insightful, sarcastic, trivial, profound. This book is the culmination of the fourteen years I spent asking questions of and listening to adolescent girls in rural West Virginia. Most of the studies and discussions of "girls" that I have encountered do not focus on poor, rural girls. But following the insights of feminist scholars of color such as Chandra Mohanty, Audre Lorde, and Barbara Smith, I understand the importance of centering one's research in the experiences and understandings of some of the most marginalized members of a group.

Because of a long history of exploitation, Lincoln County is one of the poorest areas of West Virginia, a state that is one of the poorest in the country. The girls in this community identified by teachers and counselors as good candidates for the resiliency program face some of the most severe adversity. I remember Shelley reflecting about the fear of letting the girls into her life—the risk involved in opening her heart to their stories and experiences: "I think a lot of times people put up this barrier which keeps them from being genuine, from letting other people get really close . . . because it's painful to do that when you're connecting with people who don't have happy-go-lucky lives." It is painful. And yet, I have found that avoidance of pain in ethnographic research—or in relationships generally—drains it of meaning. I believe Ruth Behar is on to something when she writes, about her own field of anthropology, that research "that doesn't break your heart just isn't worth doing anymore" (1996, 177). That said, power differentials are important here. Compared to the girls, who cannot just choose to disconnect from tough aspects of their own lives, Shelley and, for that matter, others of us who are part of this project have the luxury of more choices about making painful connections.

Scholars of this region write about Appalachians' deep connections to place. Anyone who has lived in these mountains knows the truth of this characterization, whether long-term "transplants" or natives. This holds for me, as well. These are my mountains; this is my place. Like Laurie Thorp, who conducted research with youth in her hometown—a place to which, she wrote, she had decided to "declare her loyalty"—I want to use this research to "make something happen" in a place to which and with a group of people to whom I have made a commitment (Thorp 2006, 2, 147).

Still, much work needs to be done in this country before we take the voices of Appalachian girls seriously. My part of the country is still characterized, to put it bluntly, as a bunch of ignorant hicks. "We *know* Appalachia exists because we need it to exist in order to define what we are not," argues historian Ronald Eller on the place my region holds in our national identity. "It is the 'other America' because the very idea of Appalachia convinces us of the righteousness of our own lives" (2008, 3).

The righteousness of our own lives, indeed. In 2009 TV personality Bill O'Reilly gave us a startling example of this view when he proclaimed that "the culture in Appalachia harms the children almost beyond repair. . . . There's really nothing we can do about it" (King 2012). He went on to argue, "Kids get married at sixteen and seventeen. Their parents are drunks. . . . Look, if I'm born in Appalachia, the first chance I get, I go to Miami."

So here is one story about a group of West Virginians who didn't move to Miami, who value their home, while acknowledging the challenges that come in an area of deep poverty; here is a love story about a group of teenagers and adults who understand the hurdles faced by rural West Virginia girls and reject the defeatist mind-set that "there's really nothing we can do about it."

Once upon a time, I fell in love with Shelley Gaines. Here, in a collection of prose, poems, interview clips, songs, field notes, sketches, and reflections, is the story of what happened next.

RIC.

Context Matters. Or, Lincoln County, West Virginia: "I Love It. I'll Leave Someday."

FOR THE LONG HAUL

"So, where are we now?" I squinted out the window of Ric Mac-Dowell's Prius and tried to find anything recognizable in the endless progression of trees, hills, and intermittently placed homes of Lincoln County, West Virginia. Ric was giving me a driving tour of the area, and I was starting to understand why the field notes of every member of my research team included long narratives about getting lost on curvy country roads.

You may find it odd that a book about adolescent girls opens with a chapter about a middle-aged man. Bear with me. Ric is a key player, especially in the beginning of the story, and a vocal, caring ally. After this chapter, the focus will shift to the women and girls central to the project.

"Oh, this is Route 10, Mud River Road," Ric said, with the casual confidence of a native. "One of the main roads." *Right, main road. I know exactly where we are.*

Before there was a Girls' Resiliency Program, there was a community in which Ric was an important player. A slim, gentle, soft-spoken man rarely seen without a baseball hat, Ric was—in his own quiet way—a rock in the community. Though born in Pennsylvania, Ric may as well be considered a West Virginia native at this point. In 1968, he graduated from Grinnell College and came to the state as a VISTA volunteer (Volunteers in Service to America) and never really left. An English major at Grinnell, Ric recalls he "didn't have a clue about what I was going to do when I graduated. [But] my senior year, there was a headline in the *Des Moines Register* with something like *VISTA volunteer needed for . . . West Virginia.* And I thought, 'that's what I'm going to do!' "

One moment's inspiration—glancing at a newspaper headline as a twenty-one-year-old—unfolded, ultimately, into forty years and counting of youth advocacy in rural West Virginia. Ric, who writes and speaks frequently about the importance of being committed to youth "for the long haul," has certainly lived by that belief himself. He tells me that he has lived in a house "up a rural holler" since 1972, working first as a schoolteacher and, later, as a professor and extension agent (a university employee focused on off-campus community development) for West Virginia University. Unquestionably a major voice in youth advocacy in Lincoln County, Ric has been involved in the Girls' Resiliency Program from the outset. And in his involvement, he has always been a nurturer. I have vivid memories of Ric calmly attending to noisy children at community meetings, distributing pears he had picked from the tree in his yard, sharing suggestions in a deep but quiet voice.

Ric was not the typical VISTA volunteer, at least not as many West Virginians perceived them. The VISTA program had been created by the Economic Opportunity Act of 1964, just a few years before Ric joined. The national attention President Kennedy had directed to Appalachian poverty, coupled with the "War on Poverty" subsequently launched by President Johnson, brought young activists into the region. VISTA volunteers, many of whom "displayed the long hair and . . . mannerisms of the suburban youth culture that evolved during the sixties" were seen by locals as "newcomers whose idea of community was different from their own" (Williams 2002, 349). West Virginia author John O'Brien vividly remembers his grandfather tossing sticks into their campfire and talking with irritation about "these daggone VISTA people. Who is it sends them? Where is this Appalachia place and why do they think I live there?" (2002, 115)

According to Thomas Kiffmeyer's (1998) study of the Appalachian Volunteers (AV), a regional service group that worked with the VISTA program and was committed to the idea of meaningful local involvement in social reform, the "infusion of non-native aid" was one cause of the organization's demise. Kiffmeyer writes that the AV "abandoned early on the tenet upon which the organization was founded—local people helping their neighbors—and thereby left itself vulnerable to charges that the group was controlled by outsiders" (1998, 91). Kiffmeyer goes on to argue, however, that ultimately the AV was defeated more by political actions taken by local community power brokers who were trying to avoid change than by its own mistakes (93).

As in any poor area, outsiders arriving to "fix problems" bring as much bad as good. But sometimes outsiders who come to stay, like Ric, become some of the most effective problem solvers in their communities. I am struck during this driving tour by just how spread out Lincoln County is, and I think of the rural isolation so many girls from this area speak of. After the school bus drops them off (often more than a mile from their houses), the girls are "stranded" at home until the next day. Roads are narrow and sometimes unpaved; we meet a bus and have to drive off the side of the road to make room for it to pass. As Dwight Billings and Ann Tickamyer point out in a piece exploring development in our region, "many Appalachian development issues are *rural* problems" generally (1993, 9).

On this drive I am also struck by Ric's tone of nonchalant yet sincere compassion. He is one of those rare individuals my mother would call a "good man," with a significant nod of her head. His tender concern for the youth of Lincoln County informs the entire trajectory of his adult life, personal *and* professional—though, as is true for many of us, the line between those two worlds is often blurred or irrelevant.

An excerpt from my field notes[1] of our driving tour:

At some point we saw a young boy (sixteen or seventeen, I would guess) walking on the side of the road. Ric stopped the car and chatted with him, introduced me. . . . After we started driving again, Ric said something to the effect of, "Now there's a kid who could really benefit from some services." . . . He wondered aloud if he could be more helpful by focusing his energies on working directly with individual kids like that boy or by being on the [Girls' Resiliency Program] board. This spoke volumes to me. Ric is such a committed, caring person who is devoted to young people. . . . Even with all that he does, he wonders if he's doing enough!

For Ric, commitment means longevity. "Most of the programs that we had for youth facing especially tough situations just didn't last very long," he explained. "People and programs came into their lives for a few months or a year, and then they were gone. We believed it was really important to develop *long-term* programs linking youth with adults who cared about them."

WELCOME TO LINCOLN COUNTY

Researchers Jodie Roth and Jeanne Brooks-Gunn (2003) say there is no blueprint for positive youth development programs because they should meet the needs of the communities within which they exist. Likewise, the Ms. Foundation—a major funder of the Girls' Resiliency Program—identified "cultural context" as a key factor in forming and sustaining effective, change-oriented programs for youth development. In other words, context matters.

The context for this story is, of course, Lincoln County, West Virginia—that county whose winding roads caused our research team members so much navigational grief. It is a county that is one of the poorest in a state known for being rural and poor. It is also the county that served as the setting for Jack Weller's damaging book, *Yesterday's People: Life in Contemporary Appalachia* (1965), now criticized by Appalachian historians and scholars as riddled with false stereotypes and explanations featuring "cultural deficiencies" rather than systemic exploitation. Drawing on his thirteen years as a pastor working with "mountain people," Weller outlined what he saw as southern Appalachian characteristics. In Weller's mind, people from this region, among other unflattering descriptors, are focused on "self-centered concerns" and have "no interest in long-range, careful planning" (161–63). Whatever our differences with Weller's understanding of the Appalachian region, Lincoln County rests in the heart of it.

Geographically speaking, Appalachia centers on the mountain range of the same name. However, many who live in the region wouldn't use the word themselves:

> For most of my life *Appalachia* confused me. When I met people around the country and said that I was from West Virginia, they would sometimes say, "Ah, Appalachia" in a peculiar way. . . . [But] if someone had asked Grandfather Bell what Appalachians were like, he might well have said, "Beats me, by jacks. Never run into one." In time I would learn that Appalachia was an imaginary place and that being Appalachian was imaginary but terribly damaging. (O'Brien 2002, 15–16)

What's not imaginary, but certainly damaging, is the poverty faced by rural communities—a topic that has received little attention in literature on youth development. Poverty rates in rural areas all over our country have always been higher than those in cities, and the gap between rural and urban poverty rates widened between 2010 and 2011. According to the United States Department of Agriculture (USDA), the poverty rate for the rural United States increased, going from 16.5 percent in 2010 to 17.0 percent in 2011 (Farrigan 2013). In the urban United States, however, poverty rates decreased from 14.9 percent in 2010 to 14.6 percent in 2011. The USDA report, under the heading "Geography of Poverty," goes on to say that the gap between rural and urban poverty rates varies considerably across regions. According to the report, "the large majority" (340 out of 386) of US counties with "persistent poverty"—20 percent or more of the population below the poverty level over a thirty-year period—are located in rural areas of the country, including in central Appalachia. Not surprisingly, this includes many West Virginia counties.

These urban/rural discrepancies are just one piece of the larger trend that the Occupy Wall Street movement is highlighting as I write this:

a huge gap between the 1 percent and the 99 percent. Interestingly, during the "War on Poverty" over fifty years ago, very similar issues were being raised. Flem Messer, an Appalachian Volunteer, noted in a 1965 presentation to students at Pikeville College in Kentucky that " 'the politicians and the banks . . . concentrated . . . all the money and power' of the county in their own hands and reinvested nothing in the community" (Kiffmeyer 1998, 79). This led critics of the Appalachian Volunteers to claim that the organization was trying to "redistribute wealth" (Kiffmeyer 1998, 85). I am amazed at the similarity of the rhetoric being used today attempting to counter the Occupy Wall Street protest and to discredit President Obama's efforts to increase taxes for the very wealthy. Occupy Wall Street and other similar initiatives raise crucial issues of economic inequality. Still, it is important to note that the gap between the 1 and 99 percent partly camouflages other gaps, such as those between rural and urban populations, or between children and adults.

West Virginia is a case in point. The entire state is characterized as poor in some formulations, but there is considerable variation in economic well-being across the fifty-five counties. Rural Lincoln County is near the bottom of that spectrum. The US Census Bureau reports that in 2010, more than a quarter (26.6 percent) of Lincoln County residents lived below the poverty level. Other telling numbers from the Census Bureau: in 2010, only 7.7 percent of adults (age twenty-five or above) in Lincoln County had a bachelor's degree or higher, compared to 17.3 percent in West Virginia; and the county's per capita income was $16,439, compared to $21,232 in the state overall.

For kids, the numbers are even bleaker. Poverty rates for children are higher than for the population as a whole, and children in rural regions are doubly disadvantaged. According to the 2012 West Virginia Kids Count Data Book, one out of every three children in Lincoln County is living in poverty. The same Data Book reports that 66.8 percent of children in Lincoln County were approved for free and reduced-price school meals, compared to 52.8 percent statewide. Numbers, numbers, numbers. For many girls in the program throughout the years, these numbers come to life in places like the checkout line of a grocery store. An untitled poem by GRP participant Chasity Owens (published originally in the Girls' Resiliency Program 2004 Calendar) eloquently shares her thoughts on—and firsthand experiences with—poverty in Lincoln County:

I remember when we would go to the store and
        we could never get what we wanted. And
        when we would check out we would always
        have to put stuff back because we didn't
        have enough money and everybody would
        stare at us like they were better.

Being rich is having everything you need like
        family and a house, and you wouldn't even
        have to have a car as long as you have love.

Being rich looks like a big family with a mother,
        father, and four kids; two girls, two boys,
        and a nice house with four rooms.

It tastes like sweet candy.
Smells like roses.
It sounds like laughter and love.

Being rich makes me very happy.
Being poor is not having a family or anything.
Being poor is very sad and unhappy.
Being poor tastes like it is bitter.

Chasity's poignant characterization of poverty is echoed in interviews with other community members. One woman, the parent of a Resiliency Program girl, was working for minimum wage at the time of our interview. She spoke of her experience in personal terms, telling us the hardest part of living in Lincoln County is simply surviving economically:

> Just trying to make money, live. . . . There [aren't] very many jobs around here for one thing, and you don't get [paid] much because I only get $5.15 [an hour] and I have to take care of four kids and a grandkid. My husband gets SSI [Supplemental Security Income]. He's disabled; he's got bad lungs.

Because of the struggling economy, Lincoln County has a low tax base to support public services. Roads are not maintained well; there is little in the way of public transportation; and—as community members and parents involved in the Resiliency Program pointed out—there's not enough financial support for education. In fact, in the first few years of our research in Lincoln County, the West Virginia Board of Education went so far as to declare a "state of emergency" in Lincoln County schools. According to a West Virginia Department of Education web posting on October 15, 1999, the declaration was the result of a West Virginia Board–commissioned site visit report that highlighted 213 deficiencies in "hiring practices, teacher certification, curriculum offered to students, instruction, and even the cleanliness of the facilities."

POVERTY DOESN'T MEAN HILLBILLY

I remind myself of the importance of nuance when setting this story's context. "Sometimes," Shelley Gaines points out in a piece she wrote for the Ms. Foundation, "it is incredibly difficult to talk about poverty and class disparity without invoking peoples' stereotypes of 'hillbillies,' which we find demeaning, disconnected from reality, and just plain wrong." She also reminds us of the importance of telling a balanced and complex tale: "We . . . tell stories of living poor, with few opportunities, and of systems that treat people differently based on their last name or the holler they live in. For us, it has become important to make sure that these stories are accurate, but also offer an analysis of the situation that moves beyond oversimplified explanations."

The concept of "the country" as a devalued place hits home for me, and I can remember the moment I first came face-to-face with this idea. Growing up in small-town Virginia, my grandma was one of the most important people in my life. I used to spend a few weeks every summer on her small farm in the country, doing everything from picking beans to feeding chickens. Sometimes I brought friends from school along. I loved that it was quiet; that I could hang out on the front porch swing; that we talked all day; that my grandma really listened to me.

One afternoon—when I was about the age of some of the youngest girls in the resiliency program, twelve or thirteen—my grandma informed me gently but matter-of-factly that at some point, I wouldn't want to bring my friends "out here" anymore. I was shocked.

"Why not?" I demanded indignantly. "Of course I will."

"Because you won't think it's nice," she said. "You won't want to bring your friends around." That was my first inkling that people looked down on the country and—as Bill O'Reilly (2009) reminded us in his recent diatribe against Appalachia—that they still do.

"They talk about us like we don't know [much] or you go to a different state, and they'll talk about Lincoln County like we are hicks and everything," says Becky, one of the girls in the program, in an interview. She resents outsiders' perceptions of those who live in Lincoln County—"especially the girls."

> Every time they do a report on [Lincoln County] I think they go find the worst people they can and put them on TV. They don't find the smart people. The way people look at you—it's like you're trash or something. . . . They don't think that much of people in Lincoln County, especially the girls. They think girls can't do nothing.

Beyond the negative perceptions Becky describes, it is often women and girls who bear the brunt of the state's economic disadvantages discussed earlier. The Institute for Women's Policy Research reported that as of 2004, among the fifty states and DC, West Virginia ranked "46th for women's political participation, 48th for their social and economic autonomy and for their health and well-being, and last, or 51st, for women's employment and earnings" (2004, 1). The institute reported more recently (2013) that West Virginia women are less likely than women in *any other state* to have a four-year college degree or to be in the labor force (Hess, Hegewisch, and Williams, 1–2). When they *are* working, West Virginia women face one of the worst gender wage gaps of any state, earning only 69 cents for every dollar earned by men (2). Beyond that, the report's authors point out, "the rural nature of West Virginia makes it difficult for many women to access social services such as child care, health care, and domestic violence shelters" (iii).

Looking at Appalachia overall, several studies conclude that daughters are pushed to assume traditional caretaking roles. Julia Feine's research reports that Appalachian women emphasize the importance of marriage and motherhood as the central focus of a woman's life (1991). Likewise, more recent research conducted by Miewald and McCann (2004) suggests that older Appalachian women believe that economic security is ensured by marriage rather than by education or a job. The researchers argue that "lack of education, few places for women to work outside of the home, the need to care for children and other family members, and social pressure to follow gender norms meant that there were few alternatives to the traditional role for women" (1054).

Some gender studies support the idea of greater Appalachian traditionalism, but others have not found a gender distinction between Appalachians and other Americans. In a 2002 study conducted by David Kimweli, Appalachians did not have different scores than non-Appalachians on the Bem Sex-Role Inventory, a scale measuring levels of masculinity and femininity (based on stereotypical gender norms). A study by Dorothy Stratton and Alinde Moore, also published in 2002, reports that West Virginia men do not have a greater preference for male-dominated, authoritarian marriages than other men. In my own earlier research with teenage girls in West Virginia, I learned that many girls had a well-developed gender-consciousness, recognizing gender bias in their families and schools. Girls complained that their brothers were given more freedom than they were allowed to have at the same age and about teachers who emphasized the importance of politeness for girls more than for boys (Spatig, Parrott, et al. 2001). Likewise, in a study examining gender roles among Appalachian college students, Eric Swank and his coresearchers did not find evidence of traditionalism:

> Numerous commentators and researchers have contended that gender dynamics in Appalachia tend toward traditional gender roles, increased sexual violence, and less progressive views of women. When exploring a sample of Central Appalachian college students, it was clear that these claims went unsubstantiated. . . . We did not detect any significant differences between the students who identified themselves as Appalachian and those who did not. (2011, 136)

On the basis of those findings, Swank advises that researchers "ought to be suspicious of the assertion that Appalachians are quicker to accommodate or sanction traditional gender roles" (137).

WHO EXACTLY ARE THESE
APPALACHIAN GIRLS?

Following black feminist scholars such as Kimberlé Crenshaw and Patricia Hill Collins, I know that to write simply about "girls" or "Appalachians" generally—and as if those were separate groups—isn't good enough. These scholars point out that there are intersecting identities such as race, class, and gender that cannot easily be separated in individuals' lives. For example, referencing Sojourner Truth's famous "Ain't I a Woman" speech, Hill Collins points out that Truth reveals the "contradictions inherent in blanket use of the term *woman*" (2003, 331). In other words, all women are not facing the same kinds of obstacles. Similarly, a blanket use of the phrase "adolescent girl" cannot cover the variety of life experiences and struggles faced by teenage girls of different races, classes, abilities, and so on.

The "girl box" isn't the same for every girl in this story. Sexism, classism, ageism, regionalism, and (for some girls) homophobia all come into play here. Despite these struggles, it is also important to note that the girls featured in this book, who were white girls in an overwhelmingly white state and county, were still privileged in terms of race. Explaining the "position" that various characters in our book are speaking from is important, given the feminist insight that factors such as geographic setting, historical period, and identity group memberships such as race and gender, help shape individuals' standpoints. As Donna Haraway explains it, all knowledge is "situated"; it depends on where one is looking from (2008). Further, Hadar Dubowsky Ma'ayan points out that these viewpoints are all relative: "In one school or situation a student may be seen as 'rich' and in another 'poor'" (2012, 20).

So it's hard to talk about girls as a category. Defining—or drawing borders around—any group will always bring "trouble," to borrow Judith Butler's words (1991). It will always leave some people out by creating a "normal" or typical experience of that group's identity. But there is not a singular, shared experience among women or girls. Rather than pointing out differences in experiences between groups—such as between "girls" and "boys," which I and the other characters do throughout this book—writers such as Crenshaw highlight the differences *within* groups, such as within the category of "girls" (Crenshaw 1991). There is not just one set of "girls' issues."

Further, some would question what we mean by the term *girl* in the first place. It is important to point out that this does not mean the same thing to everyone. For example, when does a girl stop being a girl and become an adolescent or a woman? As Jessica Taft points out, "As an identity category, it is in fact quite fluid and flexible" (2011, 73). Taft notes that this brings hard questions to the field of girls' studies, such as asking what it means to be a girl (95). Feminist and queer theorists draw attention to the fact that gender is a social construct. In other words, our ideas and beliefs about what it means to be a woman or a girl (or boy, or man, or person) are constructed by *people,* their ideas and actions, and by social or cultural traditions, rather than only by "natural" forces of some kind. There are also more than just two gender categories. Even though gender identity—the way individuals would self-describe their gender—varies (for example, some do not identify as a man or a woman), people are almost always *assigned* a gender at birth that is either "boy" or "girl." This could be another meaning of the "girl box"; gender isn't as simple as checking one of two boxes, and some youth do not identify strictly as a girl or a boy. In this way, gender is both self-determined *and* imposed from the outside by societal pressures. Similarly, many writers who in the social sciences would be called "postmodern" point out that even adolescence is a socially constructed idea rather than a set, biologically natural "stage" that is the same for all of us (Lesko 2001; Walkerdine, Lucey, and Melody 2001).

Despite all of these concerns, I use the word *girl* throughout the book, including right there on the front cover. I believe it is important to be able to use a word to describe a shared status—girlhood—while being careful not to assume that all girls have the same experiences or identities. The important feminist insight that the personal is political is based on an understanding that experiences in the everyday lives of individual members of a group (say, girls) often have broader, societal roots. Having a word to rally around allows for a sense of community, the ability to organize, and a way to describe how certain groups are disadvantaged

(Crenshaw 1991, 1241–42). Being able to talk about the collective experiences of girls and how they are linked to larger causes of oppression (like patriarchy, racism, or regionalism) is critically important.

WAY BETTER THAN THE CITY

Still, when writing about Appalachian girls, I am uneasy about portrayal. I worry that by frankly stating the problems facing Lincoln County, I will be painting a picture of a community of passive victims, or even of a broken Appalachia—and we know the world doesn't need more ammunition on that front. Filmmaker Isaac Julien wrote, in response to accusations that one of his films (*Young Soul Rebels*) perpetuated negative stereotypes about the gay community, that "the project of producing positive images is an impossible one." He went on to argue that "though it may have the best intentions of redressing imbalances in the field of representation, it is bound to fail as it will never be able to address questions of ambivalence or transgression" (1992, 261). In a similar vein, in advocating what he calls "critical regionalism" in thinking and writing about Appalachia, Douglas Reichart Powell says that our goal should not be "more 'positive' portrayals of regional life" (2007, 116–17). Instead, we should describe "local problems and priorities [as they are] enmeshed in broader patterns" (143), thus moving from "social construction" of a region, which can perpetuate negative stereotypes, to "social invention," which involves purposefully creating understandings of a region with particular goals in mind (24). And it's true; it is important to tell the whole story as much as we can know it. At the same time, arguing that when writing about people in a marginalized community the author has no responsibility to represent them fairly—in other words, with an awareness of past and present biases—to me, borders on the absurd. But here in Lincoln County, "the whole story" includes a whole lot of good.

Although girls, parents, and GRP staff openly discussed Lincoln County's problems and lacks, they were quick to point out the good, too—especially the beauty and the close sense of community characteristic of the county. One parent told us the best thing about living in Lincoln County is the quiet, natural beauty:

We've got a huge yard where the kids can get out and play, and we can get out and play ball with them and stuff like that. And I've got a little sort of like a gazebo . . . a little tiny building that has screen around it. . . . We go out there and drink a cup of coffee and just love it. And in the wintertime we can sit on the porch and watch the snow. We don't have to be out in it. But it is beautiful. The house is not that great but . . . I love it, and I wouldn't trade it . . . because I grew up in the city.

Scholars of Appalachia characterize the area as a place with a heavy emphasis on kinship—a place where communities are close, family bonds are strong, and people "take care of their own." In many cases several generations of family still live in the same area, or even in the same house.

Ric would say that even an area known for mistrust of outsiders will sometimes extend its definition of "community member" when someone hangs around long enough. "There was this initial, 'who is this person? This person is an outsider.' . . . [But] you become part of the community," he explains. "Soon after I moved to Sugar Camp Creek . . . the lady up the road . . . died in her home. I just happened to be passing by one morning after one of the neighbors found her and didn't want to touch the body. I ended up picking the body up and putting it in the bed—helping with that, helping dig the grave. And I think those kinds of experiences sort of made me part of the community." Or, as Appalachian historian John Williams puts it, "Genuine community is purchased through respect" (2002, 398). He writes that "an unspoken code of reciprocity [governs] routine interaction among neighbors and kin" (2002, 364). Ric was *taken* in because he was willing to *join* in—in his quiet, unassuming way.

For Ric, it was also the everyday friendliness and hospitality of the people in Lincoln County that made him decide—to borrow Laurie Thorp's words—to "declare his loyalty" here. Ric said, "I remember Gus and Frank, a father and son, who lived up the road from me. . . . Every time they'd see me when I'd be walking on the road, they'd invite me in to eat. We'd sit around. . . . I'd pump the organ, then he'd play. They'd give me stuff. I remember Gus wanted to give me his World War I coat because he thought I wasn't dressed warmly."

One community member attributed Lincoln County's low crime rate to this kind of community closeness. "You get to know more people," she said. "It is more like a family than out in the cities where you don't even get acquainted with anyone." Another community member agreed, distinguishing the intimate partner violence and drug abuse (more prevalent in Lincoln County) from the violence occurring in other communities:

> There is not a whole lot of crime like robberies. There is like domestic violence, drug abuse, and stuff, but most of these places where the girls live they don't have to lock their doors at night. . . . It is a relatively safe place to live. Lots of people have their families nearby, so there is an extended family as far as childcare and stuff goes. . . . You basically know everyone around you because you grew up with them.

One thing to note here: sometimes the girls' perceptions of Lincoln County are at odds with adult perceptions and "official" statistical data. For example, the reported crime rate in the county is relatively low, but some of the youth have concerns about their physical safety and talk about increasing drugs, alcohol, and violence in their communities. Ric says the current "big county spike in prescription drug abuse, deaths, and arrests" suggests that the young people's concerns are warranted.

As is probably true most everywhere, the youth see both the good and bad about their community. While frankly pointing out what "sucks" about their hometown (as teenagers are inclined to do—I know mine were), everything from lack of things to do and places to work to the biases held by other community members, they are quick to point out both physical and cultural aspects of a place they dearly love. Their positive comments about Lincoln County parallel those of scholar bell hooks, who came to West Virginia a few years ago and spoke about both the joy of growing up in rural Appalachian America and about how that joy is rarely mentioned publicly.

The following composite poem, "Lincoln County," captures the range and depth of the girls' varied, complex perceptions of their county home. Each line of the poem is a direct excerpt from what an individual said or wrote in conversations, interviews, journal entries, or short essays.

Lincoln County

Almost perfect
Pretty cool
Positively beautiful

Mountains, rivers
The old swinging bridge
Four Mile Road
Leaves turn[ing] colors
Deer in a field
Fishing at the dam

[It's] Small.
You get a chance to shine.
A good place to live
Way better than in the city
Close to family
Dirt bikes and dune buggies
I never want to leave.

[It's] Tough.
No work
Not much to do; I'm bored.
No hospitals
They should build a Wal-Mart.

A safe place
[Kind of] secluded from the [real] world
Back in the country
The hills and creeks block things out:
Big crime
Gang violence

[Kind of] secluded from the [real] world
Afraid of change and difference
Rebel flags all over
Racist
Stupid

Things happen, even here.
Sexual harassment
Drugs

Domestic violence
Abuse

Mostly Country
Not a bunch of hicks, just a weird accent

Lincoln County is my world.
I love it.
I'll leave someday.

A NATIONAL SACRIFICE AREA

"I love it. I'll leave someday." This is a common story here in West Virginia, and perhaps in economically depressed communities all over the world. Regardless of their assessments of the place, for those who can leave it is hard to make a self-affirming commitment to stay. It was not uncommon to hear the young people speak about their love for Lincoln County and then to declare—almost in the same breath—with regret and seeming resignation that they cannot stay because there are no jobs. According to some of the girls, their parents have the same conflicted desires for them. A member of our research team documented in her field notes a poignant moment where this issue came to the surface during a discussion at an after-school poetry-writing activity: "Shelley then asked [the girls], 'Do your parents want you to be happy?' Yes all around. 'Do they want you to stay in Lincoln County?' Vehement no's, all around."

The girls' responses are not surprising. Williams points out that Appalachia has a history of youth needing to leave the region to prosper. Preparing students for success, he writes, meant "preparing students to leave" (2002, 330). This brain drain often happens immediately after high school graduation. Williams shares the words of a student from Mingo County, West Virginia: "'It was a trend there that once you graduated from high school you went off to Chicago, Cleveland, Columbus, Baltimore, Detroit,' the student said. 'I graduated at two o'clock on Sunday, June the fourth, 1967. Two o'clock Monday afternoon I was sitting in Columbus'" (2002, 330).

This was and is directly related to economic possibilities, of course. Lincoln County, like most of West Virginia and many resource-rich areas all over the globe, has a history of outsiders taking wealth out of the area. "The perceived economic and cultural deficiencies of Appalachia allowed entrepreneurs a free hand to tap the region's natural resources in the name of development, but by midcentury the dream of industrial prosperity had produced the opposite in the mountains," explains Appalachian historian Ronald Eller (2008, 2).

Ric has seen this firsthand in Lincoln County. "We talked at one point about how county residents had thought they owned the mineral rights to their land, but somehow in the past they had lost them," I wrote in my field notes from our driving tour. "The gas company owns the rights to the gas in the property he's living on right now. . . . Ric said that a lot of people's attitudes were sort of resigned—'there's nothing you can do.' [He] said he thought that was part of the history of being beaten down by outside companies."

Eller agrees: "Much of the story of Appalachia describes the exploitation of the region at the hands of outside economic interests," he writes. But, he adds, the tale is more complex than simply outsiders taking the profits of coal, gas, and other natural resources out of the region. "Mountain residents themselves have been among the strongest advocates of growth, and they have engaged in some of the most callous exploitation of the land and of their fellow citizens that has befallen the region" (2008, 8). At the same time, other natives of this area *resisted* the exploitation of out-of-state corporations—or at least fought for better circumstances. Lynda Ann Ewen, a West Virginia sociologist, points out that federal laws about occupational safety had their origins in the Black Lung Movement of our state (1999).

Still, Eller writes, the take-away point is that we must look at the poverty of Appalachia not as a result of a backward culture, but instead as "rooted deeply in the very process of private industrial development that [has] created modern America" (2008, 4). Eller is articulating what Kiffmeyer (1998) calls the "colonialism model" of Appalachian poverty. In this model, Appalachian poverty is a result of exploitation by "outside industrial giants" (1998, 66) and "local elites" (Gaventa 1980) who support them in order to ensure their own economic well-being. As Denise

Giardina, a West Virginia writer, noted in a *New York Times* editorial about the 2010 Upper Big Branch mining disaster: "We knew then, and know now, that we [West Virginians] are [in] a national sacrifice area. We mine coal despite the danger to miners, the damage to the environment and the monomaniacal control of an industry that keeps economic diversity from flourishing here." A national sacrifice area that—as the popular billboard slogan in our state goes—"keeps the lights on" in the rest of the country. O'Brien summarizes the industrial development process in a powerful segment of his memoir that my mind often returns to when thinking about the roots of problems faced by the state:

> In the Appalachian Mountains, the golden age of laissez-faire capitalism was one of America's great nightmares. Within forty years, timber companies had clear-cut the oldest and largest hardwood forest that human beings would ever see. In that time, thirty billion board feet of quality lumber and an equal amount of pulpwood left the state, along with 98 percent of the profit.... Both coal and timber operations ravaged enormous portions of the mountain landscape as well as subsistence cultures that had survived peacefully for more than a hundred years. All of this transpired while county officials and local newspaper editors—who often became coal or timber executives—looked the other way. By the 1930s, 75 percent of West Virginia's landmass and between 85 and 95 percent of the state's natural resources "legally" belonged to outside interests. (O'Brien 2002, 63)

A *system* producing poverty and, in turn, people living in poverty. I dwell on this point because of the many blame-the-victim interpretations of Appalachian poverty, sometimes called "culture of poverty" explanations, that abound (Kiffmeyer 1998, 66). A particularly harmful one came from Harry Caudill's *Night Comes to the Cumberlands: The Biography of a Depressed Area,* which Williams points out became a nonfiction best seller in 1962 (2002, 324). His general theory, in Williams's words, was "that Appalachia's original settlers came from . . . the dregs of English society and the refuse of London's jails. Once in the mountains, Caudill argued, geography isolated these settlers, leading to a 'depleted gene pool' among their descendents, which in turn explained the unambitious and socially dysfunctional character of Appalachian people today" (2002, 325).

What all of this means for rural Appalachian youth is that the state of the economy of their community makes it hard for them to flourish here, encouraging many who can leave to do so. Still, leaving is not easy. Lawanda, the bright rural Appalachian teenager featured in George Ella Lyon's novel *With a Hammer for My Heart*, explains the situation frankly: "I'm wanting to go to college. Nobody in my family has ever done it and we sure can't pay the bills, but I'm still planning to go. Last summer I tried to get a job to save money, but I soon found out there's not enough work here . . . for grown people, much less kids" (2008, 5). Of the relatively few kids who go away for college, few return. I remember the dramatic words of a West Virginia schoolteacher from a research project several years ago. "Will they come back?" I asked her. "No," she said definitively. "No. If they're successful, they will leave" (Spatig et al. 2001, 67). In an emotionally wrenching move, even their parents seem to be pushing them away. *We want you to be happy. We don't know if it can be here.*

I love it. I'll leave someday.

COMMUNITY AND COMMITMENT

Wendell Berry, the famous Appalachian writer and activist, describes community as "the mental and spiritual condition of knowing that the place is shared, and that the people who share the place define and limit the possibilities of each other's lives" (1969, 61). In other words, he sees community as an interconnected and interdependent group of individuals—individuals who both *define* and *limit* what is possible for each other. Using this understanding of community, Ric MacDowell is clearly helping expand the possibilities for many Lincoln County youth.

He's also encouraging others in the community to make the same commitment. Ric writes: "While it is true that all children in our society are at risk, some are much more at risk than others. Those at highest risk are children whose caregivers lack good parenting skills and lack resources to support their children, especially when they need critical services." He argues that, when we're honest with ourselves, we know who these kids are: "As a community we really can identify most of these youth at an

Ric's house

early age. The issues are whether or not we choose to intervene, and what the interventions will be."

For Ric, choosing to intervene was something learned at an early age. "I had a paternal grandmother who always said, 'you've got to help people. . . . ' If someone walking down the street needed [a job], she would have them mow the grass, invite them in for a cup of coffee and some cookies. I think she modeled that for me." Many years later, Ric is modeling that for others. That twenty-one-year-old VISTA volunteer, now in his sixties, is still living in the same house he did when he first arrived.

"But, seriously, who wouldn't be?" my daughter asks, looking at the photos Ric has sent us of his place. "It's *beautiful*. It's like a secret, beautiful hideout." So in the context of what has now become Ric's home—beautiful, small, secluded, tough, safe, country Lincoln County—the Girls' Resiliency Program (GRP) began in 1996, three years before I became aware of its existence. It all started in one school with eight girls and "the woman with the vision." Cue Shelley Gaines.

2

SHELLEY.

The Birth of the GRP: It's a Girl (-Driven Program)!

LITTLE TINY BOXES

"No, I'm not going to buy you that class ring—because you're not going to graduate high school, anyhow."

As a teenager, Shelley Gaines's best friend Jamie (name changed) faced many family expectations, but not the kind that make you want to work hard, study, and go to college. "There was nobody who said, you know, 'you're cool,' or 'you're smart' [or] . . . anything other than 'you're going to get pregnant and . . . you're not going to graduate high school,'" Shelley recalled. Jamie's two sisters had had babies as teenagers. No one in her family had gone to college before. And although Jamie was in the "college track" with Shelley and taking all honors classes, no one in her family believed that she could be the first to go to college.

As it turns out, she wasn't.

"She had all these labels that she carried around," said Shelley. "She ended up dropping out of high school in her senior year and . . . went to another state with a guy." Shelley added that at that point, Jamie completely dropped off the radar. She hasn't been able to track her down since.

Petite in size but not in presence, Shelley was and is a real force to be reckoned with. In the years I worked with her, Shelley wore her fine brown hair in a youthful pixie cut and was quick to break into a broad smile. With her down-to-earth, "get it done" personality, you rarely had to wonder what Shelley had in mind. Growing up in both North Carolina and West Virginia as the daughter of a social worker mother, Shelley knew early on that she wanted to work with struggling kids. She points to her relationship with Jamie as the experience that led her "from generally wanting to work with kids to more specifically wanting to work with girls in a supportive, affirming way."

In Lincoln County, Shelley saw once again the story of low expectations shaping outcomes. "When I [started working] with the kids here I had that same feeling," she remembered. "The kids that we were working with were really carrying around a lot of labels that people gave them and that it just got perpetuated within the family, or from the community. . . . Everybody has had these girls in these little tiny boxes that were very disempowering . . . and predicted all of these terrible things for their futures." Thinking of the potential she had seen in Jamie, Shelley had different ideas about the girls' futures.

Working as an intern for high school resiliency programs established through West Virginia's Safe and Drug Free Communities program in the early 1990s, Shelley met some of the county's movers and shakers, including our chapter 1 hero, Ric MacDowell.

Ric remembers: "[It was then] that I met Shelley. One of the things we found out when we did the analysis of the data from the resiliency programs we had going on in the county's four high schools was that girls who were in the program had a much bigger increase in self-esteem [than boys]. . . . We made a decision to have just a girls' group. . . . [Shelley] thought, 'I really like this, and I'd like to stay in Lincoln County and continue doing this work.'"

So in 1996, with eight girls in one junior high school—and no support staff—Shelley became the first director of the Girls' Resiliency Program (GRP). Over the next few years, she brought in grant money and hired staff; the program grew quickly to include more than sixty girls in three schools. The GRP was selected as one of twelve youth development organizations in the United States to be supported by the Ms. Foundation's Collaborative Fund for Youth-Led Social Change program, and Shelley received the prestigious Gloria Steinem Women of Vision Award.

KIND OF LIKE MENDING BONES

One of the reasons I was drawn to this project was Shelley's vision of youth capability and her deep-seated optimism about what was possible. In a piece written for a presentation at Marshall University, Shelley reflected on the beginnings of the GRP and on the importance of the concept of resiliency in the philosophy behind the work:

> When we started the Girls' Resiliency Program, most people didn't even know what resiliency meant. At that time many youth programs targeted "high risk" youth, and they were based on the premise that youth needed particular skills and particular experience in order to succeed. Our work in Lincoln County was based on a very different model. Resilience is the concept that people—youth, in this case—hold innate strengths and natural abilities that can be used to help them not only overcome challenges but become stronger and succeed. This was a model that fit with my values about not wanting to fix youth or teach youth but to support them and challenge them—to be their best, to try new approaches, and to think more systematically about social issues that were impacting them personally. So we created a program that offered opportunities—for girls and then later, boys—to give voice to their experience, to learn new skills or practice old ones, and to develop leadership. Our core belief was that these youth were capable.

Youth are capable. Although this may not sound like a particularly radical or original idea, focusing on the strengths of young people is the basis of a somewhat controversial philosophy of youth development work. Many programs treat youth as victims or problems in need of fixing—like programs that focus on treating or preventing alcohol and drug abuse, teen pregnancy, and other "problems" that individual adolescents experience.

Given the pervasiveness of negative images of adolescents in our culture, this is not surprising. As Eve Ensler puts it in an open letter to girls in her book, *I Am an Emotional Creature: The Secret Life of Girls around the World,* "I know we make you feel stupid, as if being a teenager meant you were temporarily deranged. We have become accustomed to muting you, judging you, discounting you, asking you—sometimes even forcing you— to betray what you see and know and feel" (2010, xxiii). Indeed, Hadar Dubowsky Ma'ayan points out that "in popular culture, adolescents are typically either demonized or trivialized as dangerous, lazy, unpredict- able, defiant, and irresponsible" (2012, 19). She notes that these stereotypes about teenagers are different depending on what kinds of teenagers are being discussed, identifying common images such as "the White, rich, clue- less girl; the dangerous gangster boy of color; and the poor, Black, ir- responsible teen mother" (19–20). With the rise of problematic shows such as "Here Comes Honey Boo Boo" (a television show on TLC, whose pro- motional shirts read: "You Betta Redneckognize"), we might add to this list the poor, white, country girl.

Despite—and possibly because of—these images, Shelley aligns strongly with the theory that *positive* youth development is more effec- tive. Considerable research (e.g., Huebner, Walker, and McFarland 2003) supports Shelley's belief and shows that programs that focus on young people's strengths or assets tend to be most successful. These programs also focus on relationships and communities, within programs and beyond. Youth are seen as resources rather than as individuals in need of services; goals are broader and focused on kids' strengths.

According to Richard Lerner, the "vocabulary" of positive youth development (PYD) is still evolving, but there is growing agreement on what are referred to as the "Cs of PYD" (Lerner et al. 2005, 22). Rick Little (1993) first proposed four Cs of PYD: *competence, confidence, connec- tion,* and *character.* A fifth C, *compassion,* was suggested by Jodie Roth and Jeanne Brooks-Gunn (2003) as well as Lerner (2004). Subsequently, these researcher/theorists have suggested a possible sixth C, *contribution to com- munity,* that emerges when the "five Cs are present in a young person" (Lerner et al. 2005, 23).

In addition to different vocabularies, there are also typically struc- tural differences between so-called positive and problem-focused youth development organizations. They draw a different mix of kids. Because in a positive youth organization members are made up of all types of youth, "the stigma that often characterizes programs based on a deficit model" is removed (Roffman, Pagano, and Hirsch 2001, 86). In other words, it's not just for the "problem kids."

But, Ric asks, what *about* the problem kids? He worries that this focus on youth capability, voice, and leadership inadvertently leaves out youth with the most serious problems. In reflections on the strengths-based approach, he expressed concerns about failing to strike a good balance between caring for and assisting individual youth with problems, on the one hand, and providing programming for groups of youth, on the other.

For Shelley, the positive youth development approach is not, in fact, leaving out those most in need of support. "With struggle," she argues, "comes resilience. . . . [You] become stronger due to hurdles." She explained in an interview that "building resiliency is kind of like mending bones":

> So basically if you were to break your wrist . . . once it has healed, that particular joint would be the strongest part of your body. It's the same idea only it's around psychological issues. So you know you've been through shit, but you have these defenses that you've created— maybe it's humor, maybe it's, you know, being able to read people really well. . . . Maybe you're really good at managing other people's conflicts because you had to manage your parents' conflicts, it could be anything. But that those skills aren't going to be thrown away. They are things to be identified and used in a healthy way and in a way that can take you forward instead of keep you stuck.

We adults are good at debating questions of what works and what doesn't. Psychological growth. Best practices. What resiliency means, and what it doesn't. But perhaps the most important question here is what resiliency means to the girls whose lives we hope to affect.

To the girls, resiliency mostly means things associated with the GRP itself—friends, trust, girls-only spaces, as well as the idea of weathering storms with the ability to bounce back. In a writing exercise in which girls composed their own definitions of the word, one girl put it in very personal terms, writing "I am resilient" in large script across the top of the page. Here are a few of their comments.

I am resilient

I am resilient because I made it through
the storm. No the hurricane.
I think resiliency is so important.
Espically in todays world.
If you're not resilient, you will probably go through
very hard times.
It's a great thing, resiliency, it lets you know
you can go through hell, and pop right back
to yourself with very few blemishes.

Resiliency

I think that being resilient is being able
to be a better person. Being with friends
and having ~~fun~~ fun and learning about
things and each other. ~~No~~ I think that
I friendship is the most important
thing of ~~resilient and things life~~
being resilient and in life.

A place to get away from the hustle and bustle
of school life we you have a big household
mostly boys; it's nice to spend time with girls.

When I met Shelley in 1999, the program had been operating for three years. By that time, it had grown to serving almost one hundred girls in three schools in the county. Described by Shelley as a "girl-driven" program, it featured a huge range of activities, from white-water rafting to serving on the organization's board of directors. All girls participated in discussion meetings in their home schools every other week. During the first half of each school year, discussions were led by GRP staff; in the second half of the year they were led by girls. These were not your run-of-the-mill discussion groups. Girls talked about whatever pressing issues were facing them at the time, from how to deal with sexual harassment to how to put on a condom. They talked about summer plans, family problems, birth control, school.

But in these early years, the girls did much more than just talk. They bowled, rafted, skated, gardened, went to amusement parks, swam, rappelled, and went camping. They did arts activities almost every week. They did community service. They conducted action research on community problems. They were everywhere. In addition to having a good time, the activities were chances for girls to try something new or challenging. Rosemary, a girl in the program, explained: "Some people . . . don't really get to go out and do stuff and have fun. . . . Some people had never been skating, and they went. Like I'd never been rafting until last year, and I went, and never . . . rappelled and [now] I've done that. I've done a lot of stuff I didn't think I'd ever do." Or, as Kris explained, "It's mostly about . . . [doing] things that you couldn't do before, like your family [doesn't] have enough money [so] you can't go bowling. This group will give you a chance to do that."

The girls' activities are discussed fully—and from their points of view—in chapters 3 and 4. Here I simply want to introduce what Shelley envisioned for the program, the type of work that was happening in the early years, and the extensive scope of that work. One finding from our research was that many of the girls mainly wanted interesting activities to do. They were not thinking in terms of "leadership" or "women's liberation" when they decided to join the group. As with much youth-focused work, the growth happened in the process, but for the girls, the initial draw was the fun activities, many of which may be seen on the organizational timeline.

So far, I have been talking about the Girls' Resiliency Program history in a matter-of-fact way, but it is important to point out that the GRP—an organization led by women and focused on girls—raised some eyebrows in Lincoln County. The Institute for Women's Policy Research tells us that West Virginia women have "the lowest levels of educational attainment in the country" and that we are among the least likely in the country to be working as managers or professionals. They write: "West Virginia reflects the difficult obstacles to equality still facing many women in the United States. . . . They by no means enjoy equality with men" (2004, 1). My state, ranking last in many measures of women's equality, is not always a hotbed of feminist activism.

But I am not convinced that gender roles are narrower here than in other regions. My own prior research with West Virginia girls (not part of the Girls' Resiliency Program) suggests a more varied picture. Low-income rural and urban girls in our earlier study aspired to higher education and professional careers not necessarily associated with traditional women's occupations, such as doctors, lawyers, teachers, veterinarians, athletes, and paramedics. They favored paid labor over unpaid domestic work and viewed husbands and children as possible obstacles in realizing their life goals. They were especially adamant about the importance of avoiding early pregnancy. Also, the girls were outspoken in their critiques of gender bias in their own families and schools. The math and science enrichment program the girls participated in sent mixed gender messages. The program challenged the idea that science is for men in white lab coats, but at the same time, it featured traditional gendered activities such as quilting, folk medicine, and crafts and did not espouse an openly feminist perspective for fear of alienating families and other community members (Spatig, Parrott, et al. 2001). All that said, I also know that the GRP's very existence was viewed as radical by some in Lincoln County.

"We're intimidating," Shelley once asserted during a discussion of men's reactions to the GRP, "because we're organized." Simple as that. Not surprisingly, Shelley faced some angry reactions to the GRP. "The two most common reactions from men, whether they are boyfriends or dads or brothers, are: one, that we're all lesbians—which is difficult for the girls to deal with because [many] people in Lincoln County are really, really homophobic," she explained. "The [second] thing they say, and this is more common of dads, but I have heard boyfriends say this, is that 'Well, now you think you are better than us.' It's that whole . . . growing or moving beyond your family."

This hits home for me. At a recent family wedding, an extended family member approaches me and asks, "You're the one with the PhD, right?" and I immediately tense up. Strivers—or individuals trying to rise up, move beyond their station—are sometimes looked upon with suspicion. This is a big strand in my small-town, *non*-Appalachian childhood experience. My mother has explained to me that a major difficulty in her own youth was family members telling her that she thought too much of herself—that she was vain. Seeing this as a flaw, she was determined to raise her own children in a way that they wouldn't think too highly of themselves. She was careful not to give my brother and me too much praise. *Don't be arrogant. Don't think too much of yourself.*

I have both internalized and rejected this mind-set. I am quick and generous with praise, and yet one of the qualities I admire most in people is humility. I know it must come at least partially from that upbringing. And I get it: the suspicion and mistrust of higher education, experts, and, in some cases, professionals, in poor, rural areas is often a way of expressing personal and community pride. *I'm fine the way I am. I don't need to be like you, with your fancy degree. I am a part of the community here, and I am not above or better than anyone else.*

John O'Brien experienced something similar in his own West Virginia family. After the dinner plates were cleared, his father would often give the kids long lectures about the values he believed were crucial for them to hold. "Ultimately his message was: Keep your head and expectations down, and you might slip by unnoticed," remembers O'Brien. "Don't be making too much of yourself in your mind" (2002, 23). This is very Appalachian—and I suspect very small-town America generally. In a way, changing or "bettering" yourself is choosing to put distance between you and others in the local community. In this sense it is an arrogant breaking of connections with family and community. *She's so superior now. She thinks she's better than us.*

This has recently been documented among low-income white students who worry about high achievement in school, fearing that it will estrange them from students who view them as "attempting to assume the characteristics of the 'other,' especially an air of superiority or arrogance" (Tyson, Darity, and Castellino 2011, 291). Karolyn Tyson and her co-authors refer to this as the "burden of high achievement" (290) and vividly portray how heavy that burden can be for youth who may be ridiculed and isolated.

This is an especially acute problem for women and girls, given that being viewed as superior—or even smart—is often not seen as attractive or feminine. Economist Sylvia Ann Hewlett, for her 2002 book *Creating a Life,* surveyed 1,000 women making more than $55,000 a year. What she found: "The more qualified, the more successful, the higher earning the woman, the less likely it is she has either a partner or a child," she explained in an episode of *60 Minutes* (Leung 2009). "For a man, the reverse is true. The higher earning the man, the more powerful, the more likely it is [that he is married and has children]."

In the same episode, two female graduates of Harvard Business School recounted men's reactions when they revealed what school they attended: "Some guy turns to us and says, 'So what do you guys do?' And we're like, 'Oh, we're students.' 'Oh, great. Well, where?' . . . 'Oh, in Cambridge.' 'Oh, where in Cambridge?' 'Okay, Harvard Business School.' And as soon as you say Harvard Business School, or even Harvard, they turn around. I mean, that's the end of that conversation." *Now you think you are better than us,* say the GRP girls' boyfriends and fathers.

And "you're all just lesbians" is, of course, not a serious accusation about the sexual orientation of every GRP member. It is a statement intended to be an insult in a time when LGBT (lesbian, gay, bisexual, transgender) issues have become a major focus in both urban and rural communities—including those in Appalachia such as Berea, Kentucky, where LGBT harassment was documented in Silas House's play "This Is My Heart for You" (2012). In this context, accusations about sexual orientation, or any other controversial issue, can be a serious problem for a community organization. This has been true historically as well. Thomas Kiffmeyer (1998) explains how local county power structures threatened by the activities of the Appalachian Volunteers in the sixties launched intense smear campaigns labeling the group as outsiders and communist. In John Gaventa's (1980) terminology, they engaged in the "mobilization of bias" against communism as a way to defeat the group.

There is no evidence of a similar organized campaign to label the GRP a "lesbian group" and thus discredit it. But the first time the girls came to a workshop on the Marshall University campus, they were harassed by people calling them lesbians on their bus ride to the campus. The girls told me about the incident in a joking manner, but I sensed that it bothered them more than they wanted to let on—and I imagine similar concerns kept some girls from participating in the group at all. For GRP girls who actually are lesbian, the story is even more complicated.

Valerie, the first girl to my knowledge to openly identify as lesbian in the GRP, was met with mixed reactions. She said other girls in the program were "cool about it," but added that "they're like, not really totally one hundred percent [accepting] of it, because it's new to them." In her opinion, staff members ranged from somewhat uncomfortable to very supportive, yet she still felt isolated.

"I'm labeled as GRP's lesbian," Valerie said in an interview, very matter-of-factly.

"If you had a friend at Guyan Valley [her high school] . . . who was struggling with coming out, would you recommend them to GRP?" the interviewer asked.

"No," responded Valerie unequivocally. "Because there's not enough support there, because like none of the staff know how it is. So I'd tell them, go online [and] get you a support group." Her recommendation may be related to the small, rural nature of the context. As Layne learned in earlier research on lesbian, gay, bisexual, and transgender West Virginians, some perceived small, rural settings as more discriminatory than larger West Virginia towns and cities (Amerikaner 2005).

Valerie's recommendation also may be related to the fact that the GRP was only for girls. Some worry that gender-segregated organizations and activities run the risk of strengthening rigid gender categories. Additionally, the questions explored in chapter 1 about what it means to be a girl are applicable here. How does the presence of queer girls, especially transgender girls, complicate this simple divide? As an alternative, more "gender-inclusive" (Connell 1998, 220) approaches encourage youth to think outside traditional gender possibilities, to consider the "variety and complexity of positioning" available to human beings (Spatig 2005), and to explore behavior considered incorrect for their sex.

Despite the fact that the majority of girls did not identify as lesbians (and none, as far as we know, as bisexual or transgender), the stereotype of the GRP persisted. And despite reactions from some men in the community, the program remained girls-only—though an off-shoot Boys' Resiliency Program came into being later, which we will explore in chapter 5. A GRP brochure, written by the girls, explained the girls-only setup this way: "Girls are more likely to be open about their thoughts and ideas if the room has only girls in it."

And valuing girls' thoughts was central to Shelley's vision of the program. "We give a message every day that women are valuable, and I think that that makes them start to question some of the things they were taught to believe about women and what they are supposed to do." She went on to connect this to challenging sexism: "So if a woman is valuable, then why does she necessarily have to defer to a man and why does she have to cook dinner? So when . . . girls are at a place where they can talk about what their values are, whether they are consistent with what they've been brought up to believe, or different, or changing though this experience, then it's much easier to deal with." Indeed, other long-term research with girls has found that "girls *do* have critical insight about how things work within patriarchal societies" and can articulate those insights (Hoskins and Artz 2004, 6).

Intimidating women. Valued women.

MOTHER SHELLEY

"But how do you separate your work life from your home life?" a member of my research teams asks Shelley over tea one afternoon.

"I don't," she laughs. "I don't! And some people will say that's such a bad thing . . . but I don't think so." She pauses and then explains: "I mean, I think . . . the girls see that this is not a job, that this is much more than that—because you know, that's the kind of relationship I have with them and that's the kind of relationship I want with them."

Given her years of fierce devotion to the girls, I am finding it hard to write a chapter about Shelley that could possibly encompass every role she has played, everything she has meant in the GRP story. One description that surfaced again and again in conversations with girls was the idea of Shelley as a mother. "It's like a mother away from your mother with Shelley," one of the girls said in an interview. "She really lets you know the rules, and then she's like another mother, like she cares a lot about the kids. . . . I can sense it."

During a weekend trip, a research team member witnessed a dramatic example of Shelley's "mothering." A sixteen-year-old participant was having a heated confrontation with her husband. He threatened to have Child Protective Services take their daughter away from her before speeding away in his pickup truck. A clip from her field notes: *Shelley walked over to K and immediately asked, "What's wrong?" and then hugged her. They spoke softly, Shelley saying at one point, "He can't take your baby away from you" as she kept her arm around K's shoulders. I was relieved by Shelley's reaction, and found her statement . . . reassuring. The man seemed so sure of himself; it was hard not to believe him.* In this case, Shelley's strong assurance was comforting even to the bystander.

Researchers Barton Hirsch, Jennifer Roffman, et al., in their work with girls in the Boys and Girls Club of America, noted how frequently girls used words like *home* and *family* when talking about the organization. "Yet, little attention has been paid as to what the term *home* means to urban girls and what the significance and conceptualization of a home-place is for them," they point out. "Can the creation of a home-place be linked to the development of valued self in adolescence? . . . What are the elements that make a setting feel like a valued home, and what are the ways in which these elements can be figured into the design of successful youth programs and organizations?" (2000, 214–15).

I have wondered the same for the rural girls in this story. The GRP is "like one big family, a great big [family] to help you and support you," explained one of the girls. What made the GRP feel like a valued home, Shelley feel like a mother—and what is the importance of these ideas for youth development work with girls? Based on my experiences with the program, I know that the girls have a somewhat idealized understanding of family related to support, strong bonds, and unconditional love. One talked about the personal importance to her that, despite occasional mood swings, Shelley doesn't dismiss or give up on the girls when the going gets rough. "I mean, she has her bad days and her good days," the girl shared. "[But] she shows us respect even when she's upset about something; she [won't] just come right out and say, 'Well, you girls are just dumb.'" Shelley, like Ric—and like a parental figure—was in it for the long haul.

In contrast, some of the girls' real parents did seem to give up on them. Ashley, featured in chapter 7, and her younger sister were left on their own when Ashley was in the eighth grade. The two girls were in foster care through the rest of their school years. In other cases, parents remained in the home but seemed to give up on the girls in other ways, discouraging them from pursuing opportunities ranging from playing on a school sports team to going to college. In fact, we learned that the girls' relationships with their moms—and other influential women—were key factors in whether the girls graduated from high school and went to college.

Another issue the girls stressed was confidentiality. Like a family, they trusted the other girls and staff members enough to talk openly about even very personal issues. One girl put it this way: "I used to not, like, speak my mind or anything. But now I do, because in the group it's supposed to be confidential. What's said in the group stays in the group. But, like, if a girl does not come to one of the things we do, she's not to know about anything that [was said]." Another girl expressed a similarly high level of trust in the group: "I can go and tell them about how I feel. . . . I know I can trust them." Shelley's insistence on confidentiality created an environment where adolescent girls would speak their minds—and this is no small feat. As we learned from Carol Gilligan's research with girls (starting in 1982), adolescence often means a crisis of voice for girls, a time when many experience a loss of confidence in speaking about who they are or what they think.

Shelley is truly a tough cookie, which is one of the reasons she was so effective at this work. O'Brien called his mother "the family metal," and I can't help but think of passionate, strong, driven Shelley Gaines in the same terms. "History has made women from the Appalachian Mountains determined survivors," O'Brien writes (2002, 18) —which is probably also true in other poor, hard-living contexts.

Determined survivors. Shelley, in fact, was so determined that I was a little worried in the early years that the growth resulting from her nearly single-handed, Wonder Woman–like way of "doing" community—with new grants continually rolling in, new programs starting up in new schools, the number of girls expanding dramatically by the year—would ultimately be unsustainable. But I am getting ahead of myself. For now we are focusing on the early years; we are growing, painting, writing, traveling, interning, rafting, and learning. Shelley is drinking tea and putting into eloquent prose her vision for the program.

"How would you like to impact the girls' lives?" asks the interviewer as they are winding down, though acknowledging that this is a very big question.

"I guess I hope that they . . . have more information, that they would have relationships with people that are sustained beyond the life of the program, and that they would have skills that they use in a real way," Shelley pauses. "And that the box they have drawn, that all women have to fit in, is at least a thousand times bigger than when they started."

TERESA.

*The Girls Have More to Say Than
They Thought They Did*

THOSE PEOPLE WILL BE DEAD

When I met her, twelve-year-old Teresa was far from a boisterous, assertive adolescent girl.

One of the first and youngest members of the Girls' Resiliency Program, Teresa initially came across as quiet, defensive, and withdrawn. She had a short stature and thick, shoulder-length brown hair that she almost seemed to hide behind. My graduate student who first interviewed Teresa in 1999 returned defeated: "She [Teresa] sat in the chair with her arms folded across her chest for the first portion of the interview," my student wrote in a note attached to the transcript. "She kept trying to answer 'I don't know,' even on simple questions.... I felt like I was a failure at this interview."

Rereading the transcript ten years later, I am struck by the pessimism of a girl in an age category known for being wildly idealistic. (As a qualitative research professor, I am also surprised to see so many closed questions that could be answered with one or two words—but it *was* one of my student's first interviews.) A telling moment from their conversation:

> INTERVIEWER: Can you see yourself changing where you live? Can you see yourself making a difference?
>
> TERESA: Huh uh [no].
>
> INTERVIEWER: How come?
>
> TERESA: People around, I mean, they stay drunk and stuff all the time. I mean, they don't listen—especially to a little kid.
>
> INTERVIEWER: Then you don't think that you could change it?
>
> TERESA: No.
>
> INTERVIEWER: Not even when you get older and you are not a little kid anymore?
>
> TERESA: Those people will be dead.

After she had been in the GRP for three years, we interviewed Teresa again. Bubbly, outgoing, feisty, and confident, it is not an overstatement to say that Teresa was not the same girl.

We asked how she would describe herself nowadays. "I'm smart," she said immediately. "And sometimes I have a good attitude, sometimes I don't. I always remind people of things. I always put in my ideas." A few minutes later, she described herself as the "teacher's pet" and told us confidently that everyone liked her. As to her relationship with other girls in the program, Teresa painted herself as a leader. Many of the other girls, she said, "tell me to tell Shelley everything. I'm their messenger. 'Have any questions? Tell me!' . . . Seems like she [Shelley] looks more to us—the second- and third- and fourth-year girls—to be a good role model for the first-year girls. . . . Everybody comes to me and asks me stuff." Indeed, for the rest of her time in the program, I remember Teresa as a positive, reliable presence—and as someone who was quick to crack a joke.

Although some of this is most likely the result of becoming older and more mature, Teresa credits the GRP—especially working as a research intern—with helping her "[find] her voice":

> I've learned that I've changed. A lot. When I first got into the program ... well actually it was whenever I first became a research intern. That was when I was twelve and everybody else was like sixteen, seventeen—they were all older than me, and I finally found my voice. I was little, sweet, and innocent; nobody would listen to me. And I had to say yes to whatever they said, and one day I just got mad and told them what I thought, and it's just been ever since then.

> INTERVIEWER: Ever since then what?

> TERESA: Well, I changed. I just tell people what I think about stuff, about discussion meetings, about like the work and stuff like that. Instead of me just saying "mm hmm, whatever you say" ... I actually give out my opinion. . . . [And] I've learned how to stand up and talk in front of an audience, like I've learned not to be shy. So, I've learned a lot actually.

I call it the Teresa Transformation. It happened with many girls involved in the GRP throughout the years, yet Teresa's transformation stands out as particularly dramatic in my mind: a complete shift from silenced to vocal. From withdrawn to expressive and engaged. From believing that her opinion couldn't matter to believing that it does. Teresa stayed with the GRP all the way until the end, becoming a VISTA volunteer with the program after she graduated from high school. Even today she marvels at the strong voice she developed in her years with the GRP. After reading a draft copy of this chapter, Teresa told me in a note that she wished she could still be the "feisty girl" she was back then.

Shelley identified girls' "find[ing] their voice" as a key program goal, as a way to push the boundaries of the "girl box"—and from that perspective, the GRP is an unequivocal success story. "I want them to learn to find their voice, and use their voice," Shelley said. "And use it often, and be loud."

But what does it mean for girls to find their voices? In the 1980s and early 1990s, feminist psychologist Carol Gilligan famously raised the issue of voice as a result of her groundbreaking research featuring interviews with adolescent girls and women (1982). Yet voice is a tricky concept because it can mean different things. Does it mean to speak up, *literally,* in classes, meetings, and other group settings? To express opinions? To possess the ability to create change? To be listened to? Hadar Ma'ayan notes that in feminist research, voice is understood to be the "the opposite of silence and refers to taking up space" (2012, 10). This has often been studied in a classroom context (e.g., Fine and Weis 2003). In her famous essay "Those Loud Black Girls," Signithia Fordham describes black girls' resistance, in the form of "loudness," against the norm of passive silence—perceived to be associated with white womanhood—in schools (1993). In a similar vein, bell hooks notes that although silence may be the dominant experience for women in primarily white communities, this is not the case in some communities of color. Unlike the voices of black men in the church, which hooks describes as being valued, "the voices of black women—giving orders, making threats, fussing—could be tuned out, could become a kind of background music, audible but not acknowledged as significant speech" (1989, 6). She pointed out that for some women, the problem is not found in their own silence but instead in the process of "talking to ears that do not hear you" (6).

Thus, the concept of voice has to do with speaking but can extend beyond that to experiences of being heard, being valued, or having authority. Based on a large study of women of different ages, ethnicities, social class, and educational backgrounds, Mary Belenky and her coauthors give a good summary of their own transformed understanding of the concept:

> In describing their lives, women commonly talked about voice and silence: "speaking up," "speaking out," "being silenced," "not being heard," . . . and so on in an endless variety of connotations all having to do with sense of mind, self-worth, and feelings of isolation from or connection to others. We found that women repeatedly used the metaphor of voice to depict their intellectual and ethical development;

The Girls Have More to Say Than They Thought They Did   51 and that the development of a sense of voice, mind, and self were intricately intertwined. (1986, 18)

An interrelated development of voice, mind, and self. This makes sense to me, especially in light of the way the girls in the GRP talked about voice—for them, what they said was connected to who they were. One girl related her developing public speaking ability and her willingness to speak in meetings to her vision of herself as a leader: "I didn't think I'd ever get in front of over thirty people and give a speech, and I've done that over the summer. And talked to them—like, I never could talk to adults, like the [school] superintendent or anything, and I've done that. And I felt good about it. I was nervous at first, and then the more I talked, the better."

Another girl said that it was a chain effect. Once one girl starts speaking up, then others follow suit: "I learned, like, from other girls, not to be afraid to speak. I've learned by watching them, that the more you keep inside and don't let it out and tell, that your opinion isn't going to be heard and nobody is going to care. So that's what I've learned—to speak my mind about whatever it is." A third gave an example of how she used her voice—and used it loud—in a way that was life-changing for her family:

> Of course my step-dad, he never did like it much. After I started to speak my mind about things, then I wouldn't let him push me over and tell me what to do and stuff. He didn't like that. And then—my mom. She was always real sick, and for almost three years she didn't even hardly get out of bed. . . . I think that was one of the best days of my life. I was fifteen, and I said, "You get up out of that bed right now!" . . . She got out of bed. The first time she actually walked through the whole house in about three years! So I think that she really likes that they [the people in the GRP] helped me with that.

But how exactly did the GRP help her develop this capability? It is one thing to say, "these girls changed," and another to explore why and how this happened so that we can make use of it in other settings. Barton Hirsch hit the nail on the head when he wrote that "if the term *voice* is expanded to include a variety of aspects of the self that girls need to express, then [organizations] can provide a safe place for this expression via different activities as well as a general atmosphere where girls' opinions are listened to and valued" (Hirsch et al. 2000, 221). Likewise, in the GRP we found that the single most important factor in bringing out girls' voices is the presence of an environment where those voices are taken seriously.

There is also a question of what kinds of messages are sent to girls about their voices in the first place. In her influential book *Schoolgirls: Young Women, Self-Esteem, and the Confidence Gap*—based on interviews with public-school students of diverse ethnicities, class positions, and family structures—journalist Peggy Orenstein discusses a conversation she over-hears between two girls in which "cute" and "sweet" are understood to be equivalent to "passive" or "deferential." In the exchange, one girl declares that the other is too sweet to be a lawyer when she's older, as no one would take her seriously. Orenstein notes the pressure to be the "good girl: the girl who is nice before she is anything else—before she is vigorous, bright, even before she is honest'" (1995, 35). The pressures of being a "good girl" can affect what kind of voice a girl believes she can or should use, or even her career goals. Over all this cultural noise, it can be hard for girls to figure out who they are and what they have to say.

Brett Blake, based on an in-depth study of pre-adolescent Latina and African American girls in an urban classroom, writes that girls pick up on this pressure and develop certain "strategies" in response: "Most girls do not (and do not know how to) express voices of their own. Rather, they incorporate learned strategies such as muting their voices, silencing their voices, and/or doubling their voices for different contexts and for differ-ent audiences" (1997, 29). Speak up, but not too loudly. Express yourself, but don't make anyone mad in the process. Rachel Simmons aptly notes: "Our culture has girls playing a perverse game of Twister, pushing and tangling themselves into increasingly strained, unnatural positions. We are telling girls to be bold and timid, voracious and slight, sexual and demure. . . . In a culture that cannot decide who it wants them to be, girls are being asked to become the sum of our confusion" (2011, 157–58). Sim-mons later describes a girls' leadership workshop for twenty teenagers of various racial backgrounds. In a group discussion where girls shared their concerns about being leaders, the overwhelming sentiment was anxiety about how others would react to their words or actions. "Like the girl who will not say why she is angry because she is afraid of losing her friend," Simmons reflected, "the workshop participants predicted similar relational loss if they acted as leaders" (361). In other words, the message seemed to be that nice girls don't push the edges of the "girl box."

The Girls Have More to Say Than They Thought They Did   53

This is magnified when you factor in other obstacles facing the GRP girls as young, rural, and low-income Appalachians. Shelley pinpointed this area for growth early on, recalling that "it took an entire year to get girls to say what they wanted to do for a fun activity." I found the same reticence in our early research data. Our first-year interview transcripts with the girls overflow with "I don't knows." Hirsch found the same in his study of Boys and Girls Club of America: "Girls, themselves, often have little experience or skill in articulating their desires with powerful adults. . . . Often, simply asking is not enough to elicit genuine voice, or any voice at all" (2000, 223). Likewise, Wendy Luttrell, in her 2003 study of a North Carolina school program for pregnant teens—who were mostly low-income and African American—found it difficult to get girls to open up in interviews. She turned instead to arts activities, which seemed to be more comfortable ways for the girls to express themselves.

Once you do get girls to express opinions, though, are they taken seriously? As both bell hooks and Teresa point out, even when girls *are* speaking, they are not always heard. *They don't listen—especially to a little kid,* Teresa complained in her first interview. If they are not heard—if their input is not taken seriously—then they learn to stop speaking out.

A former GRP staff member spoke about the difficulty, despite best intentions, of honoring girls' input. "I think that yes, the program is girl-driven . . . [but] I think that the staff has, you know, a lot of control also. It's not purely girl-driven. Girls are not organizing themselves. . . . I mean, girls give the ideas and then staff does it." Other researchers have noted this tension in programs that intend to be youth-driven. In Jessica Taft's studies of girl activists across the Americas, she found that youth in these organizations often had "very strong positions about the need for adults to step back and let teenagers lead their own organizations" (2011, 187). "Girl activists want adults to treat them as equal partners," she wrote, "rather than future leaders, ignorant children, or exceptional icons" (190). Yet even when a youth program makes a conscious attempt to value girls' voices, it does not always result in a true shift in approach (Brown 2009). For their part, adult staff also experience uncertainty and frustration with their own roles in youth-driven organizations. A former GRP staff member gave an example of an activity that had to be carried out even though many of the girls had lost interest:

Poetry is something that not a lot of girls came to this year. . . . I can understand both sides. As a staff working with the budget and everything, I mean, having that money and telling grant people that we are going to spend this money on writing poetry and we are going to produce a calendar—that's something we have to fulfill. . . . But at the same time . . . we asked girls, "Why are you not coming to poetry?" and . . . a lot of them said it was boring. That they didn't like doing poetry; they were tired of it.

Despite the tensions here, our research showed the GRP to be a place where, on the whole, girls' voices were listened to and valued—a factor that undoubtedly played a major role in the Teresa Transformations of so many of the girls involved.

MORE TO SAY THAN
THEY THOUGHT THEY DID

One way girls "found their voices" was through the arts. Luttrell (2003) found in her work with pregnant teenagers that they were enthusiastic about portraying themselves and their experiences through collages and theatrical skits. Despite the ambiguous response to the poetry workshops mentioned above, for the most part girls in the GRP loved the creative arts programs. Beyond the poetry-writing workshops facilitated by a local poet, the girls also did a series of songwriting workshops coordinated by a local musician and directed and performed a play by a local playwright about sexual harassment in high school.

In the introduction to the book *She Say, He Say: Urban Girls Write Their Lives,* educator, writer, and activist William Ayers reflects about the importance of writing workshops with a group of ten-year-old, poor, inner-city girls, and I am struck by the similarity of outcomes. "As the participants begin to see themselves as the major actors and stars in their own stories, writing becomes linked to choice and action, intentionality and agency in their own lives," wrote Ayers. "A story is crafted; a life is storied. The teacher's message is this: you can write your story, and you can also author your own life" (1997, x). Similarly, Maisha T. Winn found in her work with incarcerated and formerly incarcerated girls that the arts were a way for youth to represent their experiences. Girls who had faced so many obstacles in their lives were able to create and perform new possibilities for themselves beyond their current situations. Winn calls this kind of work "a performance of possibilities"—or public performances as "metaphors for young people to make bold declarations about their current lives, historicized lives, and possible futures" (2011, 124). In the same vein, Michelle Fine calls them performances of "life in the subjunctive," or life as it should or might be for girls (afterword to Winn 2011, 145).

The GRP poetry and songwriting workshops were both opportunities to explore new art forms and also powerful vehicles for self-expression for the girls—a place where their point of view mattered. The workshops enabled them to share even their most personal concerns, fears, insights, and questions. The following poem, written by one of the girls, is an exploration of the struggle to establish a positive self-concept and the relationship between identity and pain:

Sadness

How do you show to yourself that you're someone and not a nobody?

How do you make the pain go away, when you're always in it?
And if the pain did go away, would you be happy?

How do you love someone if you don't think you love yourself?

How do you make the pain go away, when you're always in it?
And if the pain did go away, would you be happy?

There's so much pain, anger, and sadness in me.

Is there any way out,
any way to make it go away so I won't have to?

So much pain, anger, and sadness.

So please help me before it's too late.

By Jenny Porter

Originally published in *Talkin' to Myself: Poems and Stories from the Girls' Resiliency Program*

Talkin'

to Myself

Poems and Stories from the
Girls' Resiliency Program
of
Lincoln County

GRP staff members spoke about the importance to adolescent girls of expressing pain or painful experiences through the arts. Shelley identified one of the major goals of the arts projects as "dismantling their isolation—you know, feeling like they are the only people who've had [a certain] experience, which to me is really important. Because I feel like a lot of issues that are, quote, 'women's issues' are compounded by silence," she paused. "And so I think teaching girls to speak about them, first with a group of supportive peers but then just generally, I think is really powerful both as a deterrent in terms of those other things happening to them, but also just to say, you know, to this local community that *this is what our lives are like.*"

A more public forum for the girls to express what their lives are like was through the writing and recording of an original CD. Ron Sowell, musical director for *Mountain Stage* (a popular radio show on Public Radio International), met Shelley at a workshop where she asked if he would be interested in leading a series of songwriting sessions with the girls. An accomplished musician, Ron has a warm and casual demeanor—an online bio notes that "he has the gift to make a thousand people in a concert hall feel like they are sitting in his living room"—that encouraged the girls to open up to him in the writing process.

The workshops, some of which included as many as thirty girls, "end[ed] up being almost like group therapy sessions," Ron reflected. "It continually amazes me. . . . . We'll give them a wide array of options of what to write about, and inevitably they end up tackling the most—the deepest and hardest issues. School violence, you know, drugs, pregnancy . . . problems with parents—parental abuse and miscommunications." *This is what our lives are like.* One girl wrote a song about her struggle with anorexia, while another wrote about the death of her father. Ron noted that although at times a girl would be writing "from a third person [perspective] . . . you could tell she was writing about herself—about her dad coming home and drinking and beating her mom, and yelling at her." Despite initial cautiousness and skepticism, over the course of a nearly two-year project, the girls learned to trust Ron. They gradually believed that "whatever they said, I wasn't going to make fun of them," he said, adding, "which, unfortunately, happens [to them] a lot." According to other research, this sense of trust is crucial. As Mellinee Lesley notes, based on research with twenty-four "at-risk" middle school girls, "adolescent girls need to feel a level of trust with peers and teachers in order to develop as writers. They need to feel safe to make mistakes and learn how to address mistakes" (2012, 39–40).

Ultimately, the songwriting workshops resulted in two complete, studio-recorded CDs, *Deep Down Inside* and *I Want a World*—CDs that became a great source of pride for the girls involved. Girls from the program participated in every step, including the cover art design and liner notes. "It [the arts], like, makes us feel like we are leaders—makes me feel like that," one girl shared. "'Because I didn't think I'd ever be able to write a song or anything like that, and it's making me feel good." Another girl agreed: "And just reading those songs and singing those songs, they really make you feel—I don't know how to explain it. They make you feel good inside because it explains everything about yourself, you know, and how you feel about it, and just lets it all flow out.... [It] lifts you up." *And rightfully so,* I think to myself, relistening to the tracks. *These songs are impressive.* As Ron put it, "I think that they realize that they have more to say than they thought they did." About the constancy of friendship. About the shame of poverty and the kindness of strangers. About having an attitude!

from "No Matter What":

When you need money she'll help you pay
When you are lost together you'll find a way
She'll believe you when you're falsely accused
And when you're crying she'll cry with you
No matter what, no matter what
A friend will be there no matter what
You can share all your secrets, your most private thoughts
'cuz she won't betray you no matter what.

from "Not Every Angel":

Standing in the Family Dollar between the crayons and the jeans
Next to the teddy bears and costumes for Halloween.
I can smell the scented candles, the perfume and the soap.
Kids play in the aisles, country music on the radio.

The school supplies looked pretty sad, nothing much left this late.
It's just as well—we can't afford them anyway.
You know, Mom and Dad don't have much money, so what can
   you do?
But I feel so ashamed, I don't even want to go to school.
Then suddenly there she was talking to my mom.
She handed her something and then she was gone.
Just a kind-looking stranger, she didn't leave her name,
But we bought all the things we needed with the money that she gave.
An angel watches over you, there always by your side.
When you are in trouble, they'll be your friend and your guide.
They might not come from heaven, play the harp and sing,
They might be a stranger or someone you know. Not every
   angel has wings.

from "I Got an Attitude":

You think that I'm bossy
You think that I'm rude
It's how I need to be
I'm just in a mood
I take care of myself
I can't depend on you
I'm watching my back
I got an attitude

The process was transformative not only for the girls, but also for Ron. "I just thought I was going to go out and have fun and write a few songs, and it would be interesting, but I've really gotten involved with these girls and really gotten very attached to them." He shared one experience in particular that made him feel that his effort had been worthwhile: "One of the girls came to me last session and . . . pulled me aside and said, 'Oh, I'm writing my own song.' . . . She said, 'I'm having a lot of problems with my parents right now. . . . Every time we have an argument I go and put it in my song.' . . . So that makes me feel real good that I've helped her find a way to express her feelings."

GRP CDs with original cover art

Transformation is a big theme here, but it was not only the girls who were changing. In a number of ways, the girls were changing Lincoln County. Despite Teresa's initial pessimistic view that by the time she was old enough to do anything, the decision makers would all be dead, the girls tackled some tough community problems.

The idea of summer research internships was born as Shelley and I sat talking in my office about my own research on the GRP's work. "Can the girls help?" she asked brightly. I was caught off guard, but intrigued. "With the research? Well, I've never done anything like that before," I stammered, pausing. "But, um, maybe we could put something together."

What we put together was a form of Participatory Action Research (PAR) similar to what has been used in service learning projects in schools and in other organizations such as the Summer Youth Research Institute (SYRI) in Hartford, Connecticut. Like the SYRI, our goal was to involve the girls in thinking critically about their community and in doing research on community issues that concern them—in other words, in doing "research to make a difference" (Morgan et al. 2004, 1). Along the same lines, the International Planned Parenthood Federation's (IPPF) toolkit, "Explore: Ideas for Youth Involvement in Research," is based on research conducted by youth on sexual and reproductive health. The young people were involved as researchers, rather than research subjects (International Planned Parenthood Federation 2008, 3). The IPPF undertook the youth action research project based on a belief that young people should be seen as a "force for change rather than simply recipients of products from programmes" and that "young people themselves are experts on youth issues and how young people live their lives, and therefore they should be seen as stakeholders with valuable insights" (2008, 4).

Already committed to the idea of youth as a "force for change" and as "experts on youth issues," Shelley obtained a grant from the Ms. Foundation that enabled the GRP to hire six girls to conduct research during the summer of 1999. For many of them, it was their first job and an exciting opportunity. "It made me feel so good about myself knowing that someone is willing to give me a chance," one girl reflected. "It just made me feel good that I have a job—a real job to put down on a piece of paper for a reference now. . . . I was really excited. I told everyone. . . . Especially the money part made me feel good, that I'm going to be able to buy my own [things]."

In a series of summer workshops at Marshall University, I introduced the GRP girls to the distinction between quantitative and qualitative methods and to observation and interviewing techniques. The workshops featured activities designed to encourage personally meaningful understandings, rather than official academic definitions, of research. In the first workshop girls did a free association exercise and a "draw a scientist" activity where they expressed their feelings and prior knowledge about science and research. Field notes from one of my graduate students:

> Once these descriptions of a mad scientist were introduced they began to discuss stereotypes and how we can fall into the pattern of believing stereotypes. [Linda] asked, "What are some stereotypes of women?" The girls said, "Staying in the kitchen," "taking care of the house and kids." Then they were asked to think of stereotypes of people in their geographic area. They said, "hicks," "barefoot," "bad teeth," and "that they're stupid." They discussed how stereotypes can be hurtful and wrong. Linda pointed out that lots of different people do research and are scientists—women, men, people of all different races.

The training sessions were designed to engage the girls in all aspects of the research process—including selecting a topic, generating research questions, collecting and analyzing data, and disseminating findings. In the session on participating as an observer, for example, girls took turns acting out scenes while the others watched and wrote field notes. Each dramatization was followed by a discussion about what the girls observed, how they interpreted it, and what they wrote in their notes.

The training sessions culminated in the girls designing their own small-group action research projects. Like those involved in the SYRI program in Connecticut, the GRP research interns identified problems they saw as important in the local community. In some cases, they also had personal interest in issues that affected them and their peers. For example, three girls were concerned about Lincoln County children who had been mistreated in their foster families:

It is serious enough to where [we] want to learn about it because, I mean, it can be really horrible sometimes for some children. Some children might get a bad foster parent—they just do it for the money; they don't care about the child. . . . I have been trying to talk my mom into [taking a foster child] because I'm an only child that's living at my house.

Another research topic the girls had a personal stake in was sexual harassment. "I think the sexual harassment is the biggest problem, because the cops were at the school yesterday over it," said one girl. She recounted a story about parents protesting at the school because of the principal's failure to take action when a female student reported harassment from a male student. The interviewer asks if *she* ever felt harassed at school. "Yep," the girl responded. "Like when you walk guys will say 'nice butt' and stuff like that. Sometimes . . . girls will walk by and they'll say, 'I smell a slut.' Like that happened to me the other day because I was with one of my friends. . . . I just don't like them saying that to me."

Once each group had identified a research topic and formulated a question, they set off to do research with people in their schools and communities. In order to receive permission to implement the research in their schools, they presented their ideas to the superintendent of the county school system. For one girl, this was also a learning experience: "I learned how to speak out to people in meetings and stuff. . . . Like then we went to the superintendent, I talked to her . . . [about] our surveys in the school."

As the following field note excerpt illustrates, the interns used research expertise gained in their university training workshops to design their studies:

Shelley began by asking them what their [question] was. The girls said, "How do people in Lincoln County feel about foster care?" Shelley asked the group as a whole, "What kind of research is this?" The unanimous response was, "Qualitative research." Shelley asked, "Why is this qualitative?" A few people answered at once, "Because it's feelings; . . . it's asking how do people feel." Shelley said, "Okay, and what [data collection] method will you guys be using?" M said, "Interviews." Shelley asked them, "Who are you going to interview?" Someone said, "People." Shelley said, "You've got to be more specific."

This led to a discussion about who they were going to interview. . . . I believe it was M who finally said, "One professional, one child, and one foster parent." Shelley said, "Okay, now how are we going to get these people?"

After a lengthy discussion of the possibilities, the girls decided to use personal contacts to locate individuals to interview. Even so, finding interviewees was not easy. One girl explained, "There's not very many foster parents that's willing to talk."

Despite hurdles in locating interviewees and, as a result, completing the projects on the original timeline, interns learned a great deal about the topics they studied and how that knowledge could be helpful to them individually as well as to the broader community:

> I actually learned where you can go [if you're abused]. [If] I get in a relationship with someone that is abusing me, I know where I can turn. I can educate other people outside the group. I mean, I can educate . . . women out in Lincoln County . . . that there are places, people willing to help. So it makes me feel good inside that I'm actually being able to help others.

The girls also reported feeling empowered to take action on community issues—they had a new belief that their actions mattered. "I think I could change the community," one girl said, and pointed to her research internship as the key factor that had encouraged this belief. Based on the success of the pilot, we coordinated another group of research interns the following summer.

Teresa was one of the only girls to participate both years. "I'm loving this stuff," she said. "I'm learning new things every year. . . . When I get older, I might want to try to do something like this." In her interview, Teresa highlighted an unforeseen result of the research project—the use of a tape recorder for demanding accountability. In a world where girls are used to snide or belittling remarks, it can be a powerful tool for showing others that *this is what our lives are like.*

With a smile, Teresa recalled an encounter with her school principal: "I went down there [to the principal's office] to change my schedule. He said, 'Why do you want to change your schedule?' and I got mad. . . .

He'll jump all over me. But I'll just have to take a tape recorder and say, 'Come on! Say something mean to me!'"

And that's a lot of attitude from a girl who sat mute, arms crossed, for much of our first interview. Teresa, transformed.

CASSI.

"They Will Make You Eat That."
Or, Tales of New Experiences and Adventure

A "B" IN GYM DOESN'T COUNT,
ANYWAY

Cassi Adkins, an extremely conscientious and organized student, made only two "Bs" in high school: tenth-grade gym class and twelfth-grade civics. Smiley faces, A+'s, and notes of "excellent work" cover her tests and papers. A self-portrait collage she created includes cut-out magazine snippets of the phrases *follow your passion, vibrant, sisterhood,* and *best.* Cassi's self-description on her MySpace account reads simply: "If you're happy and you know it . . . *clapping.*" Cassi has a bright smile and writes with many, many exclamation marks.

As you can imagine, it's pretty hard not to like Cassi. She is a devoted friend, and has described herself more than once as "one-fourth me, one-fourth Sara [her close friend], one-fourth Jennifer [her close friend], and one-fourth Timmy [her boyfriend]." Petite in stature, Cassi frequently wore her waist-length, blondish-brown hair in a single braid. In focus group interviews—many of which began as formal interviews and devolved into prom-planning, storytelling, or gossiping sessions—Cassi showed explicit concern for the interviewer (usually LeAnne, a former graduate student of mine). *Are you getting what you need? What was your question again?* Sensitive to group dynamics and generous with smiles and laughter, Cassi appears to be the glue whose bright spirit holds her friends together. In fact, one of the only times she got in trouble at school was in order to care for a friend: "My friend . . . was crying, and I got up to give her a hug while Ms. J was gone. I got up out of my seat, and I got in trouble for that. I didn't understand why I couldn't hug my friend who was crying!"

Cassi's family lives "way out in the boonies," which means she had to wake up at 5:30 A.M. to catch her bus to high school. Their home is on a one-lane paved road deep into the hollers of the county where her dad was raised. Nearby, on a parallel road, Cassi's grandparents live in a double-wide trailer. Cassi's mom, whom she calls Super Mom, has worked a series of customer service jobs in restaurants, hardware stores, and bars. In Cassi's words, her mom "hates it with a passion, but she does it for us." Cassi's dad is an auto mechanic with an equally demanding work schedule. Because both parents had to be at work for long hours, Cassi found herself babysitting her younger siblings after school and during the summer months. One of Cassi's teachers explained that she primarily got to and from her remotely located house by school bus. "Once she got on the bus and went to the holler, she didn't come out until it was time to get back on the bus," she said. When another teacher inquired about her summer plans, Cassi replied that she would probably be babysitting every day. "Cassi is stuck up in the holler with the kids," her teacher reflected. "I hate that for her." The first teacher speculated that if Cassi had been a son, her parents may not have expected her to babysit: "If she were a boy, she would probably have her a big truck and be able to go and run and do." Cassi noted that it was unlikely that either she or her brother would ever have had a truck of their own because her family was poor (her word).

Unlike Teresa, who was one of the first GRP girls in the late 1990s, Cassi and her friends were some of the last girls to enter the program.

Joining in 2005 as an eighth grader, Cassi jumped into community service projects, anti–school consolidation activism, out-of-town trips, and—her favorite—pottery classes. But by the time she graduated from high school in 2009, the GRP no longer existed. Always relationship-oriented, Cassi said wistfully in a 2010 interview that she wished the program were still around for her little sister. "It'd be good for her," she nodded, adding that the GRP gave girls opportunities that weren't available to them anywhere else in Lincoln County. As a sophomore this year at Marshall University, Cassi is the first in her immediate family to go to college. Cassi's mom, though a strong supporter of her daughter's moving on to college, was torn about a step that she feared would take Cassi out of their county. As Cassi explained, "Mom doesn't want me to go, but she wants me to go and do something and be somebody." *We want you to be happy. We don't know if it can be here. I love it. I'll leave it someday.*

HUNGRY FOR AN US

Cassi's self-description as equal parts Sara, Jennifer, Timmy, and herself underscores psychologist Mary Pipher's belief that "with girls this age, relationships are everything. No work can be done in the absence of mutual affection and regard" (1994, 254). For Cassi, her self-identity is literally built on her relationships. In a girl world stereotypically characterized by cattiness (think Rachel McAdams in *Mean Girls*), the GRP with its genuinely supportive relationships is a refreshing alternative model. A number of researchers focusing on girls' programs have noted that overcoming assumptions about "mean girls" is an integral part of their work. Maisha T. Winn (2011) explained that in a program called Girl Time that works with incarcerated youth, many "girls had learned to loathe the company of other girls before their incarceration (which was only exacerbated in detention); they embraced an ideology that females were not to be trusted and could never want the best for you. Dismantling this deep-seated belief was hard work" (135). Similarly, Jessica Taft found in her study of girl activists that a notion of "girl solidarity" seemed nearly impossible against a backdrop of cultural assumptions about girls' competitive, back-stabbing relationships. Taft found that even the girl activists some-times expressed beliefs that girls were too accustomed to distrusting each other to work together on organizing (2011, 85). Clearly, there is much work to be done still.

In the case of the GRP, I can say with certainty that personal rela-tionships were key to the success of the program—as is the case in much positive youth development work. As Michael Resnick (2000) notes, many studies have demonstrated the protective value of nonfamily, adult rela-tionships for young people. In other words, positive, supportive relationships with one or more teachers, parents' friends, neighbors, youth organization staff, and so on can reduce the likelihood of teenagers engaging in self-destructive or risky behavior and increase the likelihood they will engage in constructive, beneficial behavior. Dana Mitra found that to be true in her study of two school-based programs designed to increase student voice. She reports that "the connection to a caring adult proved to be the stron-gest developmental influence . . . for students" (2004, 670).

These connections are especially important in the context of cur-rent societal views about relationships between adolescents and adults. According to Jean Rhodes, those of us living in Western cultures such as the United States tend to have a "blind spot," or a "cultural ambivalence" about such relationships—increasingly moving toward a view that parents are "solely responsible for their children" and regarding youth involve-ment with other adults as unnecessary, even suspicious (2004, 157). Further, Linda Camino and Shepherd Zeldin argue that US adults tend to hold relatively negative views about adolescents generally, seeing them as a "source of worry or threat, not potential" (2002, 214). Perhaps these views are a reason that many individuals report having no important nonfam-ily adult relationships during their youth (Camino and Zeldin 2002, 214). And of course, these kinds of connections with adults are critical for young people in less than ideal family situations.

Many girls came to the GRP with strained family relationships. Some girls were encouraged by parents to fight with their peers, rarely received parental recognition for their strengths and achievements, and some received little attention of any kind—good or bad—from their par-ents. One girl in the GRP who was a good friend of Cassi's, Ashley, had almost no relationship with her parents during her adolescence. With a father in jail and a mother who came home only occasionally, and usually just to drop off groceries, Ashley—our heroine in chapter 7—began raising her baby sister when she was only twelve years old herself. "I left the back door open. . . . so if Mom would ever want to come in, she could go through the back door. But she never did. She never came home," Ashley recalls. "I remember staying up until five in the morning, calling her and crying and leaving her messages: 'Get home!' . . . I mean, it was really stressful for me." Other girls described similarly absent parents, while still others described scenes of serious intimate partner violence between parents, stepparents, or foster parents. *This is what our lives are like.*

School relationships also tended to be hard for many of the girls. They described teachers who showed favoritism toward preppy students, treated other students disrespectfully, and were "always out to get you." One girl was locked in bathrooms and had to eat alone in the principal's office for protection from other students' harassment. In light of such problematic relationships at home and school, the GRP provided an important opportunity to develop strong relationships with both adults and peers. For some girls, the relationships they found in the GRP were among the only stable ones in their lives.

The success the program experienced in terms of fostering healthy relationships in the lives of participating girls can be attributed largely to the effort of the women who directed the program. In the words of Pat Macpherson and Michelle Fine, young women are "hungry for an us"— actively looking for connections with supportive women (1995). Jessica, the GRP's second full-time staff member and the woman who helped Shelley lead the program for several of its early years, agreed, reflecting that "they learn about relationships from us. I think it's that whole role modeling thing and it's . . . having a different kind of experience, having a [different kind of] relationship with a person than they've probably ever had." Jessica believed that this kind of modeling helps the girls, on a visceral level, in "learning to trust somebody, learning to be open, learning to be loved, to care about another person. . . . I think being heard and being listened to—I think those are the . . . things that really make a difference." This desire for caring connections with adults—the hunger for an us—may hold true for all youth. Writing about after-school programs for youth of all genders, Jean Rhodes says that caring youth-adult relationships are "the critical ingredient. . . .

Through consistently warm and accepting interactions [with adult staff], youth can begin to recognize the potential that exists in close relationships and open themselves up to the people around them" (2004, 145, 151).

Shelley and Jessica certainly modeled positive relationships in their interactions with each other. The closeness between the two women—and the general community-minded spirit that often prevails in West Virginia—comes to life in one of my favorite field-note clips of the project. Here, we are sitting in a board meeting:

> Jessica and Shelley work very well together. Sometimes Shelley passes Rebecca [Shelley's baby] off to Jessica without even saying a word. At the beginning of the board meeting, Shelley introduced the agenda, handed Rebecca to Jessica, and continued with the agenda items without ever missing a beat. She didn't even take a break from talking. Jessica did not seem the least bit surprised that one minute she was listening to Shelley speak, and the next minute she was comforting a small baby! . . . It's almost as if they sense when and how they can help each other.

Beyond close relationships between staff, girls came back again and again to *their* relationships with staff members as what made participation in the GRP meaningful. One girl contrasted Shelley's and Jessica's feelings—that they care "about what you do in life"—with her perception that even most girls' family members "don't care what their kids do." Another girl said she was closer to Shelley than to her mother. A third said that Shelley and Irene, a staff member featured in chapter 5, were there for her when her mother was sick and her father wasn't around: "They helped me. They did just about everything for me. I mean, everything that I've learned, I learned from the group . . . and the way I think about it, if I hadn't been in Shelley's group, then I don't know where I'd be. I'd be lost."

During her time with the program, Cassi had a particularly meaningful relationship with an adult—a pottery teacher who was a periodic, part-time GRP staff member. For her college admission essay, Cassi wrote a beautiful reflection on the impact her relationship with the pottery instructor, as well as learning the skill of pottery, had on her sense of self. Given our emphasis on listening to what girls have to say—and on girls speaking for themselves—I include it here in its entirety:

I was perched on my stool in front of the potter's wheel with my legs propped up to anchor my elbows. The clay rose and fell in my hands; turning and spinning with the wheel. What would it be? A bowl or an ashtray? Or will it go the extra mile and become that perfect vase? I bring up the walls of the clay, seeing it in my mind's eye. It would be me.

I have accomplished many things in my life. I maintained a high GPA, became a member of the National Society for High School Scholars, the National Honor Society, and even placed first in the county for the Young Writer's competition. Coming from a background of high school graduate parents, and drop-out relatives, I strived for success in academics. I wanted to make my mother proud and show that the Adkins descendants are not the unintelligent, backwoods people like we have been portrayed. Not even the members of my family believed we had what it takes. I can still see my grandmother sitting on the porch, looking out at my five-year-old brother and sighing. The look on her face was not one of sadness, but of reluctant acceptance. She looked over at me and said, "He's gonna turn out like the rest of them. He's gonna drop out and become nothing." It was then that I chose not only to make my mother proud, but to set a good example for my brother. So I did. I excelled at everything I tried. Everything, that is, except art.

Art was one of the most impossible tasks I had ever faced. No matter what I tried, I failed. I could not draw or paint to save my life. I hung my head in shame as I walked down the hallway where my rudimentary stick figures hung in between breathtaking landscapes and stunning dragons. It wasn't until eighth grade that I found I had another option. Through the Girls' Resiliency Program, I was introduced to pottery and the woman who would change the artist in me.

I watched my teacher in utter fascination. She centered the ball of clay in seconds, the walls rose before my eyes, and before I could blink she had created a beautiful bowl. I was in awe. I had never seen anything like it before. I knew this was the art for me. It was nothing like the class I had taken in school. As time went on, I began to separate pottery from art. Art was frustration and heartbreak. Pottery was freedom and joy.

Patricia Hubbard-Ragette is the reason I have excelled in pottery. I attribute all of my passion and longing for this art to her patience and understanding. When I sat at the wheel, she helped me understand that I had to brace my elbows. When we discovered that my legs are simply too short to accomplish this, she helped me to scour the room for a foot stool. If my walls were off center, she would simply point it out and guide me in the right direction. She was a coach, a critic, and a friend. This amazing woman did to me what she did to that lump of clay four years ago. She centered me, putting me on the right track. She brought up my walls, making me stand higher and stronger. Finally she shaped me into this extraordinary and confident person. Without her, I never would have made that perfect vase. I never would have unearthed the person I wanted my brother to see.

Beyond the close relationship with Patricia, Cassi was also inspired by her Aunt Rose—a nurse, whom Cassi looks to as a role model in her own career path—and her "Super Mom." As a somewhat introverted personality who spent countless hours with family, Cassi had a very close relationship with her mom. Cassi remembers, for example, how hard it was to say good-bye to her mom on the first day of kindergarten. She recalls refusing to sit in any seat other than the one her mom had been seated in when she dropped Cassi off that day. Possibly more so than her peers in the program, Cassi had already found comfort and strength in her connections with older, supportive women before even entering the program.

TALKING BACK

William Ayers, an educator and activist, argues that good teachers don't just listen to students—they "talk back" (1997, xii). Always in the context of a supportive and loving relationship, Shelley certainly did her share of talking back to the girls. In discussions, Shelley raised questions, offered ideas, and on occasion, directly challenged girls' thinking. From discussion group field notes:

Shelley discussed why parents may have rules, to protect kids from the world. To this, L replied, "My mom really don't care." Shelley said, "Yes, she does." But L said, "No, she don't." Shelley then said that when L's mom gives her rules to follow, that's a way of showing that she cares. L then began to relate a story about her brother having his gun taken away for three months because he used it while his mother wasn't home, and seemed to think that maybe her mom cared a little.

In addition to these more structured discussions, many girls talked about how much they valued being able to talk with Shelley individually about problems in their lives. Often these talks happened on lengthy car rides to and from GRP events. When a girl asked to be picked up first or dropped off last, Shelley knew the girl wanted an opportunity to speak with her one-on-one. One girl described several instances when Shelley came to her house to pick her up and talk when she was having trouble at home. "It helps," the girl said.

I was always impressed with Shelley's ability to create and navigate relationships with the girls that were both challenging and nurturing. It was a form of highly effective personal guidance similar to John Gottman's "emotion coaching" (2001). According to Jean Rhodes, such coaching involves adults who "model and teach strategies for managing feelings, including learning to approach negative experiences as opportunities for intimacy, learning, and personal growth" (2004, 151). One girl's description of the way Shelley led her to find and implement her own solutions to a crisis is illustrative: "The other day when we was having a conflict [about] one of the girls' ex-boyfriends, and she was crying a lot and we called Shelley and one of the girls goes, 'Shelley, we can't handle this.' . . . And Shelley goes, 'Well, this is what you can do. Sit down and talk to her.'" Shelley then incorporated the girls' own solutions. "And she [Shelley] goes, 'Do you have any ideas?' And we came up with some ideas that the group could do and that's what our decision was and that's what we did, and it worked out." The same girl noted that she appreciates that GRP staff members "don't tell you to go out and do this. They lead you to your own answers." The GRP girls' experiences support Rhodes's argument about the importance of "meaningful conversations" between staff and youth (2004, 152).

Rhodes points out that in the context of trusting relationships, these kinds of adult-youth conversations help teens "acquire and refine new thinking skills" (2004, 152). Put another way, such youth–adult relationships and interactions "scaffold" youth understandings of emotional and social processes. They serve as a support system—not unlike physical scaffolding in a building project—that enables young people to move from one level of knowledge and understanding to a higher one. To be effective, the scaffolding must occur in what the influential psychologist Lev Vygotsky called the youth's "zone of proximal development" (1978, 86). This is the place where there is a readiness to grow or learn, where tasks that a young person is unable to accomplish on her own *can* be accomplished with guidance from adults or more advanced peers. This certainly seemed to be the case for Cassi as she learned pottery with Patricia's support and instruction.

Of course, these kinds of trusting, close relationships—enabling adults to know a young person well enough to identify her zone of proximal development—require a huge investment of time. Researcher Barton Hirsch noted in his own work on youth programming that "not having enough time each day to form bonds with girls, or not working at a site long enough for those bonds to develop fully, can have negative repercussions for girls" (Hirsch et al. 2000, 220). GRP staff understood this and made an extraordinary effort both to spend one-on-one time with each girl and to be available to them twenty-four hours a day. As the program grew to include more girls in later years, this critical goal was hard to maintain. One staff member wistfully remembered home visits in the early years, when she was "just sitting and chatting, and not worrying about what time it is and how long we're there, and who's next, and how many people can I see today." She added that if she could change the program in some way, she would "do more of that, because, I mean, I think it helps. Because some girls—you find [out] stuff at their home that they wouldn't tell you at discussion meetings or at some workshop or something."

THESE ARE JUST GIRLS

The encouragement of thoughtful and independent decision making influenced the girls' relationships with each other, even when Shelley and other GRP staff were not around. Reading the following interview transcript, I was blown away by the maturity and leadership shown by the girls in defusing an argument between peers:

> GIRL: We have a girl with us right now that keeps going on and on about her ex-boyfriend. And we [confronted her] . . . and she got mad at us and turned red in the face and everything. We said we didn't mean to be rude. And we had to sit down and talk; there was no other way about it. We've got a problem and we worked it out. We're just too good of friends. We all sat down in just a big group, and I said, "This is what we're going to do: we're each going to say our piece, and then we're going to say we're sorry for being so rude." And we all did that and it worked out fine.

> INTERVIEWER: Was Shelley there?

> GIRL: No, we took it upon ourselves.

> INTERVIEWER: Really?

> GIRL: We have learned that we can't hold Shelley up and make her do it all. We've learned to rely on ourselves.

This example illustrates several of the five Cs of positive youth development discussed in chapter 2. The girls' positive experiences *connecting* with adult staff who provided guidance and coaching, rather than direction, enhanced the girls' social *competence* (interpersonal skills such as conflict resolution) and their *confidence* in themselves individually and collectively. These results did not happen after an afternoon PowerPoint seminar on "leadership development." These were deeply personal, gradual changes in the way girls interacted with each other and the world. *We had to sit down and talk; there was no other way about it.* One girl explained that this way of interacting was in stark contrast to the way many of her peers outside of the program interacted, never taking "time to . . . really get to know you, to understand your feelings and stuff." She went on to say that in the GRP, "everybody listens and they give you time to explain why you feel, you know, why you believe that way. . . . In the group we can talk [about] whatever we want and people wouldn't tease [about] what you are talking about. Like, if you believe one way . . . they wouldn't put you down because of it."

I don't mean to present the girls in the program as some sort of superwomen or as girls with extraordinary interpersonal abilities. At heart, these are just teenagers. One of the youngest members of our research team—a graduate student who looked only slightly older than the girls themselves—captured a moment in her field notes of the girls just kicking back between song recordings at the CD studio:

> They were talking about guys, which somehow led to a discussion about cute guys. . . . K jumped in and said, "Sisco's hot as shit!" Then a couple of the girls proceeded to describe a video where Sisco [a singer] is dancing in the dark and his hair and clothes glow because of a black light. This led to a mild argument over Sisco and his hair, whether it was white or blonde. (Girls break into the chorus of a Sisco song and dance around the room.) . . . Then the girls asked me who I thought was the cutest guy in the world. I told them that I thought the hottest guy was Bruce Willis. The girls all started laughing. R and M were making gagging noises. All I could hear was "GGGGGRooooossss." M said, "He's old! And he's bald!" The other girls chimed in, "Yeah, he's old and bald!"

Girls in the program were not only supportive and problem solving in their peer relationships but also comfortable enough with each other to just be silly. As LeAnne, a heroine in chapter 6 and a former doctoral student of mine, said of Cassi and the other fun-loving, playful girls early in her dissertation research: "I don't know what I was expecting, but these are just girls—like I was." We tend to underestimate the importance of play in the lives of adolescent girls. Based on a study of a school program for pregnant teens, Wendy Luttrell makes a strong case for the "transformative power of play" (2003, 179). From her research with the pregnant girls, she learned that play can provide "a protected space of moral and creative reflection that is increasingly at risk of disappearing in our contemporary culture and education" (2003, xviii). Clearly, challenging the "girl box" doesn't always have to be serious business.

THEY *WILL* MAKE YOU EAT THAT

Beyond personal relationships, other keys to the success of the GRP were the built-in and ongoing opportunities for new, challenging experiences. For some girls, this was the defining characteristic of the program. In explaining how she would describe the GRP to a friend who had never heard of it, Teresa summed it up with the following: "We go to new places and try new things. We eat new things, and believe me: they will make you do it! Like the last day of work, they're taking us out to eat, and we have to try new things. And I've tried a thousand new things." We saw this process unfold for Cassi, for whom art was a challenging and frustrating endeavor given her past "failures" with it. In the context of the supportive relationship and constructive guidance she got from Patty, however, she conquered that fear and accomplished a great deal.

In some cases, girls were fearful about the new experiences. One girl commented that she was "scared to death" when she went white-water rafting for the first time with the GRP. But for most, their fear came out during an annual ropes course.

"What's the hardest thing about being in the program?" an interviewer asked one of the girls.

"Oh, the ropes course," the girl responded, not missing a beat. "You have to trust people you don't even know. There's this trust wall up there—it's really high—there's a ladder you climb up on it and you, like, act like you have a penny in your butt, and you squeeze it and then you hold your hands crossways on your chest, and you fall. You're stiff, and you fall back and they have to catch you. That is hard to trust somebody that you don't even know." Other girls also identified falling backwards off the ledge as the hardest part of the program. One girl was so afraid of it that she considered quitting the entire program to avoid it. Another was terrified to rappel off an eighty-foot wall: "When I went up on the eighty-foot, I cried. I got so scared when I got to the top."

A poem by former GRP member, Kimi, captures the stifling, immobilizing experience of fear and the difficulty of overcoming it:

Fear

Fear can prevent you from doing a lot.
You could possibly conquer it.
But if you're afraid of everything,
it's hard.

If you're afraid of people,
it's hard to make friends.
If you're afraid of dancing,
it's hard to perform.

If you're afraid to talk,
it's hard to be heard.
If you're afraid of rejection,
it's hard to let your feelings be known.

It's easier to hide,
when you're so afraid.
All I want is to just conquer my fears,
yet I still seem to run away.

Fear can make you stressed out.
Fear can make you sick.
It's amazing that all of this can happen
in just one week.

by Kimi Meade

Originally published in the Girls' Resiliency Program
2005 Calendar

Knowing how fears could trap girls in the "girl box," Shelley and
other staff members responded to the girls' fears with understanding, reas-
surance, and encouragement—but also firmness. As one girl put it: "They
take you to new places and [say], 'Do you want to do this?' If you say
no, they would be like, 'It won't hurt you.' And then certain things they

talk you into it. They make you feel good about yourself." Despite initial fears, girls valued being challenged and the bonding that came with facing scary experiences together. They accomplished genuinely hard tasks and came away with a stronger sense of themselves and what they could do. Girls appreciated being confronted with problems that reflected high expectations. The girl who had cried at the top of the eighty-foot wall said later in an interview that she was "glad I did it" and happy she could prove her brother wrong—he had said she wouldn't be able to do it.

One staff member explained the "soooo important" lesson she has learned about expectations from working at the GRP:

> C stayed with me for a while when she was pregnant, and my mom knew about it because she would call me and C would be at my house. And so Mom knew she was having a baby and that her family wasn't involved. And she was like, "Gosh, I feel so sorry for her," . . . but I don't feel sorry. . . . I don't think of them as like "oh, I feel sorry for girls" or feel like they're, you know, victims or anything like that. . . . You have to have the same expectations for all—you have to set high expectations for these girls. . . . In a lot of ways, nobody sets expectations for them. They don't have expectations for themselves, and their families don't have expectations, or if they do, they are lower than what they should be—and then they've got teachers who are like . . . "Well this is so and so and she's not going to graduate— she's just going to have a baby, and why do we even try?"

The violence of low expectations. Many researchers and writers have highlighted this as a major strike against women of all races, men of color, and low-income people, and it was certainly true for these girls as well. Tammy Schilling pinpointed low expectations at school as a damaging factor in the long-term study of Tasha, a young woman of color identified as being "at-risk": "It is possible that Tasha's experiences in school actually reinforced her insecurities, as research has shown that schools reproduce social inequalities and send strong messages regarding the worth of poor and working-class youth of color" (2008, 303–4). Coming from low-income families, many GRP girls faced similarly low expectations at school. One friend of Cassi's recalled: "When I was in fifth grade, we did reading on the computer, in English and Reading. I scored ninth grade [level]. My teacher was announcing the name of who scored the highest, and everyone like pointed to the smartest guy in the class. [But] it was me. And I was like, '*What?*' " Despite being a voracious reader, her school's expectations—and even her own—had led everyone to assume that she couldn't possibly have scored the highest on a reading test. The "girl box," again rearing its ugly head.

As damaging as low expectations can be, the flip side is the huge potential benefit of high expectations through challenging activities. Psychologist Larry Brendtro and child and family services expert Mark Strother write that "when adventure experiences are skillfully managed, students meet growth needs and build resilience. . . . As students develop their talents within a supportive environment, each failure is viewed as a learning experience; each success kindles the motivation for mastery" (2007, 5). The same holds true with other kinds of activities, as elementary school teacher Ron Berger discovered. Working in a school culture that instilled an "ethic of excellence," he encouraged students to do "beautiful work" and to "care deeply about the quality of what they did" (2003, 4)—whether writing a descriptive essay, preparing slides from research on amphibians, or designing a blueprint for a new house. Yes, elementary school kids actually accomplished those things. In Berger's view, expecting youth to do "work of excellence is transformational" (8). For the GRP girls, that was certainly true.

As GRP members, girls whose teachers saw them as "at risk" students did extraordinary work that changed both themselves and the community. In 2001 they designed and created a large, permanent mosaic mural on the wall of a prominent building in Lincoln County. That same year they opened a coffeehouse in building space adjacent to the GRP office. To save money and give the shop a trendy look, the girls refurbished wooden electrical spools as tables, covering each tabletop with beautiful, handmade ceramic mosaics. The coffeehouse also featured the work of local artisans, including many GRP members. Girls worked behind the counter, serving coffee, tea, and snacks to community members who stopped by. On my first visit, I sipped hot tea and picked out colorful beaded earrings—a pair for each of my daughters. I remember being impressed that teenage girls had opened, and were successfully running, a coffeehouse.

GIRLS CAN'T BUILD HOUSES

Or can they? The girls in the program also volunteered for a multitude of community service projects, some of which were pretty ambitious. They visited hospitals and nursing homes, cleaned up lakes and parks, volunteered at shelters, tutored younger children, helped organize and run a teen center, and—perhaps most impressively—constructed an all-girl-built Habitat for Humanity house. Would the girls have participated in so much community service had they not joined the Girls' Resiliency Program? According to one girl, "probably not, because I wouldn't have known about it. . . . There was nobody to ask if we would want to volunteer to do things." Another agreed: "I've learned a lot. . . . I used to not do community service until I got into the group. . . . I used not to care about others that much until I got in the group."

I heard over and over how much girls loved the community service projects. One girl spoke proudly about how they constructed a Habitat for Humanity house despite the skepticism of their male peers: "Well the *guys*, they were trying to say, 'y'all can't build a house!' and stuff like that." The interviewer asked her how it made her feel to participate in that community service. "I feel good that I can drywall!" the girl laughed. "That's hard work! I put the holes in the wrong place and went through the other side a few times, but finally I got the hang of it."

Some of the appeal in working on community service projects was that the girls were used to being treated as if they were on the other end of that chain—that they themselves were in need of help. "I think they should drop the 'at-risk,'" Teresa said strongly in one of her later interviews. "What am I 'at risk' of? Taking drugs and killing myself or something?" When *they* were doing community service—tutoring young children, cleaning up their county, visiting isolated, elderly folks—they were not "at-risk"; they were the ones helping. They were the agents of change, not the receivers of help. Teresa's rejection of the "at-risk" label is an important reminder about grounding research and community programs in the perceptions and identifications of the youth themselves. Mellinee Lesley writes that "'at-risk' as a label has been denounced for contributing to images of feckless children and adolescents lacking in any sense of self-control or agency. Often missing from discussions of the label 'at-risk' is the resilience of students contending with social settings and school policies that serve to inhibit their learning" (Lesley 2012, 27).

Community service is a model that has worked well in other youth development programming. Kurt Hahn, the founder of Outward Bound, "believed that modern youth suffer from the misery of unimportance and need to be committed to some demanding cause beyond themselves" (Brendtro and Strother 2007, 5). Father Chris Riley, from Australia-based Youth Off the Streets, sent former "street kids" across Eastern Europe and Asia to work with families living in dumps, orphanages, or war-torn areas. "Such life events," write youth development specialists Brendtro and Strother, "cause them to look at the world through fresh eyes, think more clearly, reach out to others, and put their abundant energies to constructive use" (2007, 5). Further, Marianne Kugler notes that youth programs that feature ongoing, long-term community service projects, rather than one-time events, are particularly effective (Kugler 2001). Many of the GRP's service projects fit this criterion, continuing over a period of weeks, months, or even years. This work is also directly related to the Cs of positive youth development. Based on a large-scale, longitudinal study of youth in 4-H programs, Richard Lerner and his coauthors (2005) talk about *contribution to community* as a possible sixth C. They posit that the other five Cs (*competence, confidence, connection, character,* and *compassion*) are linked to the likelihood that a young person will engage constructively in a community.

According to our own research, community contribution (or service) also lessens the social stigma of being a member of a youth development organization. "Some of the students at school, like when we got called out of class for this meeting . . . some of them think it is like for people who are, like, dumb and need help. Some people make fun of us," one girl shared. *What do you tell them?* the interviewer wanted to know. "I just tell them, I tell them what we do, we do fun stuff and we do, like, community stuff." Because community service clubs are an established, well-known type of organization—think Girl Scouts, YSAs (Youth Service America), and religious youth groups—framing the group's work in this way made some of the girls feel it would be more acceptable to skeptical peers.

Service activities were also a key way in which the girls became leaders—organizing, working as a team, and speaking in public. Our observation of a workshop on conflict resolution for younger 4-H campers is illustrative. Two girls, L and R, with Shelley's help, planned and implemented two back-to-back workshop sessions for campers. In the first session, Shelley led the activities with L and R assisting her. In the second session, the girls took the lead, starting right from the beginning with a warm-up activity. A clip from the reflective part of that day's field notes:

> R and L seemed to bloom during this game . . . smiling often, helping with the other children, and I got the feeling they were having a lot of fun. . . . R started off speaking softly, but soon was using a clear, pleasant tone and was very well-spoken. The group responded very well to her direction and personality and seemed to have a good time. . . . I was impressed by the fact that L was leading kids who were older than she. Not only did she do it well, but the kids responded very favorably to her as a leader.

The girls also remember the community service projects as good times. One girl wrote a piece for her speech class on volunteerism, drawing primarily from her experiences in the GRP. "When I was thirteen, I helped paint the inside of the old coffeehouse building. And that same year, we went on a camping trip. It was fun! It was a sleepover, and we also cleaned up the lake. We cleaned out like fifty garbage bags full of trash." Despite the rustic living conditions, she recalls it with a smile: "I remember the girls were sleeping in this old trailer that didn't have electricity, but it was still fun."

US GIRLS HAVE AN OPINION ABOUT THAT

In Shelley's mind, community service was a first step toward the larger, but more elusive, goal of getting girls involved in social activism. She saw that as another important component of challenging the "girl box," believing that the program should involve both individual empowerment and community engagement, including critique and resistance. Jessica Taft notes that there is a big difference between community service and social justice activism: "Youth civic engagement programs, as they have developed since the late 1980s and early 1990s, primarily aim to involve young people in formal, state-based politics and/or conventional civil society activities, especially volunteering," she writes. These programs, however, do not typically feature dissident political activism (Taft 2011, 37). Though Shelley had envisioned a program that featured both community service and social activism, she perceived that the girls lacked interest in the latter. "Social change justice happened more because of me, rather than the girls, because I don't think girls here are political at all—have any notion at all about social change or even community service. . . .We have to meet them where they are, and where they are is they don't have a clue," she recalled. At the beginning, Shelley had girls pick between different service projects that might be meaningful for them. Having them choose was, in her mind, "a way to get them to say, 'oh, well, you know, I care about the way Lincoln County looks,' or 'oh, I care about, you know, I want to help a single mom repair her house because I understand what that experience is like. I can connect to that and I care about that.'" Respecting the opinions of young people does seem to be related to youth agency in this context. For example, Mitra's study of model school-based programs found that increasing youth voice also increases their agency (2004). Even in these programs, though, moving youth toward critique and change was more difficult than building their competencies in other areas.

Providing opportunities for the girls to be involved in community service and ultimately to view themselves as agents of social change is an approach consistent with recent research on positive youth development (e.g., Ginwright, Cammarota, and Noguera 2005). But the relationship between social change activism and community service or Lerner's "community contribution" is complicated. Lerner defines "youth contribution" as youth having a desire to "give back to the world around them" and as engaging in activities such as "being leader of a group, helping friends and neighbors, helping in sports activities, participating in school government and religious youth groups, volunteering in the community, and mentoring and tutoring others" (Lerner et al. 2005, 54). Although this definition captures GRP community service activities such as cleaning the lake and building a Habitat house, it doesn't captures the kind of political stance involved in the social justice activism Shelley had in mind.

Like Shelley, Jessica Taft distinguishes between girls' empowerment programs and girls' activism. As it is currently understood, she writes, "Girls' empowerment is all too often focused on incorporating girls into the social order as it stands, rather than empowering them to make any meaningful changes to it" (Taft 2011, 23–24). Whereas activism is focused on changing the *world,* Taft argues, traditional girls' empowerment programs—she offers Girls, Inc., Girl Scouts, and the Nike Foundation as examples—often focus on changing the *girls* and their capacity to deal with social issues, increasing their self-esteem, and/or making "healthy choices" (28–29). This shifts the object of change work to the girls themselves. Although high expectations for girls are critically important, claiming that girls should become empowered and achieve their dreams may be ignoring or downplaying the constraints they face. As one girl Rachel Simmons interviewed explained, "Now that it's all about girls taking initiative and power and stuff, you get all these mixed messages. The media says girls should take control, like Nike ads. . . . The people on TV, they show you these scenarios, but they never show you how life is" (Simmons 2011, 60). Simmons reflected that those of us who work with girls have focused "so fiercely . . . on winning girls the right to dream" that we have neglected the focus on how to create conditions that allow those dreams to become reality. The GRP's design, as Shelley envisioned it, focused both on girls' individual "empowerment" *and* on girls' social justice activism, defying the activism/empowerment dichotomy Taft sets up.

Shelley's vision of social justice activism had a lot in common with what took place in San Francisco's Center for Young Women's Development, where participants who had "lived the effects of oppression, be it gender, sexual orientation, economic, or racial/ethnic" purposefully acted to "change their communities" (Camino and Zeldin 2002, 217). As Shelley explained, however, it was a difficult task to show the girls that they can still have a political voice while they are too young to vote *and* when they have a history of adults not listening to what they have to say. Or in the words of Taft, "Girl activists also share a structural location. As minors, they are excluded political subjects" (9).

In addition to being formally excluded from voting, girls who are politically active are often dismissed as engaging in teenage rebellion (Burg 1998). Even girls themselves don't always have faith in girls' ability to be politically active. The girl activists of diverse racial, ethnic, and national backgrounds that Taft studied often associated superficiality, ignorance, insecurity, and other negative traits with girls, while they associated confidence, knowledge, and caring about others with activists (90). By defining girls and activists as opposites, Taft notes, "they unwittingly reinforce[d] their own gendered marginalization and collective invisibility from the terrain of social movements and social struggle" (91). In other words, they were unintentionally supporting the idea that girls can't be effective activists. This seems to be yet another aspect of the "girl box."

One of the largest "social activism" projects undertaken by the GRP was studying and resisting Lincoln County high school consolidation. The project began as a summer research internship topic, for which girls conducted surveys on community views about the consolidation plan. Based on that research, they wrote newspaper articles and made presentations to school administrators, and later on they organized protests, petition drives, and even mock funerals for the schools that would be "dying." "Well, I thought that it was pretty good, because us girls have an opinion about whether we want our school consolidated or not," Teresa said emphatically during an interview that year. "Because, you know, I mean even though I'm not going to go to that school, I'm still not up for it. I mean, I just don't think of *me*—I think about all the other girls." *Us girls have an opinion about that.*

Of course, the girls experienced the resistance to consolidation, and later, the newly consolidated school itself, in different ways. Whereas Teresa and many of the girls were against it, some—including Cassi—were quick to point out the benefits of a larger school. "Where I have been, and it's like really small; everyone has been the same," one girl said, adding that the diversity at the new school allowed students to embrace different identities. "Now, you have all your goth people, jocks, and the normal boys. Hamlin [smaller, pre-consolidation high school] was more like everyone the same. Then when everyone came here they realized there were more people like themselves. . . . And more people came out of the closet. I was like, 'Oh my god, left and right you would hear about so and so being a lesbian.'"

In order to capture the girls' complex, changing views on consolidation, I constructed the following composite poem based on interview

GRP Anti-Consolidation T-shirt

and document data from the first year of the newly consolidated school. As in the case of the composite poem about Lincoln County, in chapter 1, it consists entirely of the exact words of youth who spoke or wrote about consolidation and the new school. Cassi was a major contributor to this poem and was part of the group of eight young people who performed it for a live audience at Marshall University.

Consolidation

I was against it.
Didn't want to go.

Protest at the capital:
 March to the governor's house,
 "Stop Consolidation" signs,
 "Honk for Shorter Bus Rides."

No matter what I did, how hard I tried . . .
Consolidation.
Lincoln County High School.

I hate it.
This school sucks.
It's a prison, a jailhouse.
They lock those doors.
You can't go outside.

Photo IDs around our necks.
 ID cards are cool;
 My picture looks great!

It's too crowded.
 On the bus,
 Down the hallway,
 In the bathroom.

 Teachers put up with more kids;
 There's no time for big projects.

 Long lunch lines,
 Still stuck sharing lockers.

There were bound to be fights.
 Over basketball,
 Football,
 About girls,
 Boyfriends,
 School rivalries,

Names:
"river rat,"
"lesbian."

We need new teachers.
They don't like us.
Tell our grades out loud.
She called me dumb. I skip her class.

Different people have different privileges.
Teachers like football players,
Basketball players, and wrestlers.
Cheerleaders get away with everything.

Teachers don't care any more.
Some do.
She's a good teacher.
Makes you feel special inside.
I love her.

You can't use the bathrooms cause people smoke.
Only one is open.
They are nasty.
Cigarette butts everywhere—
Like an ashtray.

It's harder.
I've made two F's; never made an F before.
I made an F; I just don't try.
I make a hundred every time; never made a hundred before.

Goths, preps, jocks, nerds, geeks, popular kids.
    We sit at clique tables.
    Guyan Valley people sit with Guyan Valley people.
    I'm in the "leave me alone" group.

Emotional put-downs.

People considered different are the ones put down.

> This kid that's like Special Ed,
> Saying mean stuff to him,
> Picking on him,
> Kicking,
> Calling him names,
> Making fun of him.

Everybody should be treated the way they want to be treated.

Getting more friends,
It's pretty cool.
A lot of new, hot girls!

I was afraid of not having the same friends.

But it's easier to make friends here.
More people, different people.
A new beginning.
I love it.
I'm friends with everybody.

Lincoln County High School
Con-
So-
Li-
Da-
Tion.

A former staff member, who had once been a member of the GRP herself, expressed a strong preference for the community service projects over the anti-consolidation activism work. In her mind, the activism was often an exercise in futility; the community service work, in contrast, was concrete and successful:

> With the consolidation, we did petitions, and we'd [go] to the board meetings saying we didn't like it and stuff like that. But they don't have as much of an effect on me as it would, like, being able to

repair someone's roof because it's leaking and because the roof is going to fall in if somebody doesn't repair it because they don't have money. . . . The girls *want* to do that. Some girls are like, "Well, I don't *care* about consolidation. It's not something I care about. I care about . . . the road having litter . . . or the creek, all the fish and the beavers not having a home because of the garbage and the pollution and stuff like that." And when we did stuff like that, I think we had more people involved than when we do like consolidation. We've had, like, a little small group of girls in there doing the consolidation and stuff like that, but when we had community service you had a vanload of people that wanted to do it. . . . I guess they [the girls] just don't really get anything out of it, you know, "Oh, they're going to consolidate. Who cares, because they already have their decision made and they're going to do it anyway." And so I think it's different with the service because you're *doing* something.

Another girl expressed a similar view, saying that the school consolidation activism was something that adults wanted the girls to do rather than a project of organic interest. At the same time, girls like Teresa—who expressed strong opposition to the consolidation and support for the activism—challenge this type of framing. And, of course, some girls wanted to be involved in *both* community service work and social activism, and did not see them as pitted against each other as an "either/or" in the same way as the staff member quoted above.

For a few of the girls, community activism was already their M.O. Cassi, as only an eleven-year-old sixth grader, led a successful campaign to have the teaching license taken away from a middle school teacher who had sexually harassed her. "It started with a pat on the butt, and he always had me sit in his lap and there were other things. . . . He had problems going way back from when Dad had him in school," she explained. Despite discouragement from her father—"Dad didn't think it was a big deal; he was like, 'He has always done that' "—Cassi's mom "went berserk" and encouraged her to fight back. Cassi remembers how many community members came out to support her, many of whom had been sexually harassed by the same teacher in the past. "Word got out about it, and all the board pulled a meeting. So many people showed up at that meeting, community members and people who had him in the past. They didn't plan on having that many people; they had to get a big old rack of chairs," Cassi recalled, adding, "Mom went and got them."

Despite the challenges of coming from a low-income family, Cassi was raised by a supportive, involved mother. Today, as a student at Marshall University, Cassi is on track to becoming a registered nurse who specializes in obstetrics. "I really wanted to have a good job that helps people," she explained, adding that she had considered becoming a doctor but decided she'd like a job with fewer hours so that she can devote time to a family. Not quite yet, though. At this point, her plan involves having one or two kids at the age of twenty-five. Cassi took pains to point out that she was going to break the family tradition of having children at age nineteen. "All the women had kids at nineteen," she said. "I'm breaking the tradition. I'm getting on as many birth controls [as possible]."

In some ways, Cassi is a girl who had already "found her voice" even before joining the GRP. Still, her experiences in the program helped shape her, in her own words, into the "extraordinary and confident person" she is today.

Self-portrait collage of Cassi, 2009

IRENE.

VIRGINIA.

Girls Take the Lead, but "It's Hard Coming from a Participant to Staff"

HUNTED DOWN BY SHELLEY

At age seventeen, Virginia had that "I don't know" syndrome so common to young women—one of the most severe cases I've ever seen. In one interview, she responded with "I don't know" fifteen times in the course of a four-page transcript.

The interviewer wanted to know how she had changed after five years in the GRP:

> VIRGINIA: I don't know. I really don't know.
>
> INTERVIEWER: You don't know. Are there, like, any words that come to mind?

VIRGINIA: I was really, really shy. I'm still shy now, but not as shy. I mean, I don't know.

Later Virginia described herself as someone who will "speak her mind," thanks to the protection of the confidentiality rule in the GRP, as well as someone who "acts crazy . . . to make people laugh"—suggesting that her shyness dissipates when around close friends. With her easygoing, calm demeanor, Virginia had a gentle presence and a sweet smile that brought out her dimples.

Fair-complected Irene, with her light hair often pulled back in a ponytail, also described herself as becoming less quiet through the GRP: "Before I was in the program, I was shy. Didn't talk much to anybody, didn't really want a lot of friends," she recalled. " 'No use talking to anyone else because nobody cares.' That's how I felt." Irene is now outgoing and talkative. I remember her as a steady, practical "roll up her sleeves" kind of person. Confident without being attention-seeking, Irene was more likely to be found taking a group photo than posing for one. Another researcher described Irene in field notes as "very matter-of-fact, patient . . . easy to talk to, and not easily ruffled." Virginia—at least around researchers—continued to come across as quiet throughout the years, saying little in focus groups and even in one-on-one interviews.

What outspoken Irene and reserved Virginia have in common is that they both were involved with the Girls' Resiliency Program as girl participants for five years and then both became GRP staff members. They were hand-picked and "hunted down" (as Irene put it) by Shelley to work for her after they dropped out of high school. Both earned Board of Education high school diplomas while they were working as staff members. Despite the challenges of girl-to-staff transitions, for those who held the positions and for the GRP itself, both Irene and Virginia loved working with younger girls in the program. As Virginia said, "Working with girls is something . . . I think I'm good at."

BRIEF WORRYING INTERLUDE

Staying true to my commitment to be fully present—a genuine participant—in this collaborative project, I am obliged to admit here that

I spent a lot of time avoiding drafting this chapter. In the early part of the writing, the stories and ideas flowed easily as I described the program's unquestionably successful early years. It was easy to connect what the GRP did so well with outside literature and tales of other flourishing organizations. As we start to get into murkier waters in chapters 5 and 6—where the GRP makes tough decisions rife with internal debate, and, in the end, folds—I find myself suddenly interested in everything but this. Student e-mails need responses. Old articles need to be revised. My office needs to be reorganized. These plants need to be watered, right now. I worry. I avoid.

Laurie Thorp, in the final chapter of her ethnography, *Pull of the Earth*, about an elementary school garden, asked herself: "Dare I write about the failures of these teachers I hold so dear?" (2006, 125). Dare I write—and from the "outside," no less—about the failures of the Girls' Resiliency Program? Dare I disagree with decisions or perspectives of Shelley, Ric, Virginia, Irene, or other staff and board members who have given so much of their lives to working with girls in Lincoln County? Who have been "on call" twenty-four hours a day for years, just to send the message that *someone is always, always here for you*? Dare I do anything but honor their rare, incredible commitment? Our chapter 1 hero, GRP board member Ric MacDowell, sends me a message providing feedback on the first two book chapters. He writes that he thinks the portrayal so far is good, accurate—but points out that we haven't yet gotten to the rough part. He says he is interested to see how we will tell that part of the story. My daughter and I half-joke that we're interested to see, too. In we go.

GIRLS BECOME STAFF

As we saw in chapter 4, relationships between girls and staff were hugely important in the GRP, not unlike the case with other youth development organizations. Jean Rhodes identifies "caring youth-staff relationships" as the "critical ingredient" in after-school youth programs (2004, 145). As Kirk Astroth, Pam Garza, and Barbara Taylor (2004) point out, however, there is general agreement about the importance of quality staff in youth development work, but there is little consensus about what knowledge, skills, and attributes those quality staff members should possess. In response to this lack of consensus in the field, the National Collaboration for Youth (NCY) set up a task force in 2003, which, based on extensive research, developed the following list of core competencies for an entry-level, frontline youth development worker:

1. Understands and applies basic child and adolescent development principles.

2. Communicates and develops positive relationships with youth.

3. Adapts, facilitates, and evaluates age-appropriate activities with and for the group.

4. Respects and honors cultural and human diversity.

5. Involves and empowers youth.

6. Identifies potential risk factors (in a program environment) and takes measures to reduce those risks.

7. Cares for, involves, and works with families and community.

8. Works as part of a team and shows professionalism.

9. Demonstrates the attributes and qualities of a positive role model.

10. Interacts with and relates to youth in ways that support asset building.

(As listed in Astroth, Garza, and Taylor 2004, 31–32)

Since the beginning of the GRP, Shelley had wanted staff positions to ultimately be filled by girls who were once in the program themselves. Astroth, Garza, and Taylor describe a divide where "some advocate professionalizing the field of youth development through college education while others argue . . . vehemently for experience-based training and preparation" (2004, 26). Shelley definitely came down on the side of experience-based preparation. She believed that the girls' life experiences in the local community and their organizational experiences in the GRP were strong qualifications for GRP staff positions.

The idea of having former participants become staff members to increase their ownership of a program is a goal often discussed in the non-profit world, yet one that is surrounded by some tension. Do staff members who were formerly participants feel like "tokens" in organizations staffed primarily by people with more privileged backgrounds? How seriously are these voices taken given our society's deeply ingrained understandings of power, authority, and legitimacy? (In the GRP's case, girls who transitioned into staff positions were definitely *not* treated as "tokens"—in fact, in time they outnumbered those who had not been program participants.) And on the other side, what kind of unique challenges arise when former participants become program deliverers?

Because of the girls' ages, this didn't become possible until 2001, when three of the first former participants (two of whom were Virginia and Irene—the third we have given the pseudonym of Jenny) were hired part-time, and then 2002 when the same three girls were hired full-time. The girls were fresh out of the program, and some were even younger than the oldest girl participants.

Not surprisingly, the girl-to-staff transitions included both successes and struggles. Consistent with Shelley's vision, there were benefits to girls' becoming staff members—the most commonly cited being higher levels of trust and communication in girl/staff relationships, fueled by an increased likelihood that staff members have been through experiences similar to those the girls are facing. "I know how it feels to be in the positions that they are in now . . . family getting divorced . . . sexually molested, sexually harassed . . . because I've been through all that," Irene explained. In this sense, Irene had an edge in meeting the second NCY entry-level youth development worker competency about positive communication and re-lationships with youth. Virginia, however, found that the shared life experiences made it *harder* to know what kind of advice to give. If she didn't know how to fix her problems when she was living through them a few years ago, went her line of reasoning, how would she know how to fix them now? Girls primarily saw the shared experiences as positive: "I think it's a good thing because they [staff who had been girls in the program] have the experience and know what's going on," one girl said. Another agreed: "When the girls become staff, they already know the other girls, like what's going on in their [lives], so they're just more apt to help them."

But it's not just the effect on relationships that motivated Shelley and some of the youth to favor girls filling staff positions. One girl said it is simply that they are the most logical people to do the work, arguing that the fact that they had been in the program meant that "they know what to do and what not to do." Shelley agreed: "They are the best people to do it—they have the experience, and they live in this community." One of her goals for the program was that the girls would view it with a sense of ownership, and in Shelley's mind, "the pinnacle of all that is for them to take over the program."

Shelley felt that another major plus for former girl participants becoming staff was their likelihood of staying in Lincoln County, as compared with more transitory outsiders. "They live in this community, and by George, they're not going anywhere," she said in an interview. "You know, like, they're *here*." My researcher has jotted down a handwritten note in the margin of the interview transcript at this point: *Why? Does this disempower them further? This assumption that they could never leave?* A valid question, yet Shelley saw the issue as less about disempowerment and more about "nurturing what's here and . . . making places for people" here in Lincoln County.

How did these girl-to-staff transitions play out once they left the realm of the theoretical and were acted out by living, breathing people? Irene, according to everyone we interviewed, had *something* about her that made her transition successful. One former staff member said, "There were certain things about Irene that make her right for the job, and I think a lot of it is her personality. . . . She's a driven person with above average intelligence. . . . She has a lot of ambition. . . . Part of it was because she had a lot of confidence about her skills." One girl agreed that "[Irene] is a really good staff member. I think that people look up to her like they do Shelley."

But Irene was only one of three girls who became staff. What happened with the other two? Virginia and Jenny both quit suddenly over one weekend near the end of their first year of work. One striking difference between their situation and Irene's is that Irene took time off—spending a year without any involvement with the GRP after she was a participant; she also took a longer, slower path to becoming a program specialist. By her own choice, she worked first as a part-time assistant, and then for a year as the full-time office manager. Irene explained that when she began she struggled to gain respect from and authority over the girls in the program, some of whom were close to her age. "There were a lot of times that we would go to an activity or discussion meeting, and I'm like, 'We have to get ready or we have to do this,' and they would give me a hard time. And they'd be like, 'whatever' and they'd just start talking or keep talking to their friends," she recalled. "And then when the older staff would come in, they're like, 'Listen up—we're doing this,' and they'd shut up really quick and be into it. And I'm like, 'Why can't I do that?!'"

Despite the fact that Irene made the most "successful" of the three girl-to-staff transitions, even she hit a major roadblock when she tried to move too quickly from being a participant to being a staff member with a lot of contact with girls. She mourned the new responsibility that put her in the awkward position of "ratting out" friends: "Like if you catch your friend smoking, you don't want to tell on her or rat her out or get her sent home from a fun activity or something. If they're having fun and you catch them smoking, you're like, 'Should I tell on them or should I not?'" Irene finally asked if there was anything else she could do, and she and Shelley decided it would be good if she acted as office manager for a year. This helped ease her into a position of authority in the eyes of the girls. According to Irene, the situation evolved into one where, "The girls were always like, 'I like Irene; how come she's not hanging out with us?' And when I finally got out, they wrote in the newsletter, 'They finally let Irene out of the office to do what we want her to do.'"

Irene also had the chance to practice, to "try on" the job of being in a leadership position at one of the high schools—somewhat suddenly— when she began filling in for staff members who quit. She worked with girls at the school, without having to prove herself in the position. She was able to ease into the job, try it on for size, form relationships with the girls, and decide that this was something she was ready to do on a more in-depth and long-term basis—all before she ever had to commit herself to saying that she wanted the job.

Virginia and Jenny did not have such gradual transitions. Instead, they found themselves quickly moving out of their roles as youth participants and into the demanding, highly visible role of program specialist.

This fast role change "ended up hurting a lot of parts of the program," according to a former staff member who believed a step-by-step system might have been helpful—a ladder that a girl would climb on her way to becoming a program specialist or director. She suggested that the first rung might come as a girl in the program took on a title of "contact person" for her high school, who "would do most of the organizing" for that school's GRP activities. That experience then could lead to a volunteer position, then to a paid internship, then to a part-time position, and so on. The former staff member pointed out that "this is nothing new. These are things we've talked about. . . . These are things that could really work." In retrospect, Shelley seemed to agree, saying, "I wish I had allowed for a slower transition for Virginia and [Jenny] because I think that they can do this job. . . . Maybe if the timing had been different."

Even if slower transitions had meant better transitions, girls also had concerns that, in their minds, were not simply about timing. They worried about their friendships. One girl, for example, had been a close friend of Virginia's before she became staff:

> It changed my friend life and everything. You [didn't] know what was friend time and . . . what was staff time. So it was awful. Seemed like I couldn't tell that staff person that was my friend without her telling somebody at the office, even though it was supposed to be like our friend time, and it was supposed to be secret. It was just awful. You couldn't do hardly anything together. . . . [It] took my friend away from me.

On the other end of the friendship, Virginia also felt the strain, noting that it was hard to be a role model constantly and that her position prevented her from partying with her friends when she wanted to. Even Irene struggled with this. "There's stuff I can't do whenever she's at my house," she said, referring to a GRP girl who had moved in with her temporarily—a common occurrence with staff members. She agreed that it was a struggle to draw the line between friendship time and girl time. Overall, she said, "It's weird. . . . I just want to tell everybody [that] it's *hard* coming from a participant to staff."

Several girls expressed a need for maturity in new staff members and a desire to have a voice in the hiring process. "I think the girls should have an input on choosing whoever's going to become staff," one girl said, with another adding: "We don't have a say in who gets hired." Although it is true that girls who were on the board had a vote on hiring—as well as all other decisions—some girls said that even the hiring *process* was a complete mystery to them.

I came away from examining this part of the organization's history believing that two keys to successful participant-to-GRP staff transitions were timing and training. The concerns about friendships surviving such a transition might not have even *been* concerns if the girls had to wait a year or two after graduating from the program before becoming staff members in authority positions over other girls. This might also have helped with the problems Irene encountered in terms of respect and authority with the girls. It probably would have been easier for the girls to see her as a model of success, as someone who had overcome obstacles similar to their own. As Jean Rhodes notes, such role models can make particularly effective youth development staff (2004). Having a structured organizational plan, including more time for "moving up" in the organization and more robust training, may have changed the outcomes as well. Those outcomes—in terms of staff retention—ended primarily in frequent staff turnover, a serious issue for youth-oriented nonprofits.

Although Shelley agreed about the timing issue and was a strong supporter of on-the-job staff training, she was less comfortable with the role of formal education. According to Astroth, Garza, and Taylor, the youth development field is evolving and seems to generally be moving toward more formal professionalism that requires education credentials for staff (2004, 26). This is an issue I discussed with Shelley and Ric relatively early in the project. We were chewing on the question of whether there should be title or salary distinctions between staff with college degrees and those who had been girls in the program and had only a high school or Board of Ed (high school equivalent) diploma. Shelley objected to there being a distinction, arguing that such a distinction would reflect a devaluing of the life experiences the former participants brought to the position. Although I agreed with her about the value of the girls' life experiences, I argued that a staff member with a graduate degree in education had valuable knowledge and skills that deserved recognition and compensation. I pointed out that it was important for the GRP girls to see that there were payoffs for higher education. Indeed, I believe the staff's effectiveness varied in relation to the kinds of competencies they brought to the position. For example, at the ropes course outing in 2004, members of my research team noted the difference between Shelley's interactions with the "red group" (color-coded groups of girls that brought together girls from different schools as well as girls of different ages) and Irene's interactions with the "purple group," and the resulting differences in the depth of girls' reflections on their experiences.

The girls in Irene's purple group seemed to have had a good time and completed all but one of the exercises successfully. Girls who spoke up during the reflections that followed each exercise generally reported the experience as enjoyable. But missing from the reflections was a level of self-awareness—a recognition of how some of the dynamics of the exercises had affected them. For example, whether anybody felt scared or uncomfortable doing an exercise and why, how girls overcame their discomfort (or didn't), who felt unheard or forgotten, who felt included or excluded in the teamwork, and whether teamwork truly was accomplished.

In contrast, when members of Shelley's red group reflected on their final activity of the morning—an exercise that involved girls lifting each other over a string placed about five feet high in a doorway—several girls appeared to have gained a sharp sense of recognition of what they were capable of accomplishing, individually as well as collectively. Girls were able to say, "I felt ___," or "I did ___" in reflecting about the exercise. Some of them talked about the fact that they'd been forced to realize that more was being asked of them in the exercise, that they needed to "step up" to the demands of the exercise and take it (and themselves) seriously. At one point, Shelley stepped into the exercise herself, pushing them to complete it successfully. On the basis of this (granted, limited) observation, it seems that girls in the red group had an opportunity to learn about teamwork and leadership on a different level as a result of Shelley's interactions with them. Although Shelley had more experience and Irene was a much newer staff member, Shelley also has formal training in helping individuals deal with their experiences and emotions. Her education in psychology, plus her years of working with girls, enabled her to "raise the bar" for her group. She was much more demanding than Irene, and the girls rose to the challenge of her high expectations.

Thinking in terms of the NCY competencies list, the formal education that Shelley had received provided her with knowledge about child and adolescent development that was evident in her relationships and work with the girls. Irene and Virginia did not have that kind of knowledge. That said, I do not believe that formal educational credentials are the only way to get such knowledge; it could arguably be obtained without a college degree. Of course, hiring competent youth development staff doesn't make much difference if you can't keep them.

STAFF TURNOVER

It was late on a Friday afternoon of a busy week at the GRP. The plan was for Jenny, Irene, and a third staff member to attend a play at Marshall University as a stress prevention activity for GRP staff. In an ironic unfolding of events, Jenny announced that she did not want to take part in the evening designed to reduce staff members' stress levels. Ultimately, Shelley told her she had to go to the play or else she would not have a job. When Shelley left the office a few minutes later to run an errand, Jenny told the third staff member, her supervisor at the time, that she wasn't going. The staff member said it sounded like Shelley wouldn't let her come back if she didn't go to the play, and Jenny blew up: "I don't give a ****! I quit!"

This is Irene's retelling of the beginning of a weekend that would become a critical moment in the organization's history—a weekend in which two full-time staff members, Jenny and Virginia, resigned without prior notice. The sudden shift would mean a greatly increased workload on the small remaining staff. Irene looks back on that time and recalls that "it just seemed like we were not going to make it through."

From 2002 to 2004, four people were hired as full-time GRP staff, and three of them left the program in those same two years. A few years later, Irene also resigned, followed ultimately by Shelley herself. But in 2004, Shelley was understandably frustrated by the frequent turnover. "Everybody that I've had—when I hired them I felt like they were the right people and that they would stick around. And I even asked those questions, because it really mattered to me that they planned to stick around," she said. "And then for whatever reasons, all these different reasons . . . people aren't here for the long haul, and I think the program and the organization suffers because of that." The GRP was certainly not alone in facing this issue. In a project sponsored by the National Academy of Science, the National Academy of Engineering, the Institute of Medicine, and the National Research Council, Jaqueline Eccles and Jennifer Gootman conducted an extensive analysis of research on youth development programs in the United States. Their report identifies high staff turnover as a major barrier for youth development programs (2002, 268).

Irene, who was office manager at the time of the fateful double-resignation weekend, recalled what the situation was like for her: "In March, when they left, it was like, we needed somebody for the schools, and so I had to . . . say I'll do—I don't know what I'm doing, but I'll do it." Irene had to instantly change roles in the program, but even those who remained with the same official titles had more to do. "Then we only had three people, so less stuff got done and more hours [were] put in." At the lowest point, after the third staff member resigned a few months later (*with* prior notice), there were only two women on the GRP staff—Irene and Shelley. "It's really hard with just the two of us trying to have contact with sixty girls or forty-five girls, however many are in the program," Irene explained. As director, Shelley's frustration was compounded by the monetary investment that had been made in the staff members. The prior year, the organization had received a $10,000 grant for staff development, which had been spent on education, conferences, and training for the four staff members—three of whom were now gone. "It's like water going through your hands," Shelley said.

Although the girls were not too focused on wasted money for staff development, most were as upset as Shelley and Irene with the staff departures. A few girls said they didn't know the staff who left or that they had maintained contact with ex-staff outside of the GRP, but many spoke of the close, personal nature of their attachments and their sense of loss when staff departed. "I cried when [one staff member] left. . . . I didn't want her to leave. . . . She made your day," one girl shared. Another said that the departures "kind of hurt me and kind of made me not want to go back because I'm so close to Jenny. I didn't understand why, and I wish I could have. I wish I knew what all went on because I really do miss Jenny." These responses remind me of Jean Rhodes's comments about how the departure of "beloved staff" in youth programs results in serious youth disappointment and "even bereavement" (2004, 157). In contrast, Teresa responded to the turnover with anger. "You get to trust one person and they just leave," she said quickly. "Like I was mad when everybody [left]. I get mad. Like I finally just got used to you—now you gotta stay." In light of the importance of relationships between girls and women in positive youth development programs, these strong responses to the pain of staff leaving are not surprising.

One of the three staff members who left that year—the one who did give advanced notice—recalled girls talking to her about "feeling like everybody's leaving them." She felt "really bad" because though she told the girls she would still have a relationship with them, she admitted that "I haven't called them. . . . I know that they feel like I've just left them hanging." She was right that at least one girl was frustrated with her, saying that she "used to be close with [her], but not anymore because she won't call me back," but other girls cited her as setting an example for future staff members who decide to leave.

Although there are inherent negatives when staff members leave, *how* they leave may be as important as *if* they leave. As mentioned before, the third staff member differs from her fellow ex-staffers in that she gave notice before leaving. One suggestion my research team identified in a report to the GRP that year, to prevent situations like the double-turnover weekend in the future, was to include a clause in staff members' contracts requiring them to give two weeks' notice before leaving. If such a requirement had been in place in March, Jenny might have continued to work for the GRP. Soon after quitting, she stopped by the office and told Irene, "I regret leaving. I miss the girls, I miss my job. . . . If I had talked to Shelley after that . . . I would still be there today." If Jenny had legally not been able to walk out quite so quickly, she would have had more time with Shelley. Whether or not she would have remained, no one knows, but at least there would have been time for a more intentional decision-making process.

At some jobs, when employees stop working, they leave on the last day and that's it. They don't expect to hear from former coworkers or think about the office again. Not so with the GRP ex-staff members.

There is, first, the issue of keeping in touch (or not) with girls with whom they were close. One former staff member said that she "[hasn't] been able to do that, because I've been consumed with my own problems." And what do you do when you casually run into a GRP girl in this small town? "I've seen her around Hamlin, and she always waves and smiles," a girl said of one of the ex-staff members. "I think that it's good to stay on good terms with them. It's not like, 'You left so I hate you!'" Sometimes it is more than a smile and a wave. After all, these are all women who committed countless hours to working one-on-one with girls. Some girls said that even after much time had passed, if they bumped into former staff members, they would try to talk them through any problems. But all ex-staffers with whom we spoke felt awkward coming back to the office to visit—an action that could have facilitated the "keeping in touch" the girls seem to want. Virginia explained in 2004 that it was hard because she wants to know what's going on with all the girls, but the other staff can't tell her because of confidentiality. Another ex-staffer said if she had gone back to visit, she would have felt like an "outsider."

Before they became "outsiders," what happened with these women, all of whom told Shelley they planned to "stick around"? Why aren't they still working with the GRP? There is not a simple answer. "I think that one of them was just not ready for her job," one girl speculated. "She wasn't ready for the commitment; she wasn't ready for the behavior required . . . but I think for the other two, they each left for different reasons." We heard from Irene the story of Jenny leaving, although we were unable to speak to her directly about the evening of the play and the time leading up to it. We did speak with Virginia, who explained she had resigned partly because of personal problems in her marriage and partly because she had a baby and believed that bringing her to work impeded her productivity as staff. These two factors combined to make her feel she was being "hateful" to everyone because she had too much to do.

For the women we interviewed, there were not many hard feelings. "In everybody's defense—for people who left—it's really hard," Shelley reflected. "I have a lot of appreciation and respect for what they did, even though it might not have, you know, been exactly what I would have done or what I would have wanted them to do." And her ongoing relationship with Virginia—who, two years later, became director of the GRP herself—is testimony that she does not think of these women purely as "ex-staff." "Shelley was at my house, and we just talked for three hours yesterday," Virginia told us in a 2004 interview. When we met for final focus group interviews in 2006, Virginia and Shelley appeared to have remained very close. On the other hand, Teresa, our chapter 3 star, upon reading a draft of the chapter, wrote in an e-mail to me: "The only thing that I wish is that after Shelley left that she would [have] stayed in contact with me. I have [tried] a number of times."

One issue that played into staff turnover was the significant demands on staff members' maturity, coping skills, and ability to manage time. The job involves a twenty-four-hours-a-day, seven-days-a-week commitment to the girls—a commitment that can extend deeply into the staff person's time and even private life—calling for strong skills in time and stress management as well as an understanding attitude on the part of the staff's family. Staff may receive calls from girls at any time during the day or night. Staff members have housed girls in need of a place to stay—sometimes for extended periods of time (all summer during a pregnancy, for example). One girl said that in order to be a good staff member, she has to know: " 'Well, my marriage is okay, and if I go and spend two thirds of my time in the office, I'm still going to have a husband' . . . They need to be ready for that, or they just can't do it." In the end, it would be hard for many partners to be happy about this kind of setup.

Shelley also spent time thinking about what makes someone the right person to hire for this job: "Do they want this job because they are dying to work with girls, or do they want this job because they can't make ten dollars an hour with a GED anywhere else and they deserve to make a livable wage, you know?" she wondered. "And it's totally fair that's [the money] their motivation, but I don't want to hire people who have that motivation." She added that those folks probably wouldn't be around for the long term. But according to at least one former staff member, that's not necessarily a problem:

> You need to hire people who are going to be there for years, but you also need people who come in for a year and who leave, or who come for a month. . . . You need all kinds of people coming, because . . . the more experience you have meeting new people and being

exposed to new experiences and stuff, the better. . . . People come in and out of your life. And you have to be able to handle that, and it's not always easy. . . . It would be nice to have conversations about relationships and what are healthy ways of dealing with that.

These sentiments are consistent with Marianne Kugler's report that having a "mix of staff members" (2001, 7), including community members, college students, senior citizens, and some professionals such as schoolteachers, is a way successful youth organizations handle the well-documented and "serious challenge" of keeping staff turnover low. It is a fine line to walk, though, because although Kugler makes a good point, girls who have few stable, responsible figures in their lives need long-term relationships and ongoing support from staff members. Irene pointed out that staff turnover can be as dramatic and damaging for the girls as "having a mom just walking out of your life and not having them anymore. I mean, it's like somebody dying or something—they're just not there anymore."

Even Irene left the program a few years later. After spending so much time getting to know her—and believing that she was a perfect fit for the organization—it was hard to hide my surprise when I heard the news. I asked Shelley about it in our last one-on-one interview in 2006:

> LINDA: What happened with Irene?
>
> SHELLEY: I think that Irene found it really hard having Matthew [Irene's baby] at the office—very hard for her to manage both of those things. I know that she felt like he wasn't treated as well as Olivia [Shelley's daughter] was or Rebecca [Shelley's other daughter]—that things weren't fair for him. . . . I think that she felt like there was a lot of responsibility on her because G [a new staff member] was failing in her position as office manager miserably. She [G] came on . . . because Irene decided she wanted to work with the girls. We had funding for an office person. . . . And Irene and G were best buddies. G was in the program—one of the first interns.
>
> LINDA: So that was a bad hiring choice.

SHELLEY: Awful! . . . But Irene wavered between covering for her, and doing her work because she tried to train her and she couldn't be trained and then getting mad and . . . Eventually it was her [Irene] telling me what was going on that led to me having to get rid of G. . . . So I think that she felt really, really—She was trying to do the program thing, and she was trying to help G in the office.

The bottom line is that staff turnover is a critically important, but complicated, issue for positive youth development programs. As Mahoney reports in the introduction to a volume on community programs promoting positive youth development, research shows a relationship between the quality of human resources in a program and the developmental outcomes for the youth (Mahoney, Larson, and Eccles 2005). In other words, programs with enough well-educated staff to work closely with relatively small numbers of young people and that have low staff turnover rates also have better youth responses. Rhodes and Spencer, focusing on staff turnover, suggest that a program may even pose a risk to youth if the youth-staff relationships are too short-lived (2005).

What made GRP staff leave? I have already talked about the time- and emotion-related stresses of the job as well as the education and experience individuals brought to the job. Does it also make a difference whether the individuals are local, with ties to the community?

LOCAL STAFF VERSUS OUTSIDERS

The desire to have long-term staff members and avoid turnover is one reason Shelley wanted to hire girls from the program to begin with. As we have seen, both local and nonlocal staff members came and went over the course of the organization's history. Further, both local and nonlocal staff members failed to keep in touch with girls after leaving.

The question of local women versus "outsiders" as staff members was one about which there was little agreement. The named benefits of having outsiders as staff often reflected an assumption that only nonlocal individuals could have education and formal training for this kind of work.

Irene, for example, argued that "not everybody [should] be a person from the program because then you don't have somebody from the outside to help you or to provide you with [advice], like, 'Usually if you get into this situation, you do this.' . . . It's good to have somebody from the outside who's been to school about stuff like that." Shelley's comments reveal a similar assumption: "I hope that almost all of our staff positions are filled by girls that have been through the program, and that the ones that aren't filled by [former girl participants] are filled with local people, not people from Huntington or Charleston or people with, you know, PhDs in psychology or whatever." In Shelley's mind, there seemed to be a hierarchy for ideal hiring: girls who had been through the program were best, followed by Lincoln County residents who had not been in the program, followed by nonlocal individuals with degrees "in psychology or whatever" coming in last.

Interestingly, Shelley herself, who came to Lincoln County with considerable graduate education in community psychology, falls into that last category. Despite not being a native Lincoln County resident or a former GRP girl, no one could argue that Shelley did not bring incredible skills and assets to the organization—skills that came both from formal education and from extensive experience, as illustrated in everything from her success in obtaining grants to the effectiveness of her relationships and interactions with the girls.

Ric reflected that though "Shelley believed that bringing up former GRP participants and grooming them to be staff was a critical piece of the organization"—a belief that he pointed out ran parallel to her desire to employ only staff from the county—"in the end . . . [that belief] contributed to AWLP's [Appalachian Women's Leadership Project, sponsor of the Girls' Resiliency Program] downfall. . . . Though it was beneficial to have staff who understood intimately the reality our youth were facing, more experienced outsiders—even those with less knowledge of the local culture—might have helped sustain the organization." My mind can't help but add: *just as Shelley herself did.*

For me, the take-away lesson is about the importance of balance or "mix," to use Kugler's term (2001, 7). Instead of framing staffing issues as either/or, why not frame them as both/and? There is no doubt that the girls and the program benefited from both local/native and nonlocal staff.

They developed positive, supportive relationships with staff who were former participants and with staff who had not been involved, with staff who stayed many years and with staff who stayed less time, with women with graduate degrees and with those with only a high school diploma. In light of Prudence Carter's research on the experiences of black and Latino high school students, this mix of staff might have been highly beneficial to the girls. Carter found that young people who are "cultural straddlers," who can maintain close ties with more than one cultural group, tend to have more successful school experiences than minority students who stick with only one cultural identification (Carter 2011). This may hold true beyond the race and social class cultures that were the focus of Carter's study. If so, it would make sense for groups such as the GRP to take what Carter calls an "intercultural" approach, where the aim would be for girls to become fluent in more than one culture—remaining closely tied to their local rural community while interacting with people from other backgrounds as well.

Shelley pushed hard to move the organization toward being truly controlled by local girls, to be "girl-driven," as she called it that first day we met in my office. It was an ambitious, well-intentioned effort that makes sense. It was a way to guard against the tendency for social reform programs, especially those in Appalachia and other marginalized areas, to become controlled primarily by outsiders with no personal history with the community. It also makes sense in light of the strengths-based philosophy of the GRP. Overdependence on outside, formally trained individuals flies in the face of the positive youth development philosophy, whereas moving former girl participants into leadership positions is the ultimate in realizing the capabilities and assets of youth, in expanding the "girl box." I understand and endorse those stances, but my study of the GRP has taught me that it is far easier to articulate these positions than to successfully apply them. As Irene herself so simply and clearly said, "It's hard coming from a participant to staff." Perhaps that is why in a review of youth development organizations, Jodie Roth and Jeanne Brooks-Gunn found that only about a third of programs gave young people authentic leadership experiences, with only 6 percent providing employment for youth (2003a). Of course, just because it's hard doesn't mean it's not an endeavor worthy of pursuit, and there *are* examples of success. Linda Camino and Shepherd Zeldin describe an organization called Youth Force where the board of directors is 51 percent youth and more than half of the full-time staff members are young people (2002). This level of youth ownership is a goal that should be pursued carefully, cautiously, with an eye toward balance, and always mindful of the possible toll on the individuals involved as well as the health of the organization as a whole.

For Irene and Virginia, the toll of the GRP's girl-to-staff transitions was substantial. And Ric was surely right that the staffing decisions also took a toll on the GRP, playing a role in the organization's downfall. The collapse was already under way as I received a research award supporting the book-writing part of this project, a process that brought even more outsiders into the picture. In addition to me, graduate students LeAnne Olson and Betty Sias (all of us residents of nearby Huntington, West Virginia) became involved—an involvement that, for some of us, continues to this day, GRP or no.

LeANNE.

BETTY.

The GRP Collapses, but the
Learning Goes On (and On)

"GET. OUT. THAT. WHEELCHAIR."

"Well, it got a little out of control sometimes," admitted LeAnne Olson, a doctoral student of mine, breaking off a piece of her cheddar biscuit at a local seafood restaurant. Tucking a strand of blond hair behind her ear, she broke into a laugh.

LeAnne, Layne, and I were meeting to talk about GRP research—primarily conducted in recent years by two of my students, LeAnne Olson and Betty Sias. Betty, a go-getter who consistently seeks out challenges—as soon as she finished her dissertation, she threw herself into training for her first marathon—was focusing on the boys' program, and specifically on how the boys had adjusted to the newly consolidated Lincoln County High School. For her meetings with me, Betty often showed up in a suit, coming straight from her job at the West Virginia Department of Education. A hard worker, Betty was "put together" in both her appearance and her work with the Boys' Resiliency Program. LeAnne, who was focusing on the girls' program, shared Betty's work ethic and was committed to the girls in almost a familial way. LeAnne was warm and approachable without striving to be the center of attention, and the girls were immediately drawn to her. She smiled, fork in hand, thinking back to the days of driving to Lincoln County for interviews, creative projects, and hang-out sessions with the girls. With only one of her, no GRP staff, and sometimes ten or more girls, LeAnne did the best she could to not get them kicked out of the school for being too noisy.

"Being a researcher and an activity facilitator at the same time was confusing," LeAnne reflected in a recent journal article. "Was I really a researcher? An extension of the Girls' Resiliency Program? A mentor? A friend? Should I allow the girls to express themselves freely or restrict their voices when they were loud? Did I need to discipline them?" (Spatig, Gaines, et al. 2009, 205). At dinner, she retold a story about a particularly rowdy girl who was sitting in one of the school's wheelchairs (though she did not have a disability) during an activity with LeAnne when a teacher walked into the room. The teacher told the girl to get out of the chair, and the girl defiantly challenged the teacher with one of teenagers' favorite responses: "Why?" LeAnne took a stand, almost ordering the girl to get out of the chair.

"I was like, 'Get. Out. That. Wheelchair,'" she remembered as everyone at our dinner table burst into empathetic laughter. She turned to me cautiously, adding, "Um, that might not have made it into my field notes. There was a lot [of things that] didn't"—instigating a second round of laughs.

IT'S TOUGH TO BE COMPETENT

LeAnne was running those activities on her own—frantically jumping between asking interview questions, distributing art supplies, and insisting that girls get out of school wheelchairs—because the GRP no longer had any paid staff members. By the time LeAnne started her research in 2007, Shelley and Irene had both resigned, and Virginia was working as the only part-time staff member. By December of that year, the organization had lost all its staff as funding ran out. LeAnne found that if she wanted to continue her research, she had to organize meetings with the girls herself.

This chapter of the story, the part where the GRP collapses, is hard to tell without worrying about stepping on toes and possibly hurting those who made huge contributions to the work. At the same time, I know that what happened at the end of the GRP story is a common ending for community-based nonprofits, and shedding light on why it fell apart can provide guidance to organizations with similar structures and issues. Or, as Shelley said to me in an e-mail note: "Glad to know you are turning all this . . . into something that may help others."

So what happened to the GRP? The main factors that led to the program's collapse differ depending on whom you are asking, of course, but there are quite a few recurrent themes. Many of them were identified in reflective focus groups with current and former board members, staff, girl participants, and researchers. Some of these same individuals also wrote about them in e-mails later in the year. One reason for the GRP's decline is related, ironically, to the strengths and successes of the early years—when the organization experienced what some now see as too much growth that was too fast and not planned strategically enough. The early years featured strong leadership provided mainly by one woman. A former staff member described the Shelley-centered nature of the organization: "Shelley has a lot of control over the program. . . . We say that group decisions are made and [that] we all sit around and decide on things, and to some degree, that's true. But I still think that, I mean, Shelley drives the program. And her decisions obviously, you know, outweigh other people's decisions." She added, a little prophetically, that "if something were to happen to Shelley, like if she was in a car wreck or were to die, I mean, I don't know that the program could go on. . . . I think that's a little scary." She went on to emphasize that Shelley was not sitting back with an evil laugh, scheming about how to suck up all the power for herself. She "really values input," the ex-staffer explained—but often the other staff members and even board members simply deferred to her. Shelley knows best. I can't help but notice that hiring local girls without higher education or formal training (as discussed in the last chapter) only added to the dynamic where all major decisions were dependent on Shelley's expertise. Certainly "wisdom about resistance, resiliency, and compassion doesn't always come from books" (hooks and Mesa-Bains 2006, 70), but educational programs can be a source of relevant knowledge and skills that seemed to make a difference in the effectiveness of GRP staff.

In field notes written by a graduate student involved well before LeAnne and Betty were even aware of the program, there is a description of an instance in which Shelley, merely by sharing her own views, seemed to sway the opinions of all the girl participants. After an afternoon swimming in a local lake, the girls were called together to vote on a logo for the Appalachian Women's Leadership Project, the umbrella organization for the GRP. There were three design choices—two of which had been created by an artist, and a third that was Shelley's own altered version of one of the artist's designs.

> Shelley held up each design, and girls voted on their favorite ones by raising their hands. No one voted for the first two designs, although I heard a few girls whisper they liked the second one when Shelley first held it up. Shelley held up the third choice—the one she had designed herself—and all girls verbalized a resounding "yes" by raising hands, nodding heads, and verbal praises. "Okay, thanks," she said.
>
> I was surprised that EVERY girl voted for the third logo design choice because a few of them liked the second choice when Shelley first presented it. It wasn't until after Shelley explained that she didn't like the first two choices—and why she didn't like them—that all the girls voted for the third logo design. They may have all decided they liked the third choice for the same reasons Shelley liked it. But I have a feeling that the girls respect and like her so much that they would support almost any decision she makes. Granted, she seems to make decisions based on their best interests, and she genuinely seems to care about their well-being. However, I definitely think her opinion of the logo designs greatly influenced their votes.

I uneasily witnessed a similar scene in my very first meeting with the GRP girls in the late 1990s. It was a board meeting, which included Shelley and a few girls, to discuss our upcoming evaluation research. At that time, we were planning research funded by a Ms. Foundation grant. The grant guidelines provided options from which our group could choose. One choice had to do with whether to use a video camera or an audiotape recorder to document interviews with program participants. The girls, who would be involved in collecting some of the data, were excited about the video camera option, but Shelley pointed out that it was hard to get some girls to talk openly and that a camera would make it that much harder. The girls held their position for a little while, but ultimately went along with Shelley's preferences. She did, after all, make a good point.

This type of control-by-influence was pretty common in GRP decisions, creating a fuzzy line between truly "girl-driven" and driven by the influence of one. I'm sure in many ways the girls and the staff and board wanted to support and please Shelley, the Wonder Woman behind many of the program's successes. Plus, deferring to the person in the room with most experience on a certain issue often makes sense and is most efficient. I truly believe Shelley tried to practice a feminist form of leadership, focused more on egalitarian, supportive relationships than the more hierarchical forms of traditionally masculine leadership (Evans 1997). But sometimes that is easier said than done. In a study of more than one hundred feminist women leaders, Jean Lau Chin found that although these women said they preferred a "feminist leadership style which was more collaborative and inclusive," many of them felt that this was not possible in order to be "effective" organizational leaders (2011, 4–5). In the GRP, with adolescent girls being led by an experienced woman, a feminist reconstruction of leadership was not fully realized. This was related in part to the age and experience of those involved. But I wonder if there might have been a way for girls to have greater influence, at least in certain kinds of decisions, or even to be allowed to make less than ideal decisions from which they could learn. And I wonder, did the control by influence go too far and hurt the sustainability of the operation? And did it take a serious toll on that pivotal, influential person?

In a 2006 interview after she had resigned, Shelley reflected that it was extremely draining to feel that she was carrying the GRP world on her shoulders. When it became clear that some of their grant funding was going to be cut, she and the board decided to set a goal of raising 10 percent of the budget from nongrant sources. "But nobody did it," Shelley said. "Nobody did it. Not staff, not board members—nobody did it. And so, in addition to writing grants—and I don't mean to sound like a martyr, but this is like, this is how I got burned out." The "Shelley knows best" mind-set came with power but also with a lot of weight. "It's tough to be competent sometimes," she later reflected. Recently Ric confirmed this, saying that "the rest of us were used to Shelley doing the work. She created the programs, wrote the grants, set the directions, picked the board. We were used to her making things happen without us doing much."

RUBBER STAMPS, CUT FUNDS, AND NEW PROGRAMS

Still, Shelley wasn't the only competent one around. The board of directors, composed of committed, experienced community members with various kinds of expertise, was supposed to be overseeing the work and financials of the GRP. "Partly I assumed, but I definitely was given, a lot of decision-making power, authority, responsibility, and the board was really a cheerleading squad," Shelley reflected in her post-GRP days. "That was really their function. And I'm sure that that was something that [we] mutually created."

Ric agrees, calling the board—of which he was always a part—a "rubber stamp." He explained that for a long time, Shelley "was doing everything, and things just seemed okay." From Ric's perspective, having girls on the board, although positive in many ways, brought challenges that hindered the effectiveness of the board. "She [Shelley] wanted girls on the board, which was great, but it was very problematic because there were these different levels of understanding about what a board does, how finances are handled, and we struggled with that," Ric said. "I think in part because of that, it was really hard for the board to step up and take some leadership and wrestle with some real issues. We were always just trying to get to the point where people would understand what in the world we were talking about." According to Ric, one board member even resigned over the financial situation—a move about which Ric now says, "He was right, I see now in retrospect. He resigned because we were working in these deficits. We were moving forward in programs, and yet we couldn't answer where the money was going to come from. Shelley was saying, 'This is how it will work.' I didn't know, really." Even the words he used in his interview—"*her* board" (italics added)—reveal who was running the show.

Both board members and Shelley characterized the board in this way, but only when the program began to fall apart did this raise alarm bells.

There was also agreement on another key factor in the organization's decline: the loss of funding. In Shelley's final years with the program, at least three foundations that had been major sources of support for the organization either shifted their funding focus away from youth development or shut down completely. Shelley worked hard to even track down the program officers she had once worked with at the foundations and was told by at least one that funding youth activism was "no longer sexy." A fourth foundation—that had once funded youth development work nationwide, including the GRP—decided to restrict its giving to six major cities in an attempt to make a more concentrated impact. Unsurprisingly, none of these cities was in West Virginia. A major shift seemed to be happening in the philanthropy world.

"You can just see there aren't more opportunities opening up. There are fewer and fewer opportunities that are funding the little niche that we were in," Shelley explained in her post-GRP interview with me. I asked why she thought that was. "I think a lot of it—and of course, this is just my personal opinion—but I think that there aren't many people who think that activism and youth development should come together. They feel like it's more about service provision, kids doing well in school, and that these kids are not emotionally mature enough or cognitively able to engage in social change work." Back in the "girl box"—or in this case, the youth box in general. Jessica Taft's work supports Shelley's suspicions. "Throughout the Americas," she writes, "there is a powerful perception that teenagers are apathetic and disengaged from politics" (2011, 41). Among her research sites in North, Central, and South America, Taft noted that "North American adults (in both Canada and the United States) were the most likely to be convinced that girl activists are incredibly uncommon and therefore 'very special' individuals" (42). The girls she interviewed argued that statements about how exceptional they were, though well-intentioned, ultimately were grounded in the belief that, in general, youth were not capable of doing social change work.

Federal funding for children and youth has been in steady decline since 1960 and is expected to continue to decline, perhaps at a faster pace. Though grant money for children and youth programs actually increased from 1996 to 2001—during the flourishing early years of the GRP—it dropped with the US economic downturn. Even in the good years of grant contributions, there was still what Mario Morino called the "extreme under-capitalization of quality non-profits" (2002). Morino was referring to the chronic underfunding of core operating expenses for nonprofits, which makes it especially hard for small, community-based organizations such as the Girls' Resiliency Program. Unfortunately, based on successful grant procurement in the early years, the GRP had come to rely almost exclusively on temporary grant funding. Most "best practices" guidelines for nonprofits recommend diversified funding sources so that if one or two disappear, the whole organization's budget is not at risk. Some in the non-profit field say that one type of funding—foundation grants, for example—should not account for more than a third of the organization's budget. By contrast, the GRP had over 90 percent of its funding from grants.

"We had awful financial problems," Ric said somberly. "Shelley left in the midst of all this financial meltdown where [another board member] and I were trying to figure out what in the world was happening. Do we really owe the IRS $55,000? Where is the money? . . . It was a mess, and it was getting worse. And so we made the decision that we were going to shut it down. . . . There was no money."

The fact that the shutdown decision, ultimately, was a financial one is not surprising in light of what we know about the importance of funding in sustaining youth organizations. According to Tom Klaus, continuous funding is the number one (of three) critical requirements for sustainability. Although his writing focuses on teen pregnancy-prevention programs, he argues that the same requirements hold true for most nonprofits. He stresses the importance of going beyond funding for specific programming and obtaining unrestricted funds that can be used to support the organization generally. Without achieving this kind of financial stability, organizations cannot survive and grow (Klaus 2008). Unfortunately, the GRP was not able to get that kind of continuous funding, especially unrestricted funds.

Another factor that, from Shelley's perspective, played a big role in the demise of the Girls' Resiliency Program was the inception of a Boys' Resiliency Program in her last years as director. Shelley, who said that initially she was "1,000 percent opposed to starting it," called it a "very significant piece of the decline."

"Why did you all start that?" I asked Shelley in our last interview. After making clear that it was not up to her, she explained, from her point of view, what happened:

> The leaders and the political powerbrokers in Lincoln County . . . wanted something for the boys. . . . "Since there was a girls' program, let's do a boys' program." Well, there was no organization or any leadership in the county, so they looked to AWLP [Appalachian Women's Leadership Project] to do that. I was very opposed to doing that, but agreed to do it with the concept that within three years, which is a very short time, they would spin off. I caved in, really, because [a man hired to become director of the Boys' Resiliency Program] and I went—during that first year—we went to New York because Ms. Foundation had a symposium about boys. . . . I came away from that feeling like I could legitimately believe that to move the women's agenda forward we had to have a boys' program. . . . It took a huge amount of my time. . . . It was really significant—the budgeting, the fundraising, the planning, the evaluation. The problem was I was still doing GRP [programming] and staff development, so I didn't relinquish any responsibility that I had before, I just added on. And the boys' program also affected the AWLP because that grant was all reimbursable. We had not one penny in the bank when that program started. We had to spend and then get it back. And because the first eight months of it was all screwed up, we would spend and not get back what we had spent!

Ultimately, Shelley said, the boys' program was the straw that broke the already-fragile camel's back. I wondered to myself if that straw broke just the back of the GRP or also of an increasingly stressed-out Shelley, or how much of a meaningful distinction there was between the two.

SHELLEY RESIGNS

As the boys' program grew and the girls' program continued to lose funding, Shelley grew more anxious and exhausted. "She did it [all], but you could see what it was doing to Shelley," Ric remembered about the time period immediately before her resignation. "She was saying she was on the edge emotionally."

Shelley remembered a growing amount of board scrutiny and critical questioning about the finances. But in her mind, it was the same issue the organization had been struggling with for years. "'The finances are the way they are because we don't raise enough money!'" she recalled saying to a skeptical board. "'I can't do all of this.' And they kept saying, 'Oh, you're so good at it.' 'Well, that doesn't make me feel better. Help me!'"

The final blow for Shelley was walking into her office one Monday morning to find a letter from Ric, requesting a meeting with her and the board to discuss the financial dilemma. For an organization where meetings often happened spontaneously on a front porch, in the grass of a local park, or over unplanned phone calls, the formality of a written letter stung Shelley. She still recalls that morning vividly:

> I remember sitting at my desk, and I was facing Irene at that point, and I just lost it. I was just like, "Blankety blank, blank, blank, blank, blank! I have given my life, I have busted my ass . . . and now I'm going to be interrogated and accused and blah blah blah blah, and I've been trying to give them this information about the financial situation for years and years." . . . And [I said], . . . "You know what? This is the beginning of the end. I can tell you right now. This is the beginning of the end. I will not work seventy hours a week and leave my family to come here and be treated like this."

She later said that it was also a turning point for Irene and the other staff member at the time, who both resigned a few months later. And in other parts of the country, directors and staff members were resigning from other youth development organizations. "Of the organizations that went through either the first or second round of Ms. funding, many do not exist any more," said Shelley. "Two of them went to being totally volunteer-driven organizations. A couple of others collapsed entirely. They don't exist at all." Understandably, Ms. expressed serious concern about the youth development movement at the last conference Shelley attended with them. They were worried, she said, about "the leadership of the movement, and how people of our generation have—we're all burned out. . . . Of the people in that first round of funding ten years ago from

Ms.—and I could even go through the list—but I don't think any of the directors are the directors any more. I think one is still there." She paused, adding what struck me as an extremely troubling sentence for girls all over the country: "And when they left, they left the whole field." This was not a shift in position, a switch from director to program officer. This was a decision to leave the work entirely.

When they left, they left the whole field. Left it to whom?

"GET OUT THAT WHEELCHAIR," REPRISE

One person it was left to was Ric, our faithful chapter 1 man, who is still doing youth development work in Lincoln County. Other people it was left to—somewhat unintentionally—were Betty and LeAnne, my doctoral students, and Heaven Rangel, a master's student who also assisted with the project. As our research with the girls' (and now, boys') programs became more active, the programs themselves continued to decline. Increasingly, the research and programming became indistinguishable. As Ric once wrote, "I don't think we can emphasize too much the importance of Heaven and LeAnne and to some extent, Betty, in keeping the girls' program alive. During that school year, they were the staff for the girls' program. If they had not been there, there would have been no program."

Youth programming is certainly not what my doctoral students signed up for. In fact, Betty admitted later that neither collaborative ethnography nor youth development was initially a draw for her:

> When an e-mail arrived from Linda requesting assistance on a project researching youth development programs, I immediately responded. I have to be honest here. My response did not stem from my desire to be part of a collaborative effort attempting to learn about the sustainability of youth development programs; my response stemmed from my need to meet requirements in my doctoral program. Nevertheless, this was my induction to the field of collaborative ethnography. That one e-mail reply led me on a journey lasting eighteen months—a journey during which I met twelve young people, six of whom allowed me to delve into their lives as I focused more exclusively on their experiences with and perceptions of school consolidation.

Betty did her fieldwork at after-school meetings, pizza dinners, laser tag outings, and during car rides transporting individual boys or small groups of boys to and from events. It quickly became evident that this work had become more than the fulfillment of doctoral program requirements.

At one point I got an e-mail from Betty asking if I thought it would be okay if she and her husband bought a pig for a boy who needed it for a school-related farming project. His family had not purchased one for him, thus eliminating him from an important competition. Another time she came to me with concerns about a boy who was unable to play school sports because he had not been able to get the required physical examination. Again, Betty wondered how she could help out. On several occasions her field notes described deep concerns she had about a young boy whose mom abandoned him and whose father had recently passed away.

At the same time, LeAnne's research was focused on the girls' program that, for all intents and purposes, no longer existed. For her, this was not an easy or comfortable role to negotiate, especially at first. As a graduate student fairly new to ethnography and lacking experience in the whirlwind world of teenagers and high school, she struggled to balance her role and responsibilities. In her reflections, she wrote:

> When resiliency program staff was laid off due to lack of funds, I found myself alone with the girls, which at times was an uneasy, even disturbing, experience. Once when twelve girls showed up, I felt overwhelmed. They were working on their scrapbooks, and I was pulled in different directions, never really sure what was going on with all the girls as I worked with small groups of them at a time. I wanted to create an atmosphere where they had space to be themselves. . . . Some days when I left I felt I had totally lost control. I sometimes focused in on one conversation—for example, about a scrapbook issue—while all hell was breaking loose around me. When I listened to recordings of the meetings afterwards, I was sometimes surprised by the number of conversations going on around me that I had been completely unaware of.

Though all hell may have been breaking loose at times, LeAnne developed relationships with the girls that went far beyond those of typical researchers and subjects. While the demise of the program thrust LeAnne into a difficult staff-like role, it also gave her opportunities for developing close relationships with the girls and, ultimately, a deep understanding of their experiences with the GRP. She hosted girls at her house for sleepovers, helped them apply for scholarships and make sense of financial aid paperwork, and even went to college orientation with and signed off as a guardian for a girl who had been in a series of foster homes for many years.

LeAnne's fieldwork and interviews are bursting with stories that most girls would never have told someone with whom they felt less comfortable. One of Cassi's close friends—one of the five girls LeAnne focused on for her dissertation research—shared the following family memory during a one-on-one interview. The girl was eleven years old at the time of this story:

> I remember he [my mom's boyfriend] used to get drunk a lot. Her boyfriend . . . and mom would get into a bunch of yelling fights, and sometimes there would be punching. He would never hit her, but she would sometimes hit him. They were always fighting, and then he got really strung out on pills and drank on top of that without eating, and then they got into this really big fight. . . . He got ahold of a beer bottle and had her on the ground and started hitting her in the head. This was outside the trailer. I grabbed a butcher knife. I was going to go after him. She was all I had. He grabbed ahold of the blade and yanked it out of my hands and threw it over in the woods. I found it in the woods all rusted a few weeks later, but it cut his hands all up. And then he was going to go after me, and mom jumped on top of him. Then we went back into the house. We had to hold the door shut to keep him from busting it down, then he drove away in his truck. Then he came back the next day, and it was like nothing ever happened.

LeAnne and the girls would talk for hours. It is not an exaggeration to say that in her ongoing and lengthy get-togethers with the girls, she became both a researcher and the primary GRP staff member. For one of the five girls especially, Ashley (featured in chapter 7), LeAnne became an important figure of stability.

"What were some things you took from your time in the GRP?" Layne once asked the group of five girls, sitting in LeAnne's living room—fighting her way into a chaotic conversation about terrible high school teachers, ex-boyfriends, and the baby son of one of the girls. "Oh, the GRP? No, that was pretty much gone," they chirped in agreement. "But we had LeAnne!" Cassi added brightly.

AND THE LEARNING GOES ON

I'm a big believer in lessons learned sections. Partly it's the emotional relief of finding the good in a situation that, overall, is pretty sad. But more than that, I believe that as a model for youth development, the GRP is worth emulating in many ways. The fierce commitment of staff members, the "long-haul" relationships and support, the opportunities to recognize and express strengths by facing new and authentic challenges, the community service and activism, the arts experiences—all these had immeasurable positive effects on so many girls' lives. The GRP is a model program, not in the sense of being sustainable and replicable, but in the sense of showing the outcomes that are possible with positive youth development programs—and how those outcomes may be achieved.

In a national context where youth are spending more and more time on their own without much to do, after-school youth programs are increasingly important (Kugler 2001). Based on findings from a 2009 national survey, the America After 3pm Study, the Afterschool Alliance reports that 26 percent of school-aged children in the United States are on their own in the afternoon after school. This represents an increase from 14.3 million children on their own in 2004 to 15.1 million in 2009. Children are now spending even more hours per week alone than Marianne Kugler calculated in 2001 when she estimated that close to a third of the nation's youth spend "15 to 20 waking hours weekly without human contact" (2001, 4). In rural Appalachia, additional factors make the situation even harder. Many young people live in geographically isolated areas miles away from the nearest neighbors and many more miles away from close friends. Also, in rural areas there are often fewer activities for youth than in larger cities, and financial resources may be more limited as well. This was certainly the case for GRP girls.

In these national and regional contexts, then, it is not a surprise that there is considerable interest in after-school youth programs. At the same time, there is limited political inclination to support them financially. This may be related to the fact that there is not enough evidence about how, and how well, each of the programs works—in other words, their effectiveness (Roth and Brooks-Gunn 2003b). Lessons learned from the GRP story, based as it is on a long-term, in-depth empirical study, provide new knowledge about effective youth development programs—especially for girls.

Even though it closed, the GRP was a highly effective program. Applying standards used by Roth and Brooks-Gunn (2003a) in an analysis of evaluation results from forty-eight effective youth development programs, the GRP scores high. This is particularly noteworthy in light of the fact that relatively few self-identified youth development programs met basic criteria for effective positive youth development (Roth and Brooks-Gunn 2003a, 180). By basic criteria, they mean: (1) having program goals consistent with promoting the five ingredients, the famous "Cs," of positive youth development (*competence, confidence, connections, character,* and *compassion*); (2) having a youth-centered program atmosphere featuring caring, supportive relationships with adults and peers over an extended period of time; and (3) providing activities that enable youth to gain knowledge and build skills by participating in challenging projects that "broaden their horizons" (Roth and Brooks-Gunn 2003a, 176).

The GRP was successful to a large extent in meeting the first criterion by accomplishing four of the five Cs (*competence, confidence, connections, character,* and *compassion*) of positive youth development. According to Roth and Brooks-Gunn, promoting *competence,* the first C, includes "enhancing participants' social, academic, cognitive, and vocational competencies" (173). Girls who participated in the GRP experienced positive changes in interpersonal and social skills such as communication and conflict resolution. They also grew cognitively, for example in their abilities to solve problems and make decisions. For those who worked as research interns or at the coffeehouse and those who transitioned into staff positions, the program also taught new skills that could be used in future jobs. The program was least effective in strengthening girls' academic abilities. By choice, Shelley defined the GRP as nonacademic in focus. As I began to learn about the academic struggles of some of the girls, especially in math, I was increasingly uneasy about that decision. "Given the importance of academic competence for future success," like Roth and Brooks-Gunn, I also "found it surprising that only 27% of the programs [of the 48 programs they reviewed] embraced this competence goal" (173). Although no one program can do everything, the omission of academic competence as a youth development program goal is particularly problematic, especially for individuals who want to attend college.

Building *confidence,* the next C, involves program "goals relating to improving adolescents' self-esteem, self-concept, self-efficacy, identity, and belief in the future" (Roth and Brooks-Gunn 2003a, 173). This was a major emphasis for the GRP, often achieved through the arts and other activities, but also through the caring tone of the program generally. Perhaps the clearest evidence of the program's successes in promoting girls' confidence and positive sense of themselves can be seen in the stories of girls who underwent Teresa Transformations and began to use their voices. Part of what they voiced was a changing view of themselves and their places in the world, moving from shrugs and "I don't knows" to "I used to be shy," "I felt like we really made a difference," and Cassi's description of herself as an "extraordinary and confident person."

Strengthening *connections* is the third C of positive youth development. According to Roth and Brooks-Gunn, this involves program goals for "building and strengthening adolescents' relationships with other people and institutions, such as school" (173). In this regard, too, the GRP fares quite well. Using modeling as well as personal coaching, program staff consistently and consciously worked to enhance the girls' connections with caring adults as well as with peers. Our direct observations and interviews with staff and girls provide evidence of successes in this. Even with the struggle of maintaining staff stability, girls developed strong, close, and sometimes long-lasting relationships with program staff, with other girls in the program, and with researchers such as LeAnne and Betty. Girls also reported improvements in their relationships beyond the program, such as with parents, teachers, and school administrators. Going beyond individual relationships, the program's ambitious community service and activism component encouraged girls' connections with groups and institutions more broadly—though with uneven success. The community service was viewed positively by virtually everyone. Girls experienced it primarily as a way of expressing caring and compassion. They viewed the activism, however, less favorably and more variably—ranging from assessing it as pointless and personally uninteresting to important and empowering.

Roth and Brooks-Gunn's next C, *character,* is exemplified in program goals related to "increasing self-control, decreasing engagement in health-compromising behaviors, developing respect for cultural or societal rules and standards and a sense of right and wrong (morality), and spirituality" (173). Character goals were the second most common youth development goal in the forty-eight programs they reviewed. In most cases, the character-related program goals were to improve participants' self-control in order to reduce their participation in so-called risky behaviors. I considered the GRP's emphasis on community service and activism in relation to character building, ultimately concluding that for program participants those elements of the program meant something more akin to caring and compassion than to character, at least as it is defined by Roth and Brooks-Gunn.

In honesty, I am uneasy with this particular C—*character*—of youth development. It doesn't resonate with my experience of the GRP or with my understanding of the positive youth development movement generally, which is purposefully not about preventing problems (e.g., risky behavior) but about developing strengths in young people. I realize those may be two sides of the same coin, but the emphasis in this component seems to be on the risk-avoidance side of the coin, and even the inculcation of certain values (e.g., respect for, rather than critique of, "societal rules and standards"). Such an approach contradicts both the GRP's stance on strengths-based programming and its emphasis on social critique and activism. Who decides, for example, what "societal rules and standards" a youth development program should be promoting? That said, there is no question that the GRP encouraged specific values—such as respect, social responsibility, community engagement, as well as attention to inequalities of gender, sexuality, race, social class, rurality—and encouraged girls to apply them in their own lives. But Shelley viewed this as "adding skills" to the girls' "tool belts" rather than building their character.

The final component, *compassion,* is related to program goals to improve adolescents' empathy. Here again, the GRP was highly effective. In some ways, this component overlaps with *connections.* In attempting to strengthen girls' relationships with others, for example, conversations and activities often focused on listening to, understanding, and being respectful of the views and circumstances of other people. Also, community service projects gave girls opportunities to gain insights and skills with others in a broader sense. Girls spoke of those projects as being helpful to others and as expressing their "caring"—about a person, a family, a lake, a county. As Roth and Brooks-Gunn found to be true in the effective programs they reviewed, GRP participants seemed to be more favorably affected by long-term, enduring projects such as building a Habitat for Humanity house than by one-time events.

Moving on to Roth and Brooks-Gunn's second criterion for effective youth development programs—having a positive, youth-centered atmosphere featuring supportive relationships with adults and peers over an extended period of time—the GRP was exemplary. As was true for the programs rated as successful in this arena by Roth and Brooks-Gunn, the GRP atmosphere was most evident in the quality of staff interactions and relationships with the girls. Over the many years of study, our direct observations and conversations with program staff and girls consistently highlight the staff's extraordinary, twenty-four-hours-a-day relationships with the girls. Someone is always, always here for you. This atmosphere remained even at the end when the program was falling apart and only one part-time staff member was left. Perhaps as important as the quality of the atmosphere and relationships is that the program experience was a long-lasting one for girls who participated. Unlike the programs Roth and Brooks-Gunn reviewed, almost half of which lasted only a few weeks or months, the GRP was a program many girls (except those who joined in the last year of its existence) experienced over a period of years.

The final and third criterion of success, the provision of activities that allow youth to gain skills and broaden their horizons, is another area in which the GRP excelled. As we have seen, program activities were real and challenging, extending girls' capabilities in areas ranging from creating poetry, music, and pottery to conducting research to building a house. This expansion of skills and broadening of horizons was accomplished by the skillful combination of challenging tasks presented in the context of trusting, supportive relationships with adults. Staff provided guidance in the form of scaffolding, striking a balance between asking too much or too little from each girl. This kind of coaching was more effective in the early years of the program when Shelley, Jessica, and other more professionally experienced women held key staff positions than it was in later years when former participants, with less time to gain youth-development knowledge and experience, had moved into key staff positions. However, by actually hiring girls—as summer interns and later as full-time program staff—the GRP was in a very small group of youth development programs that provided youth with authentic leadership experiences. Among the forty-eight programs Roth and Brooks-Gunn reviewed, only 6 percent provided any kind of youth employment.

In addition to meeting most of what Roth and Brooks-Gunn call their "stringent requirements" for effective youth development programs, the GRP is also a model program in the sense of showing what can be learned from the real obstacles that were faced and from mistakes that were made by hard-working, competent, caring human beings. As John Dewey said many years ago, the idea of a model program is not to have others "literally imitate what we do. A working model is not something to be copied; it is to afford a demonstration of the feasibility of the principle, and of the methods which make it feasible" ([1899] 2007, 110). This is not unlike Roth and Brooks-Gunn's argument that although it is neither possible nor desirable to "design one blueprint for an effective youth development program . . . the field needs an agreed-upon set of principles" that are a little less vague than what is often seen in positive youth development writing (2003a, 171).

At the same time, we can take a focus on "effective models" too far—or fall into a too-limited understanding of what it means for a program to be "working." Maisha T. Winn writes that although educational researchers often focus on the question of what works, research with incarcerated girls begins with the question "What is the work?" (Winn 2011, 123). This is related to the distinction Jessica Taft drew between empowerment versus activism approaches to working with girls. Is the work directed at the girls, or the world, or both? Winn urges practitioners to avoid a black-and-white, simplistic understanding of problems and solutions. She reflects:

> One of the first questions people often ask me about Girl Time is how many of the girls stay out of detention centers, jails, prisons, or "trouble" as a result of this program. This question is flawed and any response I could attempt to provide would be equally as flawed. For even when girls stay "out of trouble," I cannot empirically support

their [lack of] recidivism as a result of the program. Nor could I say Girl Time failed if a girl returns to a detention center. (2011, 126)

Just as the GRP and other youth development programs can help girls develop valuable skills, expand their vision of what is possible, engage in community activism, and more, girls are still going out into a world filled with sexism, racism, regionalism, homophobia, and classism. This context makes it difficult to unequivocally measure "results" and "success." Or, to put it more positively, there are many reasons and ways girls face hardships, and many ways in which to challenge those constraints.

In addition to lessons learned about "effectiveness," we learned that one of the strengths of the GRP—its focus on activism—may also have contributed to its downfall. Partly this was related to its uniqueness and thus a lack of information about how to do this kind of programming with youth. "So much of this stuff is just really, really tricky, and . . . nobody does this. I mean, there are a lot of programs in the world—there are even some that do the kinds of things that we do—but I feel like there is nobody out there that is a good role model," Shelley lamented in 2004. "When you say, you know, you're having problems with this or that, they're like, 'Ah, that's so normal. It's a part of the stage you're in.' Well, great. What the hell do I do about it? Nobody has any answers for that."

The group's focus on activism may also have reinforced its overreliance on Shelley. Had the program featured more traditional approaches to youth programming, it may have been possible to get more buy-in, participation, and support from individuals and organizations in or near the local community and thus to have less dependence on a single individual director and a small group of board members. The relatively unusual focus on activism was part of what attracted money and recognition in the early years, but it also may have come with a steep price tag. It meant a lack of information and guidance from other programs, as Shelley notes, and perhaps less local community involvement. Of course, dropping or reducing the program's focus on activism would have meant sacrificing some of Shelley's beliefs and principles. It wouldn't have been as true to her ideal of a girl-driven, activist youth organization. Ironically, the fact that it was activism-oriented may have unintentionally increased her own control and responsibility and, at the same time, reduced that of others, including the girls themselves.

Finally, the youth activism focus likely made the loss of funding even more drastic than it was for other youth organizations in the same period. Economic decline drove much of the downturn in funding for grassroots community organizations across the board. Such economic decline might have been an impetus for greater social activism in the United States, but instead we had political shifts toward conservatism. bell hooks and Amalia Mesa-Bains have written about changing responses to activism over a ten-year period, 1995 to 2005, from a time when they (hooks and Mesa-Bains) "shared the sense that [they] were moving forward in antiracist, pro-woman struggles" to a very different time: "Since we met in the 1990s . . . the movement's work and energy has been undermined. . . . We have entered a period of grave silence, censorship, and violence" (hooks and Mesa-Bains 2006, 1). In the context of such "desperate times," Mesa-Bains notes a "deeper sense of hopelessness," especially among young people, but stands firm on her commitment to activism: "We are refusing to be silenced or pitted against each other, and so are many others who are working for peace, justice, compassion" (2006, 2).

The GRP was undergoing similar ups and downs during the same period, flourishing in the early 1990s and floundering as years passed. It might be reasonable to say that a more traditional youth development approach, with social activism as one, perhaps small, part of a broader program, would have been easier on Shelley and the board. It probably would have been more "fundable," and thus more sustainable, in this period in which there was a resurgence of emphasis on "personal responsibility," the cutting of social services through welfare "reform," and an assumption that nonprofits and individual families could fill in the gaps (Duggan 2012). In this environment, a less political, less activism-oriented program might have had a better shot at survival. But I cannot bring myself to take such a position. Instead, I find that I am in agreement with hooks and Mesa-Bains that taking an activist stance, in that particular period, was especially difficult but also critically important. Being a long-time believer in advocacy to promote equality and fight injustice, I found the activism of the GRP to be one of its strongest elements. Even though I realize that the activist nature of the program played a role in its closing, I stand with the organization on this and am honored to be connected with this important work.

Striking a more even balance between long-term, slow, planned growth and short-term, faster change in response to ideas and opportunities might also have been helpful in sustaining the GRP. My research team warned in our 2003–4 program report against the rapid expansion that was occurring because we worried that the speedy growth would lessen the high quality of the programming. Looking back, Shelley agrees that the timing of major organizational moves, like opening a new program or hiring a new staff member, wasn't always right. "I think what happened a lot with me and the GRP and AWLP is that I wanted something and then I made it happen," she said. "I mean, like youth in staff positions—I wanted that to happen, but I don't know in our development if that was the right time for that to happen." There is a danger for any nonprofit when one capable, enthusiastic individual is calling the shots with little in the way of mechanisms—a strong, active board, for example—to balance her individual influence. Finally, the importance of seeking greater diversity in funding sources, especially balancing grant support with money from individual donations and other sources, was something that was recognized too late.

For me, this analysis and reflection on what might have been reinforces a broader lesson from earlier times in my life. It may be painful, but it is important and rewarding to commit to projects and to people deeply, even while knowing they are imperfect and may not work out in the end. To be alive is to be engaged and connected, to grow, to change, and to love—in an ever imperfect world. To commit to something or someone thinking they will never change or end is simply not real.

A member of my research team asked Shelley about the biggest thing she had learned from this work. "There's like, of course, all kinds of things just like skills—how to do this, how to do that, how to lead a meeting, how to talk to a girl who is suicidal, how to whatever—all that kind of stuff," she paused. "But . . . the main thing I have learned is what girls' lives are like."

What girls' lives are like. Unquestionably, a significant lesson learned for all of us—including LeAnne and Betty, who played such crucial roles as the program was winding down. And when the program ended, the girls' lives went on.

ASHLEY.

Life after the GRP. Or, "College Is a Big Smack in the Face."

With LeAnne Olson

"JUST BREATHE,"

Ashley advised me, "Everything will be fine." Her pep talk was in response to my bad case of the jitters before a presentation of our collaborative research at my university. During the presentation, just looking at Ashley sitting by me on the stage, so calm and collected, helped me relax—at least a little.

A friend of Cassi's and one of the last to join the Girls' Resiliency Program, Ashley—who was in foster care throughout high school—is one of five girls who participated in LeAnne Olson's dissertation research. With glasses and thick, shoulder-length brown hair, Ashley has a laid-back, confident demeanor that instantly puts others at ease. In her casual style, I have heard Ashley lead into very tough stories with, "Oh, I've already told this to a million social workers"—waving her hand as if to dismiss any concerns the listener might be inclined to express. Whip-smart and quick with a comeback (or a laugh), Ashley is a true survivor.

After our collaborative research project ended and the GRP had shut down completely, LeAnne continued working with five former GRP girls who planned to attend college: Ashley, Cassi, Jennifer, Marycait, and Sara. Three aspired to medical careers—Cassi wanted to become a physician, then changed to nursing, and Jennifer a veterinarian. Ashley's initial goal was to be a pharmacist. Sara hoped to go into archaeology. Marycait planned to pursue a degree in fine arts. LeAnne's study followed them through their senior year of high school and into the first two years of college, or other postsecondary circumstances in Sara's case. Using Ashley's experiences (and those of the other four girls in this group) as a starting point, this chapter explores the legacy of the Girls' Resiliency Program. In other words, what happened next for girls who participated in the program?

For some of them, college happened next. Education is seen by many as the surest way to climb up the social ladder out of poverty and into the middle class (Clark 2006; Fine and Burns 2003). At the same time, we know that schools reinforce social inequalities related to race, sexuality, class, and disability (Fine and Weis 2003). Schools and universities play two roles, both strengthening social inequities *and* offering opportunities for upward mobility. As Michelle Fine and April Burns put it, schools and universities are places where "class, race, ethnic, and gender inequities are reproduced with little notice *and* they are vibrant places that hold out possibilities for individual and collective social change" (2003, 856). Schools, in many ways, are both problems and solutions.

Despite these contradictory roles, there is no question about the importance of higher education in increasing chances of economic well-being. In a recent *New York Times* column, David Brooks writes that in most areas of the country (everywhere but in big cities), it is obvious that "the most crucial inequality is not between the top 1 percent and the bottom 99 percent. It's between those with a college degree and those without" (*New York Times,* October 31, 2011). Although I do not agree that it is possible to pinpoint a single "most crucial" inequality, Brooks convincingly argues that the economic benefits of a college education have increased dramatically over the past few decades. Looking at figures cited by Ben Bernanke, chairman of the Federal Reserve, Brooks notes, "In 1979, the average college graduate made 38 percent more than the average high school graduate.... Now the average college graduate makes more than 75 percent more." Brooks does not comment on gender differences, but David Glenn's five-year study found a significant rise in income for women who earn a college degree, with men earning about the same income with or without college (Glenn 2004). In light of the importance of a college education, especially for girls, and in the context of the low college-going rate in Lincoln County, our research goal after the collapse of the GRP was to understand factors that were helpful and factors that were inhibiting for these former program participants as they tried to make their way from high school to college. Three of them would be the first in their families to attend college.

Richard Lerner, a psychologist and the director of the Institute for Applied Research in Youth Development at Tufts University, points out that there are "relatively few positive indicators to which people can point to reflect the desirable, healthy, and valued behaviors" they hope to see in adolescents as a result of their participation in positive youth development programs (Lerner et al. 2005). It is much easier, of course, to measure rates of *undesirable* behavior such as drug use, crime, and so on. Clearly, for former GRP girls, college attendance is a positive indicator, a sign that a girl has the competence, confidence, and resources to make a successful transition from high school to college and eventually to a college degree.

The girls' transitions to college, however, were not smooth. Given the economic and social barriers faced by low-income and working-class students who are often the first in their families to go to college, this was disheartening but not surprising. Our study provided considerable information about specific barriers, as well as about factors that were helpful to the girls in making the transition to college. Despite some family-related barriers, the girls' relationships with their mothers were helpful in many ways. Four of the girls faced serious financial problems, and all five girls faced obstacles related to mathematics. Finally, their association with LeAnne and their own agency were factors in their transitions.

For better, and sometimes for worse, the girls' mothers played major roles in the girls' educational biographies. Ashley recalled close, supportive times with her biological mom, experiences that paved the way for early successes in school. "My mom would read to me and my sister from the time we were in her belly," Ashley said. "I never remember it being hard for me to learn to read, or anything like that. I knew all this stuff at such a young age." A few years later, her mom helped her with science homework. "I remember that we would be sitting at opposite ends of the kitchen table, and mom would be sitting in the middle. She would say, 'I have one left-handed daughter and one right-handed daughter.' If we needed help she would be right there. She would not leave us until our homework was done."

The other girls also identified their moms as important to their success in school, especially in the elementary years. Sara, for example, said, "I knew most of my ABCs and was reading a few words" before entering Head Start. She recalls that her single mom "would go to work, come home, and talk to me. She didn't have anyone else to talk to, so she would talk to me constantly. I guess I picked up language easily. . . . Mom realized that I was catching on and actually learning," Sara explains, "[so] she went on to teaching me stuff and sitting down with books." Because they received personal early instruction from mom, the girls began school ready to learn and confident in their abilities. All five were strong students in elementary and middle school.

As the girls moved up in school, their moms became less involved in assisting them with academics. This may be related to the fact that only two of the girls' mothers attended college themselves. Based on a long-term study of middle-class and working-class girls, Helen Lucey, June Melody, and Valerie Walkerdine found that working-class mothers in England did not feel capable of helping their children with school work beyond the early elementary grades (2003). Perhaps because Cassi, Ashley, and Sara's mothers' formal education ended at or during high school, they used their knowledge to educate their daughters more in their early than in their later school years.

Similar to the middle-class girls in Lucey, Melody, and Walkerdine's study, the former GRP girls in our study, despite varying social class positions, received "strong messages from their early childhood that it is their identity to go to the university and become professionals" (2003, 296). Unlike Adam Howard and Arthur Levine (2004), who found that an expensive education was the last thing on the minds of low-income parents, the low-income mothers in our study held high expectations for their daughters' college education. All the girls remember that starting at an early age their mothers let them know that they would be going to college. Cassi's mom, who did not attend college herself and had been unable to attend high school full-time because she had to work to support her family, encouraged Cassi to apply to Yale University. Cassi explained that she briefly considered this but decided against it: "I'm not well-rounded. It's not just that. You have to have all kinds of extra stuff. They value people who did sports or student government and community service."

Closely linked to education, a parent's[1] occupation influences the time she has available to spend with children on homework as well as the flexibility she has (or doesn't have) to go to school events. In research comparing parent involvement across different neighborhoods—an elementary school in a working-class area and one in an affluent suburb—sociologist Annette Lareau found that parents' occupations were not related to the extent to which they *valued* education. However, their occupations did have an impact on their "flexibility and ability to attend school events during the day" (2000, 115). This was true for the former GRP girls. Marycait's and Jennifer's mothers—who had flexible work schedules—were more involved in their daughters' education than the other girls' mothers. This enabled Marycait and Jennifer to participate in extracurricular activities and to have their homework monitored. Marycait was active in school theater productions, and Jennifer participated in marching band competitions, playing baritone and tuba. Jennifer also was active in the agriculture program and Future Farmers of America, serving as the organization's treasurer her senior year. In addition to supporting Jennifer's participation in extracurriculars, Jennifer's mom served as PTA president and fund-raiser when Jennifer was in elementary school. In contrast, Ashley's and Sara's mothers and even Cassi's "super mom" were less involved in tracking their daughters' homework and less able to attend school events. When LeAnne spoke with teachers about the girls, they knew Marycait's and Jennifer's mothers, but teachers wondered about constraining factors in the home lives of Cassi, Ashley, and Sara.

Throughout their school years, Marycait, Jennifer, and Cassi received ongoing positive messages and support related to their mothers' high academic expectations. Even in their first year of college, the girls' mothers, and in Marycait's case, her father as well, provided important college-related support. Jennifer's mother took care of Jennifer's newborn baby during her freshman year. "I know I couldn't do it without my mom there. There are so many times I need someone to hold him just to be able to do anything," Jennifer said. During Jennifer's first semester in college, her mom changed her work schedule so she could take care of the baby while Jennifer attended classes on Tuesdays and Thursdays.

In contrast, Ashley and Sara heard positive messages from their mothers early in life, but later on experienced declines in their mothers' support. They got messages that it was important to go to college but received little support to help make that happen. For Sara, her stepfather's abandonment of the family twice was followed by a downturn in her school success. "I was good at math up [until] fourth grade. Then my parents split up." Sara remembers "moving around a lot, and I couldn't believe he just up and left." As Sara's mother became less financially secure, she relied more on the family, including Sara, to help out. Even as a child, Sara became a caregiver to her mother and sister, and academics were put on the back burner.

Later on, when her stepfather returned, both parents worked long hours, and Sara was left to her own devices after school. "After school, I didn't have my mom to tell me, 'Do this homework,'" Sara explains. "I would go home and start reading fan fiction or something. I would think I would do it [homework] later. It would get to be ten o'clock, and I would still be reading and would have to go to bed. Then I would have to fake a lot of essays. I made a D the first six weeks, and the other six weeks were Fs." When she turned sixteen, she started working for her stepfather, who managed a fast-food restaurant in a neighboring county. Throughout high school, she worked long hours on the weekends. Because her ride to work was her stepfather, she was frequently at work for ten to twelve hours at a time. She enjoyed the money, but the long hours meant she frequently put off schoolwork. When her parents realized she was getting poor high school grades, her mother became angry and began to question Sara's ability to pursue a college degree.

In Jennifer's mind, Sara's parents squelched her dreams by telling her she wasn't capable: "I hate seeing people like Sara. She always tells her parents she wants to do something, and her parents tell her she can't do it. Not like [they forbid it], but that she won't be able to." Jennifer remembers when she and Sara were thinking about participating in tennis, but Sara's parents told her that she "wouldn't be able to." Jennifer believes these messages damaged Sara's confidence and were self-fulfilling: "If you're always being told you can't do anything, and you're never going to succeed with anything, then it would be hard to want to do anything. If somebody tells you enough times that you're stupid or you can't do something, you eventually think it and can't do it because you've got to be able to think you can before you can do anything." The "girl box"—and its ability to influence what is perceived to be possible—rears its head again. Or as the novelist Chimamanda Adichie warns in a TED Talk about the "danger of a single story": "Show a people as only one thing . . . and that is what they become" (2009).

Sara, too, faults her parents for not supporting her with tangible assistance or even with encouragement. "They expect me to do stuff, like go to college, get a car, but there is not really any help. They will tell me that I need to do this, but they wouldn't push me," Sara explains. "I have to do it all myself."

For Ashley, as well, school difficulties began when problems emerged at home. She said, "I had straight As up until sixth grade. That was when everything with my parents started going downhill." Although she "can never remember back to when it [her family life] was normal," she divides her childhood family experiences into those *before* and those *after* her father was arrested and her mother left. In the "before" period, there were good times. In addition to memories of her mom and the two sisters doing homework together, Ashley recalls comfortable living arrangements and big family shopping sprees. "My dad had really good jobs, plus burglary, so we had a lot of money," she said. "Mom didn't ever have to work. . . . We would go to Walmart once a month and spend $1,000. We would have like four or five buggies." Then everything changed.

A major turning point in Ashley's life happened in August, just before she started seventh grade. Ashley recounted this event in her own words:

> Me and my mom were looking on the Internet for school clothes. We were just going to order them on the Internet. I didn't know it

was with a stolen credit card, but it was, I found out later. . . . We [Mom, Dad, and I] all got hungry and went to KFC to pick up food. We went past . . . a big parking lot . . . and [saw] all kinds of cops. I thought, "Well, they are getting ready to go bust somebody." It was us. We drove to KFC and got everything. . . . We came back, pulled in, got all the food out. We didn't even get to open it before there was a bang on the door. Bang, bang, bang! There were all these red and blue lights going crazy in our front yard. I guarantee you ten. They were all in the front yard and in every driveway across the street. It was bad, like he had killed someone. They come in and are pointing guns at us. . . . My mom is freaking. She said, "Why are you here?" Then there went Dad. They were at our house for hours. They searched everything. They took everything that had been reported stolen from all these burglaries that he did. . . . He was arrested for burglaries. He was a felon, and he had, like, three pistols. He has been in jail ever since.

Not long after that, things started getting to Mom, and she'd leave. That is the time that I started raising Lilly [my younger sister] myself. She [Mom] wouldn't come back for days. It was right before school started. When school started, I started taking care of Lilly. My grades went way down. It was so bad. I had, like, Fs in all my classes. Somehow I managed to pass seventh grade. . . . . I left for school 20 minutes before she [Lilly] did. My bus ran at 7 and hers ran at 7:21. I would set the alarm and I would tell her that whenever the alarm went off, "Switch it over to this, get dressed, and be out of the house by 7:21. . . . The door is not locked. Don't lock it; just shut it because we don't have a key. . . . I will be here when you get home."

Mom would go buy groceries and leave them there. We would see her twice, maybe three times a week. She would never stay the night. . . . Mom said, "You are old enough to raise your sister."

By then, we hadn't paid our bills, so our gas was off. Our water was on. We had electricity. . . . We would have to get some pots and boil the water and pour it in the bathtub to get hot water in the bath. . . . I would lock the doors at night, [but] I left the back door open . . . so if Mom would ever want to come in, she could go through the back door. But she never did. She never came home. I remember staying up until five in the morning, calling her and crying and leaving her messages: "Get home!" She could have a cell phone but she couldn't pay the gas bill. I would stay up all night crying.

In the summer after Ashley's eighth-grade year, her mom was arrested for drugs. "My mom was in jail, and my dad was in jail," Ashley said, "and there was no one to take care of us." That is when Ashley and her sister went into foster care, moving from home to home throughout the remainder of her secondary schooling. Her four years in foster care were uneven. At times she struggled: "If you are, like, eleven [years old] and up, you are automatically the 'bad' kid. That is how they treat you from the get-go," Ashley explained. "You are not in your natural habitat. You don't know anything. You don't know them. You don't know what the rules are in the house. It is like you are staying in a really bad hotel for a long, long time." In one long-term foster home she described her foster dad as being sick of her because she was not doing enough housecleaning. "He wanted a servant, not a daughter," she recalled. And yet in earlier years in the same foster home—before the couple split up—she was comforted by the words of her foster mother who said, "I am going to take care of you."

As was also true for Cassi, Jennifer, and Sara, Ashley witnessed her mother struggle with financial dependence. Jennifer's and Cassi's moms had regrets about their experiences as young adults and wanted better for their daughters. They were especially eager for their daughters to go to college for future financial security. These mother-daughter dynamics are not uncommon. Lareau's research shows that low-income parents value education and frequently regret their own educational decisions as students (2000). Also, Erica Chenoweth and Renee Galliher found that "for females, college may be viewed as the only option for obtaining financial security and independence" (2004, 12). During their senior year of high school, the GRP girls were eager for independence, and college represented a way to become self-sufficient and meet their career goals.

But first the girls and their families had to figure out how they would get admitted to and then pay for college. According to Sara Hebel of the *Chronicle of Higher Education,* in rural populations, fewer parents have college degrees, leaving their children with less college-going advice about admission and financial aid procedures (2006). I found this to be true in earlier research with low-income girls in West Virginia where "parents had uneven resources to help their daughters achieve school success" (Parrott et al. 2000, 54). For the former GRP girls, the same thing held true, for the most part. Girls with college-educated parents, Marycait and Jennifer, received college-going advice at home. Ashley worked closely with her social worker. But Cassi and Sara relied more heavily on LeAnne for college-going advice, especially in relation to applying for financial aid. More so than the other girls, they were expected to negotiate the transition to college themselves, not unlike the low-income students Janice Bloom, a City University of New York researcher, describes, who had to "shoulder the weight on their own" (2007, 356). Despite the lack of family financial resources for three girls, all five of the girls' mothers encouraged their daughters to attend college.

"IT'S ALMOST BETTER TO NOT HAVE MONEY"

More students in high school aspire to attend college than actually enroll every year, most often because of financial reasons (Fine and Burns 2003; Porter 2006). The primary barrier to college attendance is lack of money (Gorard and See 2008; Plimpton and Quint 2007). The former GRP girls in this study voiced the same issue. When we asked them early in their senior year what might keep them from going to college, they overwhelmingly mentioned the cost. Costs include tuition and books, of course, but also room and board and all the preliminary expenses of college entrance exams and application fees. Cassi was surprised to receive a $200 bill for a dormitory deposit at the end of her senior year of high school. Her parents could not come up with the money, but her Aunt Rose offered to pay the deposit and to purchase dorm supplies as well. Cassi later said that her mother cried after she had moved into the dorm because she was not able to buy Cassi new clothes for college.

For Ashley, initial college costs were covered by Chafee, a federally funded program created under P.L. 106-169 and administered by the West Virginia Department of Health and Human Resources Bureau for Children and Families. The Chafee program provides financial support to foster kids. Because of Chafee, during her senior year Ashley was unconcerned about college costs, knowing they would be covered for her. As the time for college neared, Ashley's social worker informed her of options for college room and board through Chafee. "She explained that my monthly subsidy is $650 and they take out $600 for rent." When Ashley found out she had a choice about whether or not to live in the dorm, she opted to live in an off-campus apartment.

Other former GRP girls did not have similar programs to cover college costs. In addition to academic advising, the girls looked to the counseling office at their high school for financial aid advice but found it difficult to get one-on-one attention from school counselors. Cassi, for example, was aware of curriculum requirements in high school but was not aware of the West Virginia PROMISE Scholarship (a merit-based source of aid for state residents) requirements until LeAnne brought in paperwork during the girls' senior year. This is exactly what Bloom is referring to in saying that in order to receive financial assistance, low-income students "must make their way through *more* paperwork than middle-class students, with *less* knowledge and support" (2005, 72). Problematically, the increase in paperwork for first-generation, low-income students must be negotiated by students and families with the least college-related experience. Or, as DeNeen Brown of the *Washington Post* puts it, "The poorer you are, the more things cost. More in money, time, hassle, exhaustion, menace" ("The High Cost of Poverty," May 18, 2009).

For girls, financial aid information related to teen pregnancy is another important piece of the picture. When Jennifer became pregnant, she began looking into her financial options as a single mother. She encountered problems getting benefits because she was viewed as a dependent based on her age and living arrangements at home. She learned that if she were classified as an independent, single mother, she would receive more federal assistance to attend college. In order to dispel her confusion with the policies and procedures, Jennifer continued to contact the university's financial aid office to determine her dependent/independent status. Based on Jennifer's experiences, Cassi believes that high school and college counselors should give pregnant teens information so they can make better college-going decisions. "Jennifer lost all of her aid, pretty much," Cassi reports. "The FAFSA [Free Application for Federal Student Aid] people told her that when she was pregnant, she needed to file as independent, [but the university] wanted her to file as dependent because she does not provide half the care." Ultimately, Cassi continues, "They took her whole Pell Grant away. She just has a little bit of aid now because of that whole screw-up. No one explained it to any of us. That is big because there are a lot of teen mothers who think that they can't [go to college] because they have babies. Jennifer is one of the ones, and I am very proud, who is still going. I was really worried about that. They aren't making it easy for her by not explaining things."

The girls' parents' financial resources varied from the ability to pay for extensive private tutoring (in Marycait's case) to the ability to qualify for low-income waivers for testing (in Cassi's case). The girls who experienced successful transitions to college found ways to pay for college with minimal use of student loans. Marycait was the only one whose parents paid for her college attendance. Jennifer, Cassi, and Ashley were able to acquire financial aid because of their low-income status, receiving Pell grants and student loans. The financial aid process was difficult, but the end result was college attendance for three low-income girls.

Sara, who has not yet attended college, names money as the main reason she did not enroll, despite being accepted and attending orientation. She did not qualify for financial aid because her parents made too much money, even though they did not have the disposable income to financially support Sara's college attendance. In reflecting on her own financial situation and those of her friends, Jennifer concludes that it is better to be at one end or the other of the financial spectrum than to be in the middle:

> It's almost better to not have money because then you have all that help. Whereas if you're really rich then you don't have to worry about it, and if you're right there in the middle where you have a good bit of money but it is all going to something else like the bills you have, so you're stuck there in the middle where you need help but you can't get it because you make too much. . . . It's almost better to be at the extreme ends.

In Sara's case, another major factor is looming dental bills. "I want my teeth fixed because they are just so bad," Sara explains. "I don't like to smile because of my teeth. I hate my teeth! They are just so nasty. When I was at Cassi's house, I bit into a celery stick and broke a tooth. They are so brittle. I am afraid I am going to lose this front tooth because it is bad off. I will die if I lose a front tooth." During the summer after her junior year, Sara planned to have all of her teeth, some of which were abscessing, removed and a bone graft to reinforce her gums so that she could have permanent dentures implanted. She was excited about having a pretty smile. Sara began the procedure by having her back teeth removed and the bone graft completed on her back gums, but when her parents realized that their insurance would not cover the entire procedure, the work was stopped and Sara entered her senior year with no back teeth. Understandably, having her teeth fixed is a top priority for Sara. After that, "I think I could save up for a car by myself [and] I could fight my way through college." Also understandable is her belief that she will be on her own in paying for both. After all, her parents had previously promised to pay for dental work, only to stop payments in the middle of restoration procedures. "Money is a real issue with me," Sara says. "I want to be 100 percent positive in my college choices, so I don't waste any money because I don't have it to waste."

Just as Jennifer theorized, the lowest-income girls in this study were able to obtain loans and grants to cover the cost of attendance, and the higher-income student relied on her parents for college costs, but the middle-income student who was left to shoulder the total cost of attendance did not end up going.

Recently there has been an increase in merit-based, rather than need-based, college scholarships (Gorard and See 2008). The irony of receiving a scholarship for exemplary academic achievement is that often the merit has been achieved in large part because of resources available to wealthier students who would have attended college anyway (Howard and Levine 2004). In other words, privileged students are increasingly receiving more scholarships based on their merit, while students with fewer resources have to take out loans to pay for college. The sad result is that lower-income students end up paying more than middle- and upper-income students for a comparable education because of interest on the student loans (Howard and Levine 2004). This is particularly troublesome in light of recent increases in college tuition rates, which are expected to continue to increase (Clark 2006). Since the 1980s, college enrollment and tuition have increased while federal need-based grants have decreased (Kettley, Whitehead, and Raffan 2008).

I find myself agreeing with Howard and Levine, who argue that financial aid policies of college and universities have deviated from their original intention to provide accessible education to all students, primarily those in need. They note that when President Truman commissioned a study of higher education institutions in 1947, the study results identified five barriers to higher education access: "race, gender, income, religion, and geographic location" (2004). According to Howard and Levine, progress has been made in regard to every category except income, which continues to discourage postsecondary attendance. They conclude that institutions of higher education are not committed to providing opportunities targeted at low-income, first-generation college students.

This seems to be true in West Virginia where we have the PROMISE Scholarship, a merit-based program initiated in 2001 for West Virginia residents. The goal of the program is to keep high-achieving students in the state and avoid the brain drain discussed earlier. Regardless of income, West Virginia students with a high school GPA of 3.0 (a B average) or higher and certain ACT scores (initially a 21 composite was required) or SAT scores (at least 1020 combined score) are eligible for a scholarship covering the full cost of tuition for four years at any state college or university. This kind of statewide merit scholarship program, increasingly popular throughout the early 1990s, has been contested by those who claim that the scholarships go against the goals of the Higher Education Act (1965) to increase access to higher education through *needs*-based assistance (Dynarski 2002; Heller 2002; Baum 2006). Critics suggest that the funding goes disproportionately to middle- and upper-income students, "who are naturally predisposed to college participation [and] are far more likely to benefit from scholarships like the PROMISE" (Defrank-Cole, Cole, and Garbutt 2009).

Because of the large number of students taking advantage of the West Virginia PROMISE Scholarship, and the limited funds available to support the program, the initial scholarship eligibility requirements were increased. As of 2008, the required ACT composite score was raised to 22, with no subtest scores of less than 20. In a study of the effects of the

PROMISE Scholarship, Lisa DeFrank-Cole, a West Virginia University professor, found that the new criteria "exacerbated the lack of diversity in PROMISE Scholarship recipients" (DeFrank-Cole, Cole, and Garbutt 2009, 61). The researchers found that enrollment in the honors college at West Virginia University increased sharply with the implementation of PROMISE. At the same time, however, a lower percentage of low-income students have enrolled in the honors program since the initiation of the PROMISE Scholarships. The study authors explain that "as PROMISE has increased requirements, fewer low-income students receive it" (DeFrank-Cole, Cole, and Garbutt 2009, 62–63). This is exactly what happened with Cassi. With a 4.0 high school GPA and an ACT composite score of 26, she should have been a solid contender for the PROMISE Scholarship. Her verbal score was an exceptionally strong 32, but because of a math score of 18, even after taking the test three times, she was denied the scholarship.

Math. In one way or another, it was a barrier for all five of the former GRP girls.

MATH. OR, "I FINALLY JUST GAVE UP ON IT"

I was "pretty good in [math]," Ashley recalled. "I was in advanced math classes when I was in elementary school and middle school, but . . . I finally just gave up on it." Sara recalled excelling in math until about fourth grade, and Cassi used to be a strong math student, as well. In fourth grade, she competed in math against the smartest boy in class: "Once you were finished with your work, you got to help other people. We would race. Nobody else knew we were racing, but we were racing to see who could get up first and help somebody." Cassi, along with Jennifer, Sara, and Ashley, were assigned to advanced math classes in eighth grade, yet for all of them, math was an obstacle in getting to, and succeeding in, college. Why? One reason is that although the expanded curriculum of their consolidated high school provided more class options, the lack of advising and inconsistent instructional quality were obstacles. All five participants scored low on math sections of the ACT or SAT, requiring them to enroll in developmental math courses in college and costing all of them a shot at the West Virginia PROMISE Scholarship.

Currently the United States is ranked twenty-fifth out of thirty-four so-called developed nations in math literacy for fifteen-year-olds (Fleischman, Hopstock, Pelczar, and Shelley 2010). In West Virginia, the situation is especially bad. Headlines in our local newspaper announce in large, bold letters: "W.Va. near bottom in national test scores" (Bill Rosenberger, *Herald-Dispatch,* November 2, 2011). In the fine print, we see that the worst score was in "eighth-grade math, in which students scored lower than 44 states or jurisdictions."

We know that math achievement is a predictor of college completion (Cho 2007; Trusty and Niles 2003), but we don't know much about reasons for US students' deficits in math comprehension. We do know that on the ACT and SAT, both of which are used as gauges to judge the likelihood of college students' academic success, US women typically lag behind men in math scores (Halpern et al. 2007). Despite the low standardized test scores, girls earn higher math grade point averages (GPAs) than boys. The former GRP girls confirm these statistics. They earned high grades in math, though they did not complete advanced math courses in high school. Their math difficulties were related to two factors: advice, or lack of it, from school counselors and the poor quality of math instruction.

School counselors play an important role in matching students with classes that lead to their desired goals after high school. We know that college prep curriculum requirements can allow students to transition to college more smoothly. Specifically, more math and science courses in a girl's curriculum are associated with an increase in the likelihood of college attendance (Cho 2007). For the GRP girls with science-related majors, a math background was particularly important. Typically, advanced math students can begin high school math requirements in eighth grade, as three of the former GRP girls did. Jerry Trusty and Spencer Niles found that "eighth grade math ability affected math course-taking in high school, which in turn affected bachelor's degree completion" (2003, 102). Curricular guidance is particularly important during these early adolescent years. For the GRP girls, instead of being informed about and carefully guided into rigorous, college preparatory course work, especially in math and science, the girls' scheduling was hit or miss depending on which counselor they happened to see. They also received incomplete guidance about scholarship requirements, as noted earlier.

At the beginning of her senior year, Cassi was registered for AP calculus, but by October she decided to drop the class, saying, "I don't need AP calculus. It's bringing down my GPA." Her GPA, with her weighted AP courses, was 4.0. She received two Bs during high school, one in a physical education class and one in her senior civics class. Although Cassi was concerned about her GPA for college admissions, she was not advised about the GPA requirements for the West Virginia PROMISE Scholarship, which she thought were higher than the 3.0 minimum.

Sara, too, had less than adequate guidance counseling at school. "At the beginning of ninth grade, they gave us this little yellow book you can look through," she said. "I was in the science department to be an archaeologist, but I wasn't taking any of the right classes for that. I was taking all the right classes for hospitality, so I had to get my paper switched to the hospitality thing, Pro-Start [a non-college prep program]. If you had classes picked out where you couldn't graduate, they [counselors] would just change it for you." So although Sara was interested in going to college, her schedule was not planned accordingly. She changed her major, deviating from the archaeology/science track during ninth grade, partly in an effort to take classes with her friend Cassi. "We sat down with [a teacher filling in for a school counselor] during our first week of class, and he worked with us to get our schedules together." It seems that the teacher/counselor helped the girls plan a schedule focused more on their friendship than on their career and college plans. In describing her schedule, Sara explained that the school had classes for archaeology, "but I never took them. I was just picking classes to take. During the middle of my junior year, I decided to go into Pro-Start, and then I finally figured out how to get it switched around to take the classes I needed to graduate. I was on the professional pathway," she went on, "but I'm on the skilled pathway now, and I don't have to take a second foreign language class, or four sciences, and I don't need a lot of electives, only a few." In addition to getting little direction from counselors and teachers, Sara did not discuss academic advising with her parents. She figured out her academic curriculum for herself.

Ashley's class scheduling advice also was problematic. When she spoke with a school counselor about registering for junior-year classes, Ashley requested taking two years of Computer Assisted Drafting (CAD) in one year. Ashley describes her junior schedule as "just an accident. [The school counselor] wrote down what I wanted, and they put me in both [CAD classes]." Ashley took the CAD program in two blocks, two classes in the morning and two in the afternoon. "At the beginning of the day, he [the teacher] just wanted everyone to run to [a local breakfast restaurant] and come back and we would watch movies." She had been excited about CAD, but she quickly realized it was not a serious class. In addition to poor advising that allowed her to sign up for two years of the program in one year's time, the CAD teacher was not highly qualified. Ashley explained that the teacher "was working in computer science in North Carolina, but when he came here they made him a teacher. He was never taught to be a teacher. He wasn't a teacher; he just knew CAD." Stories like these concern and sadden me, especially since increased academic rigor in high school is associated with girls' college attendance (Plimpton and Quint 2007).

In reflecting on the assistance she received from school counselors, Cassi wrote out her recommendations for counselors: "Know what you preach. When I come to you for help, don't point me to a drawer and dismiss me. Be able to answer my questions. Don't hand me the documentation and say, 'Good Luck.' Actually *HELP* me when I need it." Such advice is important, given the fact that students' academic tracks are more likely to predict their college attendance than their parents' education or income (Plimpton and Quint 2007). To advise, or even allow, high school students who plan to go to college to follow a course of study other than college preparatory is unconscionable. I might even argue that allowing *any* high school student to follow a course of study other than college preparatory is problematic, given what we know about the importance of a college education for economic mobility. To do so may well be "to consign [them] to a future of dead-end jobs" (Bloom 2005, 66).

But lack of advising was not the girls' only math-related problem. Cassi traces the onset of her math problems to the loss of two good math teachers in the middle of the year during eighth and ninth grades. They were replaced by permanent substitutes. "We started out with good teachers, but they left," Cassi reports. "All this started way back in Algebra 1 and Algebra 2. We didn't really get good instruction since both of our teachers just left halfway through the year and were replaced by incompetent teachers." This is not surprising in light of the common practice of using permanent substitutes to replace qualified teachers. Richard Ingersoll, a professor of education and sociology at the University of Pennsylvania, found that "if a teacher suddenly leaves in the middle of a semester, a principal may find it faster and cheaper to hire a readily available but not fully qualified substitute teacher, rather than conduct a formal search for a new teacher" (2001, 45). In earlier research with girls in West Virginia, we learned that in math classes in both rural and urban low-income schools, substitute teachers were often used to fill long teacher absences, and that content coverage and instructional quality often suffered as a result (Parrott et al. 2000, 53). In the current study, former GRP girls describe their substitute math teachers as unable to cope with classroom management and unable to teach math concepts. Cassi, who ended up with As in all her math classes but struggled in understanding math concepts, wrote, seemingly to teachers everywhere: "If you went to college for English, do *NOT* try to teach me math." Likewise, Sara pleaded, "Know your subject." Four of the five GRP girls were taught by out-of-field math teachers during both of those critical eighth- and ninth-grade math classes. Looking back now, I can't help but think of these classes as a terrible turning point in the girls' lives.

Sadly, such occurrences are not uncommon in rural areas such as Lincoln County, West Virginia, where school resources are limited (Thomas 2008), and teachers are known to teach out of subject more frequently than in other areas (Truscott and Truscott 2005). Susan Ansell and Melissa McCabe report that in high-poverty schools, "32 percent of students are taught by at least one core-subject teacher without at least a minor in the subject" (2003, 57). In fact, the "only schools that have few problems finding and keeping [qualified] teachers are those located in suburbs with ample resources and stable populations" (Truscott and Truscott 2005, 127).

Whereas the school might employ college-educated teachers, out-of-field teaching changes their status as "highly qualified." As Ingersoll notes, "Data clearly show that the typical out-of-field teacher has both a bachelor's and a master's degree, is fully certified, and has substantial coursework in an academic specialty" (2001, 44). However, "highly qualified teachers may actually become highly unqualified if they are assigned to teach subjects for which they have little training or education" (42). In other words, although teachers might be certified to teach, in order to be "highly qualified" they must teach in their primary field.

The experiences of the former GRP girls suggest that lack of teacher quality in math is particularly problematic because students are expected to build on a prior knowledge base. Even for strong math students, having a poor teacher in one or two years can hinder progress in the years to follow. Trusty and Niles found that in the United States, "31% of high school students were taught by teachers who did not have both a major and a teacher-certificate in math teaching"—in other words, teachers who were not highly qualified (2003, 103). In addition, Ingersoll reports that "one-third of all secondary school math teachers have neither a major nor a minor in math or in such related disciplines as physics, engineering or math education" (2001, 43). Xuejin Lu, Jianping Shen, and Sue Poppink report that only 59.5 percent of high school math teachers are highly qualified (2007). *How many studies do we need to realize there is a problem with math instruction?* The GRP girls' math problems were related to the school's failure to find and employ highly qualified math teachers. These math difficulties had serious negative influences on their transitions to college.

Because Jennifer and Ashley have college majors in science fields, they are required to successfully complete a college math course before enrolling in science courses for their majors. The delay of completing their developmental math courses cost them extended time in college and the expense of paying for additional credit hours. Several girls had to enroll in developmental classes numerous times to pass them. As a result, some are even considering lowering their career aspirations. After enrolling in developmental math for three semesters, Jennifer began taking biology and chemistry courses designed for nonmajors because the science courses for her major required college math as a prerequisite. As a result, she is considering changing her major and transferring to a different college in order to become a veterinary technician rather than a veterinarian. In fairness, this change is also related to other factors. As Jennifer balances single motherhood and schoolwork, she recognizes that a shorter school program would be more manageable and still provide a stable income. She is also unsure of her mother's ability to continue providing care for her young son if she were to move out of her parents' home to attend vet school.

LEANNE. OR, "YOU HAVE EARNED A SPECIAL PLACE"

The GRP offered middle and high school girls many kinds of challenging opportunities and a great deal of personal support, but academics were not emphasized in the program. This was by design. As we have seen, the program emphasized leadership as well as social justice and community activism. At the same time the girls were coming into middle school and participating in the nonacademically oriented GRP, their mothers, who had worked with them extensively in kindergarten and elementary years, began to provide less assistance with schoolwork. The fact that during this critical period neither the GRP nor the girls' families, for numerous reasons, focused on girls' academic successes—particularly in math—put the girls at a disadvantage in transitioning to college.

When the GRP ended during Ashley and her friends' junior year in high school, LeAnne became the one and only (de facto) program facilitator. The safe space girls had with LeAnne was similar to what they had experienced in the GRP, but the emphasis changed to include academics as well as family and social issues. For the three who attended college at Marshall University, LeAnne also became a math tutor, but this may have been a case of too little, too late. That said, the girls identify LeAnne as an important factor in their transitions to college. Her long-term immersion in the field throughout three and a half years of data collection, analysis, and writing enabled her to develop close relationships with the girls and deep understandings of their lives and college transitions.

One of the main roles LeAnne played was that of an information provider. In their senior year, she asked the girls about their high school classes and college-going plans during regular visits to the school. As the girls ran into roadblocks, she answered their questions. Because there were three first-generation college-going students in the group, she provided information that was lacking from their parents' experience. "As a former academic counselor at a nearby state university, I understood the process of applying to college, from immunization requirements to terminology that was unfamiliar to the girls," LeAnne recalled. "For example, Cassi was not going to apply for a scholarship because she [incorrectly] did not see herself as a first-generation college student because a cousin had attended one year of college. After our lunch discussion about scholarships, Cassi went home, wrote an essay about her financial need, and applied for a scholarship, which she received." Saba Ali, a professor of education at the University of Iowa, found that in rural Appalachian areas, students are more dependent on the advice of family members, and when family members have experienced academic failure, they are unable to provide the needed academic advice to their children. In addition, she found that parents were unfamiliar with the academic preparation needed for college as well as the application process (Ali and Saunders 2006).

In addition to college-going information, LeAnne provided other kinds of support. She acted as a parental figure for the low-income girls during college-going events and college orientations because of their parents' inflexible work schedules. She attended college orientation with Jennifer the day before Jennifer gave birth to her son. She frequently took Cassi to college events, such as the governor's symposium for West Virginia GEAR UP! (a US Department of Education program preparing low-income students for college) and her college orientation. She attended Ashley's college orientation at a distant state university and joined their university-sponsored program for parents.

For the three girls attending Marshall University, LeAnne's job on campus also allowed the girls to stop by for social support as well as information and academic assistance. "Cassi relied on me the most," LeAnne recalls, "as she was experiencing her first time away from home. We frequently went to lunch close to campus, or she would stop by work to tell me about her day. When Jennifer needed someone to watch her son, Cassi and I were both available to provide support."

For Ashley, also, LeAnne was an important player in the transition to college, "being there" with support and encouragement throughout. "You helped me emotionally more than anything," Ashley said, "coming to visit me and being there for me on parents' weekend. That was just great. You are still on my FERPA [Family Educational Rights and Privacy Act] if you ever wanted to call and check up on me. There was just you, my social worker, and my real mom. You have earned a special place."

When Sara expressed an interest in culinary education, LeAnne told her about a program at a nearby community college. LeAnne found out from a community college admissions officer that Sara's fees could be waived if a high school counselor wrote a letter stating her financial need. After Sara received that information, she filled out an application and had a counselor write a letter. LeAnne hand-delivered the application and letter. Sara was accepted and made plans to attend their orientation. Because Sara did not have her license or a car, she asked LeAnne to take her to the orientation. "I picked her up early, and we had lunch at a local restaurant," LeAnne recalls. "Sara was excited and wore the T-shirt the community college had sent her."

In addition to providing information and being there with other kinds of support, from emotional to mathematical, LeAnne was an Appalachian female role model. The girls developed close, ongoing relationships with a West Virginia woman with advanced educational degrees. This is important because for first-generation college-going students, role models who are "like them," who have earned a college degree, and who can provide guidance are lacking in low-income communities (Bloom 2007). It follows that this lack of role models and realistic visions of college education may hinder college attendance for students who have not seen success stories within their own communities. In Lincoln County, the population of bachelor degree holders is below 6 percent, providing few college role models. Female college role models are especially important for giving first-generation, college-attending rural girls the sense that achieving academic goals is possible (Alloway and Gilbert 2004).

The connections between LeAnne and the former GRP girls are strong and enduring, perhaps strong enough to pass Ric MacDowell's "long-haul" test. Together, LeAnne and the girls made presentations at two annual conferences of the Appalachian Studies Association. They also met with members of the Lincoln County Youth and Prevention Coalition (a group Ric chairs) to share their high school to college transition experiences and recommendations. In preparation for the meeting, they collaboratively decided which issues to emphasize and what recommendations to make to the school and local community. LeAnne's reflections, written near the close of her dissertation research:

> As I met with participants one final time as a group, two weeks before my dissertation went to my committee, I was impressed by how far we had come in our educational journeys. I passed out a final writing prompt about my findings and their recommendations. As I distracted

Jennifer's son with drawings, I noticed the rare silence as the girls completed their writing. When I returned home and gave the writing prompts my full attention, I was impressed with the girls' honesty and surprised by some of their responses. Would this study ever end? No, I will continue to be involved with my participants and continue to accompany them on their educational journeys. I want to acknowledge the strong bonds I have formed with my participants. They are all intelligent, strong females who are capable of earning a college degree.

LeAnne is continuing to follow the girls as they make their way toward and through college.

AGENCY. OR, "MY MOM PLANTED THE SEEDS, BUT IT WAS ALL ME"

The factors explored in this chapter—moms, money, math, and mentors (i.e., LeAnne)—can be thought of as elements of social systems or structures, primarily the family and the school, that influenced the girls' transitions from high school to college. Of course, it is important also to consider individual acts of human agency that were involved in the girls' transitions, in both intended and unintended ways. In her dissertation, LeAnne used structuration theory to interpret her findings. For Anthony Giddens, "Structuration theory is based on the proposition that structure is always both enabling and constraining, in virtue of the inherent relationship between structure and agency (and agency and power)" (1984, 169). This is not unlike feminist scholar Lisa Duggan's concept of individual agency within "a limited range of very constrained choices in a sexist, capitalist economy" (2006, 8). Or as Karl Marx famously put it: "Men make their own history, but they do not make it as they please; they do not make it under self-selected circumstances, but under circumstances existing already, given and transmitted from the past" (1852). It's the same story for these West Virginia girls. They choose, but they don't choose without constraints.

The systems that seemed to most strongly influence the former GRP participants' transitions to college were their families and their high school experiences, but it is not possible to understand how these systems contributed to the girls' college outcomes without taking a look at the girls' own agency, their ability to make choices and follow through with action. The girls made decisions about college, their career, and family plans—and acted on them. When we met with the girls in their junior year of high school, they excitedly talked about their plans for the future, which featured attending college. During their senior year, we asked them about how they saw their goals playing out in five years. Again, all of them mentioned college, but they also mentioned plans for a family. Marycait said, "Hopefully I'll find someone and get married and have children in my midtwenties." Similarly, Jennifer responded, "My baby starts kindergarten! I'll be in veterinary medical school, living in Virginia. Maybe have another baby." Cassi, who initially planned to become a doctor, decided that nursing was more practical because, like Jennifer, she was interested in starting a family.

Given their young ages, LeAnne was surprised at the importance the girls placed on starting their own families. As the girls made high school curricular choices and college major choices, they assumed they would be wives and mothers. Their career choices reflected their expectations of fulfilling traditional motherhood roles. I was surprised as well, especially in light of earlier research I had done with low-income West Virginia girls who made it clear that they did not want to have kids at a young age, fearing that could prevent their realization of career goals. Undoubtedly traditional social systems, both family and school, influenced the former GRP participants' understandings of gender roles and relationships. Perhaps the girls' ideas and goals might have been different had they been part of the GRP in its earlier years, when Shelley, an ardent feminist who challenged traditional gender expectations, was more directly involved. When these five girls joined the GRP, their primary staff association was with Virginia, a former GRP girl who dropped out of high school and started a family at about the same time.

Whatever their career and family goals, all the girls planned to go to college and demonstrated agency in high school when they registered for particular classes. These choices affected their transitions to college. In some cases, their decisions were enabling, such as when Marycait and Cassi selected AP or dual-credit classes for which they earned college credit. In other cases, girls' curricular choices were constraining, like when Sara chose to schedule classes with Cassi during her junior year and as a result, switched out of the college preparatory track.

Beyond changing tracks, Sara did not apply herself to her high school work. Even one of Sara's favorite teachers described her as a "classic under-achiever. I could not pull her through." Despite her intelligence, Sara and her teachers agreed that she lacked the motivation needed to be a successful student. One of her teachers said that Sara "would say, 'Oh, I just didn't do it.'" Likewise, Sara admits to LeAnne: "I just didn't do any of the work." She explains, "I slacked off a lot. I am lazy." Although her teachers did not identify specific reasons for Sara's behavior, they speculated that either work or something in her home life was keeping her from spending time on assignments. Sara was working long hours on weekends and on weeknights was home alone with no one monitoring her schoolwork. But ultimately, Sara made choices about what she spent time on outside the classroom, and more often than not, it wasn't school assignments.

Cassi, in contrast, made many choices that helped in reaching her goal of attending college. "She is a very ambitious student," her twelfth-grade AP English teacher remarked. "She is very bothered if her work is not to her level of perfection." Describing Cassi as "task-oriented," "responsible," "focused," and having a "good work ethic," another teacher said that "Cassi is not shy about asking questions and asking for help." In reflecting on her transition from high school to college, Cassi acknowledged what she gained from her mother, but she also knew that it was up to her to act. "My mom planted the seeds," she said, "but it was all me." Even when she ran into unexpected roadblocks with advanced calculus, low math ACT scores, and the subsequent denial of the PROMISE Scholarship, Cassi was determined to fulfill her college-going plans. "It didn't matter if I had to take out millions in loans," she said. "I was going to go to college."

Similarly determined to go to college, Jennifer also faced unexpected obstacles related to choices she made in the context of family and school structures. Although she demonstrated responsibility in most areas of her life, Jennifer did not always make good personal decisions. During her senior year, she and her boyfriend stopped using birth control, and she became pregnant. Her relationship with her boyfriend deteriorated after he was arrested for theft. He was in jail when she had their baby. It is unclear why Jennifer made the choices she did about sexual activity and birth control, but she was not alone in doing so. The 2012 West Virginia KIDS COUNT Data Book focuses on the rise in teen birthrates between 2005 and 2009. During that period, West Virginia's rate of teen pregnancy and the gap between the state and national rates of teen pregnancy both grew steadily. In response, the Data Book recommends fully implementing the state's sex education curriculum. As Jennifer's experiences show, that may not be as simple as it sounds.

Jennifer was uneasy discussing sex with her mother. In seventh grade, she forged her mother's signature on a consent form that granted permission to attend a sex education class. Jennifer describes the interaction this way: "I asked my mom, and she asked if I wanted to [attend the sex education talk]. I was not going to tell her that I wanted to. It would have been a really awkward conversation. So I told her that it didn't matter, so she put no [on the consent form]." Jennifer continued to avoid sexual discussions with her mother. In eleventh grade, when Jennifer's mother found out that Jennifer was sexually active with a man who lived in her hollow, she took her to the doctor to be tested for sexually transmitted diseases and pregnancy. She threatened to have the man arrested for statutory rape if Jennifer did not end the relationship. In twelfth grade, Jennifer began to date the boyfriend who was to become the father of her baby.

During her senior year, Jennifer participated in a panel sponsored by the Youth and Prevention Coalition to come up with solutions to teen pregnancy. Her recommendation, to "have the family planning in the schools and make it more available," suggests that birth control information and materials were not readily available to her.

Despite boyfriend problems and a new baby, Jennifer perseveres in pursuing her goal of college attendance. She admits that having a baby while attending college makes studying more difficult. "It's harder to get my homework done. Mom works Friday, Saturday, and Sunday, and that's when I do the bulk of my big work, and the first weekend he would not let me set him down, all Friday and all day Saturday." Jennifer has to be more responsible than traditional college students because she is raising her son. "I put him [the baby] in bed at 8 P.M., and I can't go in my room [which is the baby's room, too] and study," she explains. "But I've been going in my mom's room and studying after he goes to bed." Jennifer is successfully attending college, going on her fourth semester. She does well in most subjects, but she struggles with math.

Reflecting on her choices and her experiences transitioning to college, Jennifer believes she "focused too much on my boyfriend, which made it harder to do everything I needed to do." On the issue of teenage pregnancy, she wrote, "USE PROTECTION!! Kids aren't as easy as you may think." Jennifer went on to write that her son "was screaming most of the time I have been typing because he hasn't had his nap and has a red bottom."

Ashley, too, has regrets about what appear, in hindsight, to be poor choices related to her transition from high school to college. Her decision to go to a large, distant state university instead of a university closer to home was one of those mistakes. Ashley's expectations of the more distant university did not match her experiences once she started her freshman year. She found it hard to make friends. She put up a brave front, but her experiences at the distant university were difficult because she was isolated from friends who had become like a family to her. Because she was lonely for friends and a new boyfriend in Lincoln County, Ashley missed classes for extended periods of time during both her fall and spring semesters. "In the middle of November, I was stranded [in Lincoln County] because no one would take me back to [school]. So I missed at least three weeks of class. My grades were good before I left. I didn't know that I was failing all my classes because of too many absences."

A second poor choice, as Ashley sees it now, was the decision to live off campus in an apartment rather than in a dorm on campus. Her advice for future college freshmen is to live "in a dorm because I think I would have done a bit better had I had friends." Cassi agreed, saying that "living in the dorm helped. Not that I made any relationships because of it, but because it helped me be close to my classes." In addition, Ashley allowed her biological mother, now out of jail, to live with her in her apartment starting in November and through the spring semester of her freshman year. Although she appreciated the chance to have a relationship with her mother after a long time without her, she says that spring break, when she went back to see friends in Lincoln County, was a "retreat. I was so sick of my mom. After a while, I just wanted her to go."

After successfully completing only three hours of credit during her freshman year, Ashley was placed on academic probation and lost her Chafee scholarship. The following semester she lived with her boyfriend's family in Lincoln County and worked at the local newspaper. This year she transferred to a nearby state university, where she feels she has a "fresh start." She is optimistic about her chances in the new university, saying "I know I am going to do a hundred times better [here]." To pay her tuition, she got a Pell grant, but because of her late financial aid application, she was still waiting on her loan to buy textbooks as of the fourth week of classes in the semester.

Recently Ashley made another choice, to be featured in this book chapter, and to continue working with us in research that seems to have no end. As I anxiously mull over the never-ending project, I hear Ashley telling me to "breathe, Linda, just breathe."

Self-portrait collage of Ashley, 2009

LINDA.

LAYNE.

There's a (Research) Method to Our Madness

FROM PROGRAM EVALUATOR TO COLLABORATIVE ETHNOGRAPHER, OR, LINDA'S JOURNEY

"I don't want to sit next to him," Billy announced as he stood up and brushed himself off. Jordan had just given him a friendly punch in the arm, which resulted in Billy's chair turning over to considerable laughter. "Okay," I responded, not sure how to proceed as I continued to arrange chairs. "Would anyone else like to sit here?" No volunteers—just some nervous chuckling and horsing around as Jordan gave Wesley a shove and tossed a small beanbag across the room where Anthony and Billy struggled with each other to get it. "Whoa, guys, take it easy!" cautioned Betty. Meanwhile, Ashley said, "Kelli's not coming today. Can I do her part?" Almost simultaneously, several other girls asked to do Kelli's part as well.

Such was the lively, chaotic, nature of our collaborative research including high school students, local community adults who work with youth, and those of us from the university. The scenario above took place at the high school as we rehearsed for a public presentation of our research—the culmination of over a year of work together. With the presentation, to be held at Marshall University, just one week away, we were having our first rehearsal with both girls and boys together. We were all pretty excited and nervous.

The first I remember hearing about this kind of research—research that includes participants as an integral part of the study design and purpose, research *with* people rather than *on* them—was when I read Patricia Maguire's *Doing Participatory Research: A Feminist Approach* (1987). Drawing on Paulo Freire's concept of dialogues, Maguire interviewed women who had survived domestic violence and reflected with them about their own words (interview transcripts) and experiences—all in an effort to address the problem of how to move forward after the nightmare of living with violent partners. I was inspired by her work, by the possibility of research with genuine "real world" meaningfulness, especially around social problems such as intimate partner violence. I decided right then that my future research would be participatory, that I would do research in partnership with individuals and groups who would identify research goals to meet *their* needs rather than as a lone ranger who conducted research to create new knowledge that *I* determined was worthy.

Fast-forward fifteen years and several *non*-participatory research studies later. I met Eric Lassiter, at that time a new professor on our faculty, read his *Chicago Guide to Collaborative Ethnography* (2005), and renewed my commitment to research that "involves the side-by-side work of all parties in a mutually beneficial research program" (American Anthropology Association El Dorado Task Force Papers, in Lassiter 2005, ix). Although I had worked collaboratively as a facilitator of several research teams and had considered issues of power in my analyses, they were very much *my* analyses. Despite my initial excitement about Maguire's participatory work, I now realize that my own work—much of which came out of qualitative program evaluation research—was not participatory in the way that Lassiter describes. I had taken responsibility for creating the research designs, doing the fieldwork, analyzing the observation and interview data, and writing. I had considerable assistance with the fieldwork but did much of the analysis and most of the writing single-handedly, seeking feedback from research assistants and participants on fully formed drafts. Based on that feedback, I made revisions and then distributed completed manuscripts. Clearly, I had the power of "the last word," as Lassiter puts it.

Nikki Jones, a qualitative researcher, describes a telling moment that highlights this power of the last word. After submitting an article about her work with urban, African American girls for publication, Jones got feedback from a journal reviewer who suggested she situate her work within crime studies rather than the black feminist and sociological literature she had used. She rejected the suggestion, fearing it would "label the girls in this study as offenders, victims, delinquents, or criminals," and did not reframe the work (2010, 181). Following the insights of scholars such as Barbara Smith, Chandra Mohanty, and Patricia Hill Collins on the importance of centering research in the experiences and understandings of marginalized groups, Jones went on to note that the identities that the girls claim for themselves—"good girls, pretty girls, sometimes violent girls, and fighters"—are far more useful than those that a racist society puts on them (2010, 181). At the same time, Jones was *still the one deciding* how the girls would be represented; she had the power of the last word.

As was the case with my own research in this period. In my defense, most of the research I had conducted—including my work with the GRP—was for the purpose of program evaluation. In each case, I was hired to design and carry out qualitative evaluation research that would focus on the experiences and perceptions of program participants. Although my role was that of an "external" evaluator, I followed case study research expert Robert Stake (2004) and instead of judging the quality of programs from an external position, tried to experience them through the eyes of participants, taking pains to be responsive to their ideas and concerns. Like Carol Mullen and Frances Kochan, our teams studied programs "from the inside out" (2000, 184). The designs of the studies differed, but all featured three strategies for generating qualitative data: observations, interviews, and the collection and analysis of written documents. Also, in each case the research was done by an ethnographic team rather than by just me as an individual. In the teams, I played the major leadership role. In most of them, I—as the only doctoral-level university faculty member—worked with three or four graduate students. I designed the research, recruited team members, and facilitated the teams' work.

In qualitative and ethnographic research literature generally, "teaming" is often discussed in a taken-for-granted way, the assumption being that each team member plays a separate role for the good of the team. Although the teams I worked with experienced teaming in this "everyone does her individual part" sense, often over the course of the research we became more collaborative ethnographers and sometimes formed close-knit, caring learning communities focused on egalitarian relations and processes. In one long-term project, our four-woman team evolved from a "loose alliance" (Erickson and Stull 1998, 14) to what we called a feminist learning community as we became "explicit about power relations, equity, [and] social transformation" (Spatig, Seelinger, et al. 2005, 103). Looking back on these research experiences, I wonder if my focus on and enjoyment of the collaboration *within* ethnographic teams caused me to lose sight of the importance of collaboration *beyond* the team—in other words, with research participants.

Before the current study, perhaps the closest I came to Lassiter's collaborative ethnography was an earlier phase in the GRP research—the 2000–2001 GRP evaluation research described in Teresa's story—where program staff and girls were involved in research design and data collection. In this work, six GRP girls helped formulate research questions and conducted interviews. In our first meeting with the girls, we warmed up with team-building activities and then brainstormed ideas about GRP activities and concerns that might be important to consider in the evaluation research. The hard part was prioritizing or narrowing the list. Despite much encouragement and many invitations, the girls *would not say* which issues they thought should be selected for the final list of research questions. Finally someone suggested that the adults leave the room and let the girls talk by themselves. While Shelley Gaines and I went out for a short walk, the girls decided that each of them would name a first choice for an issue and that each of those six issues would be included in a research question. Rejoining the group, we followed their lead, and Shelley then selected an issue, and I did as well. In this collaboration we each had a voice, but we were not able to put our voices together in a dialogue, at least as a mixed adult/youth group. Instead, each person had a separate, equal say in making the decision. Although the girls helped develop research questions and generated some interview data, the analysis and writing were done by those of us at the university.

WHAT WE DID. OR, SPEAKING TRUTH TO FRIENDSHIP

I always feel reassured when I remember Michael Patton's assertion that naming a research design is not as important as carefully describing what the researcher actually did (2003). In that spirit, I will describe what happened during this last, most recent phase of the GRP research, exploring several naming possibilities.

In spring 2006, I went to Lincoln County and met with Ric MacDowell and Nona Conley, the only remaining board members of the Appalachian Women's Leadership Project (AWLP)—the umbrella organization for the Girls' and Boys' Resiliency Programs—to explore the idea of doing additional collaborative research that would culminate in a book about the youth development work (what ultimately became this book). Over lunch, they sadly confided what I had feared, that the programs were in danger of dying and might not be good candidates for the project. After more discussion with them, and later with Shelley, we decided to move forward with the study anyway—mainly because we wanted to understand what happened. How did programs with such a strong beginning end up in such a vulnerable position? Would the programs survive, and if so, in what form?

At one level, the purpose of this phase of the research was to answer these kinds of questions, from the points of view of those who had been (and some of whom still were) directly involved in youth development work—especially the youth themselves. In addition to these pressing local purposes, we hoped the study would be significant more broadly, especially by providing frank, useful information to assist others engaged in, or contemplating, similar youth development work. So in the fall of 2006, board members, program staff, and youth participants joined graduate students and me in beginning a collaborative study to figure out what went right, what went wrong, and how to strengthen and sustain these fragile programs.

Our research was a form of collaborative ethnography. We used observation, interviews, and collection and analysis of written documents to generate data. Seventeen teenagers, four university-based researchers,[1] and five adults who worked with the resiliency programs joined this community-university partnership in which all parties were to participate in everything from study design to analysis and writing. In the earlier research (e.g., Spatig and Amerikaner 2005) girls had never participated in the analysis and writing. The responsibility—and power—of those aspects of the research remained mostly in my hands. The current project, by contrast, involved both program participants and university researchers in each stage of the research, including analysis and writing, though not without some roadblocks.

Another goal of the project was to explore collaborative ethnography with youth as a research method. In this chapter, I describe the ups and downs of the collaborative processes. In doing so, the other collaborators and I insert ourselves into the story by writing openly and vulnerably, as Ruth Behar (1996) described it. We do this not just to see ourselves in print but to be strategically reflexive. We acknowledge and reflect on our own subjectivities—who we are and how we see things—as a means of making the research "more accurate . . . or valid" (Glesne 2011, 151). In other words, by making our presence in the research process clear and explicit, we are better able to fully understand and communicate about issues of interest in this study.

We began the collaborative work by developing a plan and making agreements with each other. The plan called for university-based researchers to observe all remaining aspects of the youth work—including program activities and board meetings. We decided that university-based researchers would interview board members, program staff, and young people currently involved (as well as some involved in the past); would assist in collecting and analyzing past documents (photos, brochures, etc.); and would work with current youth to create new documents including journals, photos, poems, essays, and life-story scrapbooks. A wrench was thrown into our plan when, as we saw in chapter 6, the girls' program closed and there were no more GRP activities to observe. After that, when we wanted to meet with the girls, we had to arrange and facilitate the get-togethers ourselves. These usually took place at the high school during the girls' lunch period. Often LeAnne Olson brought pizzas, and the school staff kindly arranged places for her to meet with the girls.

Also, we decided to conduct a series of reflective discussions about the GRP and its work historically. The idea here was for current and past board members, staff, and youth—along with university researchers—to participate in tape-recorded discussions, organized as focus group interviews, where we remembered and reflected on particular periods in the organization's history. We analyzed them in terms of key people and events; accomplishments and successes; and regrets, obstacles, and lessons learned. We also discussed how each period of the organization's history should be represented in our writing.

Finally, we agreed to use the information we would amass to produce a book telling the story of the program. We made the following agreements about the book we hoped to develop together:

1. The story must be real/true (not just the "good stuff") as perceived not only by university researchers, but by those who are and have been closest to the work, such as youth, staff, and board members.

2. The story must not be harmful to the young people, the programs, the community, state, or region (not reinforcing negative stereotypes of Appalachia or West Virginia, for example, or engaging in destructive rather than constructive program critique).

3. Proceeds from the book should go to the AWLP or similar youth work in the county.

4. The story should be written in an interesting format for a broad audience—not for an exclusively scholarly readership. Ideally, it would be appealing to young people as well as adults interested in youth development.

Although some of us, including me, did not anticipate this initially, during the course of our work together we realized that collaborative research and performance can *themselves* be forms of positive youth development. A public presentation of our research was the culmination of the year-long collaboration. As the first occasion where we would formally articulate what we learned from the research—our findings—it became a driving force for our work.

The presentation, especially in the sense that it was a *performance,* became a central feature of our collaboration and, as will be evident later in the chapter, of the youth development work as well. It was actually fun, though at times difficult, preparing together for the presentation—figuring out who would say what and when, practicing, and performing it together to a small but receptive university audience. For adult participants as well as youth, that afternoon was an emotional high point as we combined "ethnography and performance into a common thread of reciprocal and collaborative practice" (Papa and Lassiter 2003, 162). We experienced the joy that comes with engagement in a project worthwhile to us individually and more broadly. As Ashley noted in written reflections afterward: "My favorite part was reading out loud in front of everyone. I really like it that I made a difference."

In the act of speaking aloud, first to each other in practice sessions and then to a larger live audience during the university presentation, the girls engaged in what Wendy Luttrell calls "showing and telling" their stories (2003, 113). Just as the pregnant girls Luttrell studied were drawn to performing scenes from their life experiences, the young people in our project, while eager to participate in other activities, were especially enthusiastic about speaking onstage. Perhaps as important as the opportunity to *speak* about their lives and viewpoints, the presentation enabled them to experience *others listening* and responding to what they had to say. Like the girls in Luttrell's study, our girls used the presentation preparation and performance to make connections with, and seek recognition and support from, others. Or to borrow Maisha Winn's words, it was a "performance of possibilities"—an opportunity for the girls to make public statements about their lives and "possible futures" (2011, 124). *This is what our lives are like.*

Another thing I didn't realize initially was that the postpresentation reflections we sent to each other in e-mails would be a primary vehicle for collaboratively analyzing and writing. In reflective e-mails to each other, we wrote individually about our perceptions and experiences. We talked honestly about satisfactions as well as disappointments and concerns about the program, about the research—including the culminating presentation—and about our individual and collective roles in both.

The act of writing (in separate voices) to each other was an opportunity to pay attention to difference, even disagreement, among us. Tensions that had not been obvious with one or two researchers speaking for everyone were illuminated when we wrote individually to each other. Perhaps this happened because it can be emotionally difficult to speak frankly, especially face-to-face, against the ideas or feelings of a valued friend or colleague.

Anthropologist David Gow (1991, 10) writes about the difficulty of "speaking truth to power" in research. We found it also can be painful to speak truth to friendship, especially in the context of a regional culture that often prizes polite, respectful demeanor and dialogue. On top of emotional and cultural barriers, I felt constrained by my self-identification as an outsider. The technology of e-mail enabled us to overcome cultural, emotional, and political barriers, making us bold enough to communicate even uneasy insights and sentiments, what Peter Senge (1990) refers to as "undiscussables," with more honesty and comfortableness than might have been possible in other forms of communication. The resulting e-mail dialogues were enlightening and productive, allowing us to explore tensions and share discoveries about the youth work and about our collaborative methods.

TENSION ONE: VOICE

Qualitative methods, especially participatory approaches, are said to provide "voice" to research participants. Given the absence of youth voice, even in research and writing about positive youth development programs, in this study I was especially eager for the girls to speak and be heard (Anderson-Butcher, Stetler, and Midle 2006).

As we saw in chapter 3, prior work with the GRP's summer research internships taught us that including youth voice is sometimes difficult. It was a challenge to encourage youth voice in the current phase of the project, too. In groups consisting of both youth and adults, but mostly adults, the girls were fairly quiet in discussions. They were invited to express their views, but they rarely spoke. Their voices were considerably stronger in groups consisting of mostly youth, for example in after-school meetings with one or two graduate students, as well as in interviews and in journal and essay writing. It was primarily from these sources that we took the girls' words and ideas used in the presentation and in our subsequent writing—as excerpts from interviews as well as in individual and composite poems, song lyrics, and the like. This is an important lesson for collaborative researchers including youth—and theoretically, any group feeling marginalized or simply uncomfortable. Building in safe spaces for youth to express themselves may dramatically improve the level of real collaboration. Also, shifting the center of power in a specific context made a difference. When an event was dominated by youth, as opposed to dominated by adults but with youth *added* to the adult framework, they were more likely to participate. This supports Linda Camino and Shepherd Zeldin's argument about the importance of adult-youth partnerships that give young people a chance to "bring their own beliefs or lifestyles into a setting where such an orientation dominates" (2002, 215).

Featuring their voices in the presentation was an important part of the experience for the girls. It honored them and their ideas and, perhaps as important, made a positive difference in their school. According to Sara, "I loved being able to voice my opinion and be with friends while being taken seriously." As Cassi points out, it was not only speaking, but being heard, that was important:

> Getting to present those poems in front of those people was just awesome. It made it all more real. What we had to say was really getting heard. That hadn't really happened in that big of a scale before. Sure, some of us had been a part of the protest against consolidation at the capitol, but that was different. With that we were promoting something that the adults said would help make our inevitable transition easier. We weren't really expressing OUR views about it. With this project, it was totally different. We were saying what WE had to say, and people were there to hear it. I loved to be able to voice my opinions and have people listen. It was wonderful. We are better now. The school is a lot better.

Not surprisingly, individuals involved in the project, including adults (some with graduate degrees) as well as high school students, spoke and wrote in different ways. In sharing our findings, in presentations and writing, it was hard to use language that was clear and comfortable for everyone. In the composite poetry and in excerpts taken directly from interviews or from material written by young people, their words are their exact words. But in other narrative about the project, the authorial voice is, in honesty, much more Layne and me and (to a lesser extent) other adult participants than it is the youth. This was an issue identified early in the year by Shelley, who commented that girls might be more comfortable with terminology such as "teamwork" and "partnership" rather than "collaborative ethnography" or "collaborative inquiry." At the same time, I believed it was important to my professional reputation to have a project and presentation that would be recognized as rigorous scholarship. Ultimately, the presentation and writing, including this book, use some combination of everyday language (which may be different for youth and adults) and research language. The resulting combination, or hybrid, reflects tensions between speaking and writing in our own individual voices and in a collective voice. It also reflects tensions between speaking, and especially writing, in ways that are widely accessible and speaking and writing for a narrower, academic or scholarly audience.

Also, in writing the presentation script, I now realize that I edited what other participants wrote with an eye toward smoothing out or even avoiding conflicts in understandings. For example, in Ric's first draft of his presentation comments about Lincoln County and how the youth programs began, he used the term "high-risk" in describing young people he and others in the community were concerned about. Knowing this wording was inconsistent with Shelley's commitment to positive youth development, I asked Ric if I could change his wording to "youth facing especially tough life situations" instead of "high-risk youth." Ric accepted the revision and used the modified wording in his part of the presentation. It was not until later, in individually written postpresentation e-mails, that the different ideas about youth development reemerged and became more visible. This visibility was partly a result of all of us writing in individual voices rather than in a collective voice authored by me. The written reflections spontaneously became a dialogue where we voiced our ideas *in our own words* about the collaborative research and about the youth development program. Through this, we learned about differences in understandings we had not acknowledged or perhaps even been aware of.

I am left with questions about what kind of balance—between individual and collective voices—makes sense in this kind of collaborative work, especially when the goal is "public ethnography," what sociologist Herbert Gans describes as "relevant ethnography . . . written in non technical English" (2010, 97). What experience and knowledge are sacrificed when individual voices are replaced with a group voice? When working on projects including both adults and youth, with some adults in positions of authority/responsibility for those youth, what balance—between youth and adult voices—makes sense? And how is it possible to achieve that balance? In switching back and forth from individual to collective voices, trying to include both, did the presentation do neither well, leaving audiences unclear and unconvinced?

Another voice tension emerged recently as Layne and I began writing this book. I had been doing the research for over ten years. Layne was coming into the work after the fact to take a major role in writing the book. Whose voice should be used in narrating the story? At first I thought the writing should be in first-person plural, using "we" to acknowledge both of us, but Layne convinced me that using "I" would be more interesting and compelling for readers, and perhaps more honest as well, given my long history with the research. At the same time, we both wanted Layne to be credited for the writing she actually did (much of the original book narration, with the exception of chapters 7 and 8, is indeed Layne's voice), so we agreed that she would be listed as coauthor. The fact that Layne, as a late-arrival participant, stepped in when other participants had neither the time nor resources to take on more of the writing than they had already done, worked out well. Layne enthusiastically agreed with our initial commitment to write the book in a way that would be widely accessible, and she regularly kept my feet to the fire on that, encouraging me to "just write the way you talk, Mom." The result, a truly coauthored book written in the single, informal voice of one author, is an unusual, but to us reasonable, compromise. It reflects the complexity of voice decisions researchers make all the time but rarely acknowledge publicly. In the next section, let's hear from Layne directly about the writing part of the project.

LAYNE: FROM ANTHROPOLOGY
UNDERGRAD TO BOOK WRITER

I did my portion of the writing for this book in air-conditioned coffee shops and libraries. I think that's important to note right up front—that it's symbolic of my privileged position in this project. In rural contexts, university libraries and wi-fi-connected coffee shops can be hard to come by. Whereas others highlighted in the book spent years living through the challenges that can come with being rural, low-income, Appalachian girls—or years working long hours that they chose to dedicate to the Girls' Resiliency Program—I swept in at the end and pulled a lot of stories together, sipping hot tea as I did it. I had comfortable physical spaces and adequate resources—important information to remember regarding the balance of power in telling the story.

I am an insider in this project to the extent that I am a girl who was raised in West Virginia. As a former grassroots nonprofit staff member, I am also an insider to the world of small, ambitious, understaffed organizations that are trying to remake the world using only their own sweat and a few thousand dollars. But I am lying to myself and everyone involved if I try to position myself as anything but an outsider to the programs and life experiences described here.

What happens when outsiders tell stories? As a West Virginian who moved to Pennsylvania for college and subsequently to Washington, DC, I know what usually happens when outsiders tell stories about Appalachia. In college, I remember encountering a blog post written by a friend of a friend who had come to West Virginia during a summer vacation to help build homes for a few weeks. His post, called "My Time in West Virginia," described "the people" of my state as grateful, friendly folks who were thrilled to have outsiders come and help them. Despite his good intentions, I was appalled at his post. "The people?" I remember thinking. "Are we one people? You 'discovered' our culture after two weeks here?" More important, I remember being indignant at the suggestion that we needed him to come build us homes, to save us.

At the same time, I chose to study anthropology in college. Unquestionably, anthropology is a discipline featuring countless "outsiders" barging in to write about groups they are not a part of—groups that have in many cases been oppressed, exploited, or even colonized by the anthropologist's own cultural group. I spent a lot of time thinking about who had the "right" to tell whose stories and toward what end. A passage from my favorite anthropology book, Ruth Behar's *The Vulnerable Observer*, surfaces in my thoughts frequently: "Nothing is stranger than this business of humans observing humans in order to write about them" (1996, 5). What are the potential dangers—and benefits—of outsiders telling stories? How much of it will we simply get wrong?

Straddling the line between an outsider and an insider, being what Patricia Hill Collins calls "the outsider within," can have its advantages. As she writes, "outsiders within occupy a special place—they become different people, and their difference sensitizes them to patterns that may be more difficult for . . . insiders to see" (2008, 317). Additionally, as an outsider, I had the time to do much of the compiling and writing part of the book project. Most of the legwork was already done. In the first meeting between my mom and me about the book, I asked if I would need to collect any new data. "Data? More data?!" she responded incredulously, flinging open a filing cabinet stuffed from end to end. "We have eleven years of data. We're drowning in data! Now we need to tell the story." With little connection to the project (except, of course, years of hearing about it at the dinner table) I became a big part of that storytelling.

I frequently referred to the four-part list of goals for the book project that girls, staff members, and researchers had put together at the first planning meeting. It became an important checklist, grounding and regrounding me in the spirit of the project as determined by those most central to it. I would ask myself: Am I choosing to highlight the "real" stuff as opposed to just the good stuff? Am I careful not to reinforce damaging and false stereotypes about Appalachia? Am I writing in a way that will be understandable and also, you know, not putting people to sleep? My peripheral role in the project may have made it questionable that I often had the power of "the last word;" that said, it is my hope that by staying true to the goals determined by the larger group, the story has been told in a way that those in the past or present GRP world find engaging, useful, and real.

TENSION TWO: BALANCE OF PARTICIPATION

As Layne's passage and the previous section highlight, we tried to think of voice as a question of *balance* rather than either/or. We knew that in youth-adult partnerships generally it is important to acknowledge age differences and avoid "one size fits all" approaches that can result in adults providing less guidance and support than youth want and need—that "youth rarely can, or should, go it exclusively alone" (Camino and Zeldin 2002, 215–16). This is also true in youth-adult research partnerships. That said, it is also important, especially in work with youth, that adult researchers not jump too quickly to their own analysis of what participants are experiencing, that they listen deeply and "stay in the moment" (Hoskins and Artz 2004, 6). In our research with the GRP, we struggled with achieving a balance in participation—a tension we explore in this section.

Trying for a fair and reasonable balance of participation in the research *process* was especially troublesome to me, as is obvious in my post-presentation reflection:

> The construction of composite poems was one of my favorite parts of our collaboration, though I'm uneasy about the balance of participation in the process. After reviewing observation, interview, and document data about how the youth perceived Lincoln County, I drafted a poem capturing what seemed (to me) to be the essence as well as the range of their views. I shared the draft with graduate students working on the project. In turn, they shared the draft with the youth. At several points, I made changes in the poems—sometimes adding lines to strengthen various parts. For example, in the verse in "Lincoln County" about the value of living in a small place, I added the line, "You get a chance to shine" that was part of a paragraph one of the girls had written. I made that addition, and some others, as a result of continued perusing of the data and discovery of material that seemed to strengthen the "truth" of the pieces. Like Drew Chappell (2006) who collaborated with eighth graders in research on banned books, I prioritized fidelity to the youth's understandings and perceptions over aesthetic considerations.

My uneasiness with the balance of participation has to do with the fact that I am the one who put the poems together in this form even though the ideas and words came from the youth. Unlike Chappell's project in which youth participants analyzed their own interview data and turned them into scripts to perform, in this project *I* turned the data into poetry for the youth to perform. Each of the other speaking parts in the presentation was written by the person who spoke them, though I edited the text, as mentioned above.

Even with a history of collaborative work with the girls, I found it difficult to remain as collaborative as I had hoped in the first year of the current project. We started off strong with mutual agreements and several meetings and discussions about our goals and plans. We also ended up strong as we worked together to prepare and perform a collaborative public presentation of our work. There were times, however, when we resorted to more traditional divisions of labor with the university-based researchers taking the lead on generating data as well as analyzing and writing it without always including others in the process. My role in developing the composite poems is illustrative. I unilaterally forged ahead with those rather than facilitating group discussions of the data and broader participation in the creation of the poems.

Looking back, I wonder if my lack of experience with collaborative analysis and writing, combined with the pressure of a public presentation, was a key factor. Having limited prior experience with collaborative research and even less with participatory research writing, I was less sure of my ability to facilitate a high-quality, collective analysis and writing experience than of my ability to do the task single-handedly. I was more comfortable tackling the work independently and seeking feedback afterward. Also, this task came toward the end of the year when I felt pressed to prepare the culminating presentation and didn't want to take time to organize a series of meetings. It seemed more efficient to do the writing myself. By that time we were focused, perhaps too narrowly, on the public presentation for which I felt responsible.

For her part, Shelley focused in postpresentation reflections on how and why the balance of participation in the research had shifted over time as a result of changes in program staff and resources: "It is hard to separate my own earlier collaborative research experience with Linda from what you all did after I left." She went on to specifically respond to my concerns: "Linda talks about feeling uneasy about the balance between the university team and the [GRP] team on the research project. I think this balance was a little more even when she and I did research together in earlier years. One reason I think it might have been different this time around is lack of time on the part of . . . [limited program] staff—this is huge. . . . Also, I had a background doing research and so was much more comfortable [than current staff] sharing decision making with Linda."

For Ric, the imbalance in research participation was related to dwindling program resources as well as other contextual factors, as he explained in a postpresentation e-mail: "As far as the process of collaborative research, I'm not sure given time and energy constraints and the distance between the county and Marshall University, how things could have really been different. All of us were scrambling and trying to keep the program from falling apart. It was hard enough to get a group meeting of youth to happen, let alone schedule an event to work on the collaborative research. It's just the reality of the beast we wrestled with."

Clearly, this kind of collaborative work is especially difficult when resources, namely time and money, are scarce. As a program staff member said at one of our meetings, "I really want to collaborate, but it's hard," referring to finding time to do interviews, locate program documents, and respond to e-mail. My work on the project was supported by a fellowship that paid for me to be released from teaching responsibilities and provided a research assistant. The GRP, however, had no similar support. They were trying to run a youth program and to find funding to keep themselves afloat. During the time of this project, money for rent and utilities on the office space ran out, and they had to leave the building. Also, money for all but one half-time position ran out.

The level of Betty Sias's participation was related directly to her circumstances as a doctoral student at dissertation stage. In postpresentation writing she reflected on her shifting priorities and involvement:

> As we began work on our initial project, the university members of the research team met frequently. We transcribed interviews, discussed findings, and planned for our upcoming presentation. In that respect, this truly was a collaborative project. But once that presentation was

finalized, and I began collecting data solely for my dissertation, I admit that any effort on my part to collaborate essentially ceased. I am left with questions about that shift. Did I fulfill my obligations as a member of the research team? I interviewed, transcribed, collaborated with the team, and participated in the presentation, but could I have been a more active participant? Was I too focused on my ultimate personal goal—my dissertation?

Resources (e.g., money, time, knowledge) were important on all sides, not just for those at the university. Also, prior research experience and confidence (especially on the part of those in leadership positions) on all sides affected the balance of participation. But questions remain. Whereas Shelley, Ric, and Betty wonder about how it might have been possible for them to play larger or different roles, I wondered (in post-presentation reflections) if I played too big a role and if the project was overly focused on outcomes, especially the presentation:

> Did I do too much myself? In a sort of ironic replay of Shelley's initial leadership role with the Girls' Resiliency Program, . . . did I believe in and talk . . . about the importance of collaboration while at the same time playing a too-major role as an individual? How can this kind of imbalance be avoided, especially when resources are imbalanced with some individuals having financial support for their participation and others not?

> Did we focus too much on products or outcomes instead of processes? The presentation we made in April drove much of our work especially in the second half of the year. Did we focus on the wrong products—a university presentation required by obligations to *my* funders rather than on grant proposals and presentations that might have more directly benefited the . . . youth programs?

TENSION THREE: RESEARCH AS YOUTH DEVELOPMENT

As our collaborative research became more active throughout the year, the resiliency programs continued to decline. Increasingly, the research and the program became indistinguishable, as Ric noted in post-presentation reflections recorded in chapter 6.

For LeAnne, as we also saw in chapter 6, this was not an easy or comfortable role to negotiate, especially at first. As a graduate student fairly new to ethnography and lacking experience with adolescent groups, she struggled with balancing her role and responsibilities as youth group leader—since more often than not she was alone with the girls and responsible for them—and her research role.

For their part, the girls enjoyed interacting with LeAnne and appreciated the chances to express themselves, have new experiences, and develop new relationships. Cassi wrote in a postpresentation e-mail to LeAnne:

> What do I remember about the presentation? Well, for starters it was really fun. I liked the whole thing—not just the presentation, but everything leading up to it too. Getting to work with you and Heaven [Rangel, a graduate student] was really cool. It's hard to think you guys got any research done at all during the meetings! It hardly seemed like an interview was really going on. Your questions were just part of the conversation. It made it so much easier to do. And in the end we had these really amazing poems that truly expressed our ideas about what was going on. Throughout all of this, I've been given chances to visit the campus that I'd never been given before. Seeing as this is probably where I'm going to school come next fall, these visits were invaluable. Plus, I got a new friend—you.

From her vantage point, Shelley had seen the youth programming and research as part and parcel of the same thing all along. She approached me about the initial research years ago partly as a vehicle for youth to be involved as coresearchers and as social change agents: "I think I had a different perspective on the research than those leading [the youth programs] after me did. I have always thought of our work with Linda as research AND intervention. I remember talking about this with [Linda] the first time we met, but I think it was a little overwhelming to consider doing research about doing research, if that makes sense. Anyway, without this as a premise, the research becomes something 'extra' or 'necessary for funding' but not seen as a change agent/development mechanism."

Shelley's comments were a painful reminder that my research with the Girls' Resiliency Program had indeed always been a part of the youth development work and that I had lost sight of that in the current collaboration, perhaps to the detriment of the project—at least in terms of its potential for benefiting the programs. I reflected at length about how and why this happened.

Looking back, my greatest regret is that we were not able to do more in the way of strengthening and sustaining the . . . resiliency programs. In some ways, the programs *were* strengthened and sustained. As Ric noted, had it not been for Heaven and LeAnne's work with the girls, for example, there would have been a drastically curtailed girls' program in the spring semester.

Our project might have been more successful in strengthening the organization, however, had I and others realized earlier that the collaborative research was itself a form of positive youth development. . . . I recall attending a presentation that several girls—along with LeAnne and Betty—made about rural school consolidation at the annual meeting of the Appalachian Studies Association the spring following our collaboration year. During the discussion period, I (as an audience member) asked the girls what it was like for them to do this research together. They responded that it was fun to meet with LeAnne and Heaven, do life-history scrapbooks, and especially the presentation at Marshall. They also spoke about their trust in each other, and in LeAnne and Heaven as well, saying they could talk about anything with each other. Just as was true of their feelings about the . . . resiliency program, they valued the collaborative "research" because it involved interesting, fun activities and because of the caring, trusting relationships it nurtured—among the girls as well as with the adult graduate students. I put the word research in quotes because the girls' answers suggest that they did not think of the collaborative experiences as research as much as fun, interesting activities, and chances to express their views and be heard.

A second, and related, insight for me came as a result of rereading Shelley's presentation remarks . . . about the "core belief"—the foundation for the resiliency programs initially—in the capability of young people. As an example of that capability, she mentioned the girls serving as research interns and doing program evaluation research as well as community action research. I had been involved in that prior research with the girls and knew they were capable. I also knew that a goal of the current research was to sustain and strengthen the programs. But I did not put it together that the two were, or could be, so closely aligned. . . . Had we been clearer about this, perhaps we could have challenged the young people involved in our year-long collaboration by asking them to join with the adults in direct efforts to sustain the [resiliency] programs. For example, perhaps they could have joined us in writing grant applications or in speaking with individuals and community organizations and agencies about sponsoring the group in some way. This might have been a better use of their time and talents than focusing on their experiences with school consolidation, creating life-story scrapbooks, and preparing and participating in a presentation/performance.

Early in the school year I applied to the Ms. Foundation for funds to support the program's work in the collaborative project, but was not successful in getting financial support for them. That was the extent of our involvement in directly seeking funds for the organization. By the end of the summer following this year's work, the program had to close its office; there was no girls' program; and one part-time staff member continued with the boys' program.

As we have seen, there were not always answers, much less resolutions, for the tensions about voice, balance of participation, and youth development that emerged in our collaborative research. That said, I believe that naming and exploring them in this text is important. It has been helpful to us—individually and collectively—in understanding this project more fully, even the parts that were painful. Frank, detailed description of the tensions also provides knowledge for others engaged in similar community-based research.

BRIEF PERSONAL INTERLUDE. OR, THE MOTHER-DAUGHTER REUNION

An unanticipated, and very personal, aspect of this collaborative project is the way it transformed my relationship with Layne. I was relieved, and if I'm really honest, I was also pretty thrilled when Layne agreed to join me in writing the book. The relief was because I knew that with the two of us committed to it, it would actually get done. I was thrilled because I hoped the project would be a fun, interesting, and perhaps important new part of our already strong mother-daughter relationship.

Backing up a little, I should explain that when Layne, our youngest, went away to college and then, after graduation, moved to Washington, DC, to work as an AmeriCorps VISTA volunteer, it was a hard time for me. I had always been a working mom, having started to work full-time when our oldest daughter was four years old and Layne was only one. But I am one of the lucky ones whose work—as a university professor—involves flexible hours that I have considerable say about. So even while working full-time, I could spend most evenings and weekends, even many late afternoons, with the girls. Having grown up with a strained, somewhat distant relationship with *my* mother who was in her own way a version of Cassi's "super-mom"—teaching full-time and very active in her church while maintaining a household with little day-to-day assistance from my dad—I worked hard at having close, positive relationships with my daughters. I wanted to be there for and with them—perhaps as much for myself as for them, I realize now.

Even with a busy, rewarding job, I had what I call a "quiet breakdown" during the transition from having children at home, or at least in college, to having none left. I've heard people speak lightly, even fondly, about the "empty nest," but for me it was not light in any way. My feelings at that time are captured by Sue Monk Kidd's words about her adult daughter not long after her daughter's college graduation: "She seems lost to me now. Because she is grown and a stranger. And I miss her violently" (Kidd and Taylor 2009, 3). Believe me, I know that heartache.

In honesty, the breakdown also was related to getting older. Just as Kidd describes in *Traveling with Pomegranates: A Mother-Daughter Story,* I hate to admit it, but I'd begun to be bothered by new "lines and sags" I noticed in the mirror and by other signs of aging. It seemed that in addition to losing my girls, I was losing my looks, my health, even my strength.

In that context, the book in and of itself was a rejuvenating new project for me. Cowriting it with Layne, though, made it something more; it was a way for us to come back together, to be on common ground again—but this time, as two adults, two women. This was not always comfortable. The mother-daughter relationship tends to have a "blurry interpersonal boundary," as Mellinee Lesley (2012, 105) describes it, and I would say that is true of my relationships with my mother as well as with both daughters. We tend to see our past and future selves in each other. And we experience the tension of continuing to separate and seek autonomy from each other while searching for new forms of connection with each other (Lesley, 106).

For Layne and me, working on the book together was a new way to connect—albeit with some interesting role reversals. Especially at first, I was hesitant to criticize or edit Layne's writing. Speaking truth to dearly loved family members may be the hardest thing of all. Falling back into my prior mothering role, I sometimes found myself viewing her words as too precious to change (kind of like all those poems and stories she wrote in first grade, carefully kept in a box in my bedroom closet). Or in a protective turn, I worried that if I questioned her words, she would feel censored or judged by me in a way that might limit her sense of self-efficacy or her autonomy. For her part, Layne seemed totally comfortable criticizing *my* writing. I can still hear her saying, fairly early in the process, as she read a piece I had written on the project, "This is good, but you should have led with this part. That would have made a much better opening paragraph." She also became my instructor about gender. Having completed a master's degree program in women's studies during the same period we were working on the book, she was up to date, much more so than I, about recent thinking and writing about gender identities and the like. I have always respected Layne, but this work allowed me to know and respect her in new ways.

The bottom line is that for me, the experience has been the impetus for considerable reflection on mother-daughter connections, "pondering the lost daughter [*daughters* in my case] . . . but also the one inside" (Kidd and Taylor 2009, 268). As a *daughter,* I easily picture my mother, now well into her nineties, pushing her walker around the house in her stylish flats (clunky lace-up shoes are out of the question) where she still lives alone; playing piano and teaching Sunday School classes in weekly church services; singing solos at too many funerals of friends; working crossword puzzles in the daily newspapers; laughing out loud at silly sitcoms. She is full of life, as she always has been. Like Sue Monk Kidd says of her own mother, I can only hope that "I will grow young like that" (270).

As a *mother*, though, this project is mainly a reunion with a daughter. Admittedly, I have moments of feeling old and drab compared to Layne, but mostly I experience the reunion as an exciting invention, a creation of a new version of my relationship with Layne, and even a new version of myself. Kidd's description of her reconnection with her initially estranged adult daughter, with whom she traveled and wrote a book, resonates strongly with me:

> It's the channel where the souls of a mother and a daughter open and flow as two separate adults, woman to woman. It is, I know now, a place created through necessary loss and necessary search, and a reinvention of the whole relationship . . . the essence of Young and Old coming together in a woman to create new life. A new self. (273)

RESEARCH, WITH A SOCIAL JUSTICE TWIST

While my relationship with Layne was transformed, we continue to share a long-standing commitment to social justice that has remained unchanged. I'd like to think our research is an example of the "socially committed" inquiry Michael Apple calls for—"research that can function as part of a larger set of movements for social justice" by documenting examples of "counter-hegemonic possibilities" (2004, x, xi). A lot of big words, but more simply put: our research shines a light on intersecting oppressions in the lives of adolescent rural girls, but it also highlights people and a program that opposed those oppressions, what Lois Weis and Michelle Fine (2004, xxi, xxiv) call "sites for possibility—for hope." The Girls' Resiliency Program was a site for hope. In light of the relative absence of research about poor and working-class youth critique and resistance (Fine et al. 2004), this study of a program focused on social justice, a program explicitly designed to engage rural Appalachian girls in dialogue and activism, is itself an effort toward social justice.

The stories featured in this research are important in and of themselves, but another social justice aspect of the project is that connections are made between the stories of these girls, this program, and this community and broader social inequalities—whether related to gender, age, geography, social class, sexual orientation, or some combination. In making those connections, I followed Weis and Fine in using social identity categories—such as Appalachian, rural, girl—but without "essentialist" assumptions about these categories (2004). In other words, I know there are real, lived experiences of being an Appalachian girl, or a rural girl; at the same time, I do not believe in the idea of *the essential* Appalachian girl or rural girl; I know that all Appalachian or rural girls do not share the same basic characteristics. In fact, challenging such boxes, such stereotypes, is part of this project.

Also, the methods we used go against traditional research power hierarchies. Though we only recently identified it as such, I also see our research as feminist—in my mind, a subcategory of Apple's "socially committed research." Writer and professor Cynthia Enloe says that a feminist inquiry is one where the researcher is "tracking down what sorts of power are at work, in whose hands, and with what consequences" (2008, 258). In other words, in a feminist study, there is always an eye toward power relations. Who has the most power? Are some voices in the research processes louder than others? Are some people serving only as "examples" and not as analyzers or researchers? Or, to borrow the words of critical theorist Gayatri Chakravorty Spivak, are some participants only "the known" and never the ones who "know"? (1990, 66). Although completely equal power relations in research may not be possible, as was true in our own collaborative project, I agree with the philosopher Linda Alcoff that the response to this problem is not to simply avoid writing about groups unless you belong to them. In regard to communities more marginalized than her own, Alcoff asks: "Is my greatest contribution to *move over and get out of the way?*" (1991–92, 8). I join her in believing that this "retreat response" is not the best approach feminist researchers can offer. Rather, feminist researchers working with more marginalized groups can try to openly address the unequal power dynamics in the process—and work to make relationships more equal—without abandoning the work completely. In the GRP research, for example, the decision to use everyday language and an informal writing style was a purposeful attempt to be inclusive, to be in the game, so to speak, with a broad audience. From the beginning when we wrote up our initial agreements, we have hoped to eventually share these stories and what we've learned from them beyond the university walls. We want to continue to engage with, and be helpful to, young people and the adults who work with them—in classrooms, in communities, in homes.

At a most basic level, is it also a feminist project because we are studying girls—girls whose voices are not often taken seriously. Feminist scholars such as Patricia Hill Collins and Alison Jaggar emphasize putting women's lived experiences, especially those women (or girls) who have been understudied and undervalued, at the center of research practices. We attempted to do that every step of the way. Our methods are also consistent with Mary Alm's (1998, 124) call for "critical self-reflection" in feminist collaboration and with Sandra Harding's claim that "the best feminist analysis . . . insists that the inquirer her/himself be placed in the same critical plane as the overt subject matter" (1991, 9). In other words, we are always part of the research story. Most feminist researchers, though often taking a systematic approach to their work, do not claim to be *objective*. Many have questioned whether any research is purely objective, or free from all ideological or cultural influences (Ramazanoglu 2002). In line with this, we collectively and consciously reflected on ourselves as part of the research process.

Also, within the diverse strands of feminism, there is some agreement about the value of horizontal, rather than vertical, organizational structures with broad participation in planning and decision making. For the most part, this is a fair description of our research partnership. Our work together featured broad participation, including teenagers, multidirectional communication, and power based on situational expertise rather than hierarchical position (Karsten 1995). That said, our feminist methods are not based on a "belief that women are 'natural' or 'better' collaborators than men" (Ervin and Fox 1994, 54). After all, it is sometimes women who maintain the status quo "even while instituting supposed reforms" (Henry 1996, 145). Even teachers involved in "anti-oppressive education" practice (Kumashiro 2001, 3) may use their power to silence certain perspectives (Butin 2002). Similarly, Patti Lather's (2001) caution against the use of overly certain, prescriptive, supposedly "liberating" practices is one I have endorsed in my own argument against the idea that "empowerment is something done by enlightened . . . [individuals] to or for unliberated" others (Spatig 2005, 315). I tried not to be one of these dogmatic "enlightened" women, but I still worry about the possibility that I marginalized other participants—even as I articulated a feminist, social justice stance—by putting forward my own version of the GRP story and of our research methods. Because when all is said and done, I know that I may have done too much, played too dominant a role, and unintentionally left my "heel-print upon another woman's [or girl's] face," as activist and writer Audre Lorde (1984, 132) put it.

As is obvious from our reflections and critiques, we have no illusions about the shortcomings of our project. Nonetheless, I believe the research we conducted is stronger because of its collaborative nature. I'm convinced that the knowledge we produced is more valid—closer or truer to the experiences and perceptions of those involved in the program as well as in the research, if those can be untangled—than had we used a more traditional ethnographic approach. Perhaps even more balanced collaboration would have strengthened the work further still, yielding more and possibly deeper insights into the organization and what it meant to individuals as well as to the local community. This is an important outcome and provides a strong justification for engaging in collaborative ethnography despite its challenges.

CONCLUDING THOUGHTS. OR, CRYING AND ETHNOGRAPHY

There is a lot of truth to Peter Woods's reminder that "people, and the bonds between them," are more important than "abstract issues" (Woods, Boyle, and Jeffrey 2000, 6). And this brings us back to Wendell Berry's notion of community as people—individuals who both define and limit possibilities in a shared place. It is important to recognize and honor the women and men who have been involved with this resiliency program. Their commitment and hard work, their dedication to and love for the young people, the program, and the Lincoln County community is remarkable. But perhaps even more important is to honor the girls and *their* strong spirits by focusing on *their* lives and *their* understandings. To a large extent, this is their story in their words, and we hope it will speak to the hearts and minds of other young people and adults who care about them.

Recently I've been thinking about the relationship between crying and ethnography. I've read about the emotional dangers of qualitative research (Hubbard, Backett-Milburn, and Kemmer 2001) and the ill effects of "emotional stress" that can accompany research on painful topics (Campbell 2002, 146), and I've experienced that aspect of ethnography. However, for me tears often signify deep, positive feelings, as when I'm "touched" upon encountering something that seems eminently good—that resonates with me in an almost bodily way about what is possible. I cried when I read the last chapter in Laurie Thorp's garden ethnography. She was open, direct, and personal in research recommendations formulated "in the spirit of making the world a better place" (2006, 146). For her part, Thorp cried when she read qualitative research expert Harry Wolcott (1990) because of the revealing, frank way he spoke about "what really matters" in research.

My heart is broken by the demise of the Girls' Resiliency Program, a program I came to respect and love. Yes, love—though I know bell hooks is right that "a woman who talks of love is still suspect" (2000, xxv). I am sad about what the girls and the community have lost. But my heart is also deeply touched by what the program represents. It's not that I don't have the courage "to tell a bad story, to refuse a happy ending" (Fine in Winn 2011, 150). It's because I have seen the good that is possible when women and men come together to support and challenge young people to recognize and build their strengths, to speak and be heard, to engage critically and actively in the world.

The GRP is a model program, and there is a positive legacy from it that continues today. In addition to a generation of young women who benefited from directly experiencing the program, former GRP board members such as Ric MacDowell have continued to do youth development work in the county. Following in the footsteps of earlier GRP efforts, there is a teen parenting program at Hamlin High School. Also, a national Department of Education grant put counselors in every school in the county, and a local youth coalition meets monthly at the high school. In addition, many of the characters you met in this story—LeAnne, Ric, Ashley, Jennifer, and I (Linda)—are now board members of the Appalachian Women's Leadership Project. In important ways, the story is still being written.

The insights gained from examining the GRP's successes *and* challenges in its efforts to push the boundaries of the "girl box" helped all of us understand what happened with our own beloved program. My hope is that they will inform and inspire others as well. If this collaborative ethnography—our love story—is written in words that are true enough, it will touch the hearts of our readers in the same profoundly personal way my own heart has been touched by this work.

Notes

Chapter 1: Ric

1. Many individuals wrote field notes over the course of this research. As mentioned in the text, I authored this particular excerpt, but many other excerpts throughout the book were authored by graduate student research assistants who were involved in the fieldwork for a period. In each phase of the study, the research was undertaken by an ethnographic team led by me and consisting of two to four graduate students. Except for field notes I wrote and those attributed to LeAnne Olson or Betty Sias, graduate student researchers featured in chapter 6, the field notes throughout the book are attributed more generally to "a student" or "a researcher." I elected to do this to avoid the confusion of including the names of so many different individuals throughout the story. Also, in team ethnography, when field notes and interview transcripts are considered shared property, often data excerpts are not attributed to a particular researcher. Following standard guidelines for qualitative fieldwork (e.g., Bogdan and Biklen 2007), we included both description and reflections in our field notes, making sure to distinguish between descriptions of what we saw or heard and our own reflections.

Chapter 7: Ashley

1. The girls in our study spoke almost exclusively about their moms when talking about care work and academic support, so we have focused on mothers in this section. At the same time, we know that not all families include mothers. Many of the issues discussed here may be applicable to dads, guardians, grandparents, and other primary caretakers.

Chapter 8: Linda and Layne

1. Many more than four university student researchers were involved in the GRP research in earlier years. Four, including LeAnne Olson and Betty Sias, were involved during the last phase of the research when, in addition to generating new data with current program participants, we reflected on the project historically, identifying and analyzing major obstacles and successes.

References

Adichi, C. 2009. *The Danger of a Single Story*. Retrieved from http://www.ted.com /talks/chimamanda_adichie_the_danger_of_a_single_story.html.

Alcoff, L. M. 1991–92. "The Problem of Speaking for Others." *Cultural Critique*, no. 17 (Winter): 5–32.

Ali, S. R., and J. L. Saunders. 2006. "The Career Aspirations of Rural Appalachian High School Students." *Journal of Career Assessment* 17 (2): 172–88.

Alloway, N., and P. Gilbert. 2004. "Shifting Discourses about Gender in Higher Education Enrollments: Retrieving Marginalized Voices." *International Journal of Qualitative Studies in Education* 17 (1): 99–112.

Alm, M. 1998. "The Role of Talk in the Writing Process of Intimate Collaboration." In *Common Ground: Feminist Collaboration in the Academy*, edited by E. Peck and J. Mink, 123–40. New York: State University of New York Press.

Amerikaner, L. 2005. *Stonewall City: Voices of Gay West Virginians*. Huntington, WV: Center for the Study of Ethnicity and Gender in Appalachia. Film.

Anderson-Butcher, D., Gwyn E. Stetler, and T. Midle. 2006. "A Case for Expanded School-Community Partnerships in Support of Positive Youth Development." *Children & Schools* 28 (3): 155–63.

Ansell, S. E., and M. McCabe. 2003. "Off Target." *Education Week* 22 (17): 57.

Apple, M. 2004. Series editor's introduction. In *Working Method: Research and Social Justice*, edited by L. Weis and M. Fine, ix–xi. New York: Routledge.

Arhar, J., M. Holley, and W. Kasten. 2001. *Action Research for Teachers: Traveling the Yellow Brick Road*. Upper Saddle River, NJ: Prentice Hall.

Astroth, K., P. Garza, and B. Taylor. 2004. "Getting Down to Business: Defining Competencies for Entry-Level Youth Workers." *New Directions for Youth Development*, no. 104 (Winter): 25–37.

Ayers, W. 1997. Foreword to *She Say, He Say: Urban Girls Write Their Lives*, by B. E. Blake. Albany: State University of New York Press.

Bailey, T., and S. Cho. 2010. "Developmental Education in Community Colleges." *Community College Research Center*, 46–51.

Baum, S. 2006. "Fixing the Formula: A New Approach to Determining Independent Students' Ability to Pay for College." National Association of Student Financial Administrators Research Report for the LUMINA Foundation for Education.

Behar, R. 1996. *The Vulnerable Observer: Anthropology That Breaks Your Heart*. Boston: Beacon Press.

Belenky, M. F., B. M. Clinchy, N. R. Goldberger, and J. M. Tarule. 1986. *Women's Ways of Knowing: The Development of Self, Voice, and Mind.* New York: Basic Books.

Berger, R. 2003. *An Ethic of Excellence: Building a Culture of Craftsmanship with Students.* Portsmouth, NH: Heinemann.

Berry, W. 1969. *The Long-Legged House.* New York: Harcourt.

Billings, D., and A. Tickamyer. 1993. "Uneven Development in Appalachia." In *Forgotten Places: Uneven Development in Rural America,* edited by T. Lyson and W. Falk, 7–29. Lawrence: University Press of Kansas.

Blake, B. E. 1997. *She Say, He Say: Urban Girls Write Their Lives.* Albany: State University of New York Press.

Bloom, J. 2005. "Hollowing the Promise of Higher Education: Inside the Political Economy of Access to College." In *Beyond Silenced Voices: Class, Race, and Gender in United States Schools,* edited by L. Weis and M. Fine, 63–82. Albany: State University of New York Press.

———. 2007. "(Mis)reading Social Class in the Journey Towards College: Youth Development in Urban America." *Teachers College Record* 109 (2): 343–68.

Blount, J. 1994. "One Postmodern Feminist Perspective on Educational Leadership: And Ain't I a Leader?" In *Postmodern School Leadership: Meeting the Crisis in Educational Administration,* edited by S. Maxey, 47–59. Westport, CT: Praeger.

Bogdan, R., and S. Biklen. 2007. *Qualitative Research in Education: An Introduction to Theory and Methods.* MA: Allyn & Bacon.

Brendtro, L., and M. Strother. 2007. "Back to Basics through Challenge and Adventure." *Reclaiming Children and Youth: The Journal of Strength-based Interventions* 16 (1): 2–6.

Brown, R. 2009. *Black Girlhood Celebration: Toward a Hip-Hop Feminist Pedagogy.* New York: Peter Lang.

Burg, D. 1998. *Encyclopedia of Student and Youth Movements.* New York: Facts on File.

Butin, D. 2002. "This Ain't Talk Therapy: Problematizing and Extending Anti-oppressive Education." *Educational Researcher* 31 (3): 14–16.

Butler, J. 1991. "Imitation and Gender Insubordination." In *Inside/Out: Lesbian Theories, Gay Theories,* edited by Diana Fuss, 13–31. New York: Routledge.

Camino, L., and S. Zeldin. 2002. "From Periphery to Center: Pathways for Youth Civic Engagement in the Day-to-day Life of Communities." *Applied Development Science* 6 (4): 213–20.

Campbell, R. 2002. *Emotionally Involved: The Impact of Researching Rape.* New York: Routledge.

Carter, P. 2011. "Straddling Boundaries: Identity, Culture, and School." In *The Structure of Schooling: Readings in the Sociology of Education,* edited by R. Arum, I. Beattie, and K. Ford, 295–312. Los Angeles: Sage.

Chapell, D. 2006. "Banned Books Ethnographies: A Project with 8th Graders." *Teaching Artist Journal* 4 (3): 182–89.

Chenoweth, E., and R. Galliher. 2004. "Factors Influencing College Aspirations of Rural West Virginia High School Students." *Journal of Research in Rural Education* 19 (2): 1–14.

Chin, J. L. 2011. "Women and Leadership: Transforming Visions and Current Contexts." The Forum on Public Policy.

Cho, D. 2007. "The Role of High School Performance in Explaining Women's Rising College Enrollment." *Economics of Education Review* 26 (4): 450–62.

Clark, K. 2006. "How to Pay for College." *U.S. News & World Report* 140 (14): 56–61.

Connell, R. W. 1998. "Teaching the Boys: New Research on Masculinity, and Gender Strategies for Schools." *Teachers College Record* 98 (2): 206–37.

Crenshaw, K. W. 1991. "Mapping the Margins: Intersectionality, Identity Politics, and Violence against Women of Color." *Stanford Law Review* 43 (6): 1241–99.

Defrank-Cole, L., R. Cole, and K. Garbutt. 2009. "Does Broad-based Merit Aid Affect Socioeconomic Diversity in Honors?" *Journal of the National Collegiate Honors Council—Online Archive* (University of Nebraska—Lincoln): 61–64.

Dewey, J. [1899] 2007. *The School and Society.* New York: Cosimo.

Duggan, L. 2006. Introduction to L. Duggan and N. D. Hunter, *Sex Wars: Sexual Dissent and Political Culture,* 10th anniversary ed., 1–15. New York: Routledge.

———. 2012. *The Twilight of Equality? Neoliberalism, Cultural Politics, and the Attack on Democracy.* Boston: Beacon Press.

Dynarski, S. 2002. "The Behavioral and Distributional Implications of Aid for College." *American Economic Review* 92 (2): 279–85.

Eccles, J., and J. Gootman, eds. 2002. *Community Programs to Promote Youth Development.* Washington, DC: National Academy Press.

Egan, M. 1993. "Appalachian Women: The Path from the 'Hollows' to Higher Education." *Affilia: Journal of Women & Social Work* 8 (3): 265–76.

Eller, R. 2008. *Uneven Ground: Appalachia since 1945.* Lexington: University Press of Kentucky.

Enloe, C. 2008. "Feminism and War: Stopping Militarizers, Critiquing Power." In *Feminism and War: Confronting U.S. Imperialism,* edited by R. L. Riley, C. Talpade Mohanty, and M. B. Pratt, 258–63. London: Zed Books.

Ensler, E. 2010. *I Am an Emotional Creature: The Secret Life of Girls around the World.* New York: Random House.

Erickson, K., and D. Stull. 1998. *Doing Team Ethnography: Warnings and Advice.* Thousand Oaks, CA: Sage.

Ervin, E., and Fox, D. 1994. "Collaboration as Political Action." *Journal of Advanced Composition* 14 (1): 53–71.

Evans, M. 1997. "Shifting the Leadership Focus from Control to Empowerment—A Case Study." *School Leadership and Management* 17 (2): 273–83.

Ewen, L. A. 1999. "Tiny Steps and Giant Leaps." Paper presented at the annual meeting of the West Virginia Sociological Association.

Farrigan, T. 2013. "Geography of Poverty." United States Department of Agriculture Economic Research Service. March 26.

Feine, J. 1991. "The Construction of Self by Rural Low-Status Appalachian Women." *Affilia* 6 (2): 45–60.

Fine, M., and A. Burns. 2003. "Class Notes: Toward a Critical Psychology of Class and Schooling." *Journal of Social Issues* 59 (4): 841–60.

Fine, M., and L. Weis. 2003. *Silenced Voices and Extraordinary Conversations: Re-Imagining Schools.* New York: Teachers College Press.

Fine, M. A. Burns, Y. Payne, and M. Torre. 2004. "Civics Lessons: The Color and Class of Betrayal." *Teachers College Record* 106 (11): 2193–2223.

Fleischman, H. L., P. J. Hopstock, M. P. Pelczar, and B. E. Shelley. 2010. "Highlights from PISA 2009: Performance of U.S. 15-Year-Old Students in Reading, Mathematics, and Science Literacy in an International Context." *NCES 2011004* (December).

Fordham, S. 1993. "'Those Loud Black Girls': (Black) Women, Silence, and Gender 'Passing' in the Academy.'" *Anthropology and Education Quarterly* 24 (1): 3–32.

Gans, H. 2010. "Public Ethnography; Ethnography as Public Sociology." *Qualitative Sociology* 33:97–104.

Gaventa, J. 1980. *Power and Powerlessness: Quiescence and Rebellion in an Appalachian Valley.* Champaign: University of Illinois Press.

Giardina, D. 2010. "Mourning in the Mountains." *New York Times,* A27 of New York edition, April 7.

Giddens, A. 1984. *The Constitution of Society: Outline of the Theory of Structuration.* Berkeley: University of California Press.

Gilligan, C. 1982. *In a Different Voice: Psychological Theory and Women's Development.* Cambridge, MA: Harvard University Press.

Ginwright, S., J. Cammarota, and P. Noguera. 2005. "Youth, Social Justice, and Communities: Toward a Theory of Urban Youth Policy." *Social Justice* 32 (3): 24–40.

Glenn, D. 2004. "Helping Students Go to College: The Value of a Degree." *Chronicle of Higher Education* 50 (34): A18.

Glesne, C. 2011. *Becoming Qualitative Researchers: An Introduction.* 4th ed. Boston: Pearson.

Gorard, S., and B. H. See. 2008. "Is Science a Middle-Class Phenomenon? The SES Determinants of 16–19 Participation." *Research in Post-Compulsory Education* 13 (2): 217–26.

Gottman, J. 2001. "Meta-emotion, Children's Emotional Intelligence, and Buffering Children from Marital Conflict." In *Emotion, Social Relationships, and Health,* edited by C. D. Ryff and B. H. Singer, 23–39. New York: Oxford University Press.

Gow, D. 1991. "Collaboration in Development Consulting: Stooges, Hired Guns, or Musketeers?" *Human Organization* 50 (1): 1–15.

Halpern, D. F., C. P. Benbow, D. C. Geary, R. C. Gur, J. S. Hyde, and M. A. Gernsbacher. 2007. "The Science of Sex Differences in Science and Mathematics." *Psychological Science in the Public Interest* 8 (1): 1–51.

Haraway, D. 2008. "Situated Knowledges: The Science Question in Feminism and the Privilege of Partial Perspective." In *Just Methods: An Interdisciplinary Feminist Reader*, edited by Alison Jaggar, 346–52. Boulder: Paradigm Publishers.

Harding, S. 1991. *Whose Science? Whose Knowledge?: Thinking from Women's Lives.* Ithaca, NY: Cornell University Press.

Hebel, S. 2006. "In Rural America, Few People Harvest 4-Year Degrees." *Chronicle of Higher Education* 53 (11): 22.

Heller, D., ed. 2002. *Condition of Access: Higher Education for Lower Income Students.* Westport, CT: American Council on Education/Praeger.

Henry, M. 1996. *Parent-School Collaboration: Feminist Organizational Structures and School Leadership.* Albany: State University of New York Press.

Hess, C., A. Hegewisch, and C. Williams. 2013. "The Status of Women and Girls in West Virginia." Institute for Women's Policy Research.

Hill Collins, P. 2003. "The Politics of Black Feminist Thought." In *Feminist Theory Reader: Local and Global Perspectives,* edited by C. McCann and S. Kim, 318–33. New York: Routledge.

———. 2008. "Learning from the Outsider Within: The Sociological Significance of Black Feminist Thought." In *Just Methods: An Interdisciplinary Feminist Reader,* edited by Alison Jaggar, 308–20. Boulder: Paradigm Publishers.

Hirsch, B., J. Roffman, N. Deutsch, C. Flynn, T. Loder, and M. Pagano. 2000. "Inner-City Youth Development Organizations: Strengthening Programs for Adolescent Girls." *Journal of Early Adolescence* 20 (2): 210–30.

Hollister, R. 2003. "The Growth in After-School Programs and Their Impact." Paper commissioned by the Brookings Roundtable on Children. Washington DC: Brookings Institution.

hooks, b. 1989. *Talking Back: Thinking Feminist, Thinking Black.* Cambridge: South End Press.

———. 2000. *All About Love: New Visions.* New York: HarperCollins.

hooks, b., and A. Mesa-Bains. 2006. *Homegrown: Engaged Cultural Criticism.* Cambridge, MA: South End Press.

Hoskins, M., and S. Artz. 2004. *Working Relationally with Girls: Complex Lives/Complex Identities.* Binghamton, NY: Haworth Press.

House, S. 2012. "This Is My Heart for You." Play premiered at Berea College Theatre, February 22–26.

Howard, A., and A. Levine. 2004. "Where Are the Poor Students? A Conversation about Social Class and College Attendance." *About Campus* 9 (4): 19–24.

Hubbard, G., K. Backett-Milburn, and D. Kemmer. 2001. "Working with Emotion: Issues for the Researcher in Fieldwork and Teamwork." *Social Research Methodology* 4 (2): 119–37.

Huebner, A., J. Walker, and M. McFarland. 2003. "Staff Development for the Youth Development Professional: A Critical Framework for Understanding the Work." *Youth and Society* 35 (2): 204–25.

Ingersoll, R. 2001. "The Realities of Out-of-Field Teaching." *Educational Leadership* 58 (8): 42–45.

Institute for Women's Policy Research. 2004. "The Status of Women in West Virginia: Highlights." http://www.iwpr.org.

International Planned Parenthood Federation. 2008. "Explore: Ideas for Youth Involvement in Research." Toolkit.

Jones, N. 2010. *Between Good and Ghetto: African American Girls and Inner-City Violence.* New Brunswick, NJ: Rutgers University Press.

Joyce, B. 2004. "How Are Professional Learning Communities Created? History Has a Few Messages." *Phi Delta Kappan* 86 (1): 76–83.

Julien, I. 1992. "Black Is, Black Ain't: Notes on De-essentializing Black Identities." In *Black Popular Culture,* edited by M. Wallace and G. Dent, 255–63. Seattle: Bay Press.

Karsten, M. 1995. *Management and Gender: Issues and Attitudes.* Westport, CT: Quorum.

Kettley, N., J. M. Whitehead, and J. Raffan. 2008. "Worried Women, Complacent Men? Gendered Responses to Differential Student Funding in Higher Education." *Oxford Review of Education* 34 (1): 111–29.

Kidd, S. M., and A. K. Taylor. 2009. *Traveling with Pomegranates: A Mother-Daughter Story.* New York: Viking.

Kiffmeyer, T. 1998. "From Self-Help to Sedition: The Appalachian Volunteers in Eastern Kentucky, 1964–1970." *Journal of Southern History* 64 (1): 65–94.

Kimweli, D. 2002. "The Relationship of Gender-Role Development, College Level, and Subjective Well-Being Among Appalachians." PhD diss., University of Kentucky.

King, L. 2012. "Bill O'Reilly's Scorn for Appalachia Still Echoes in the Mountains (Video)." *Washington Times.* April 24.

Klaus, T. 2008. "Ensuring Organizational Sustainability: A Guide for State Teen Pregnancy Prevention Organizations." Washington, DC: Advocates for Youth.

Kugler, M. R. 2001. "After-School Programs Are Making a Difference." *NASSP Bulletin* 85 (626): 3–11.

Kumashiro, K. 2001. "'Posts' Perspectives on Anti-Oppressive Education in Social Studies, English, Mathematics, and Science Classrooms." *Educational Researcher* 30 (3): 3–12.

Lapan, R. T., B. Tucker, S. Kim, and J. F. Kosciulek. 2003. "Preparing Rural Adolescents for Post–High School Transitions." *Journal of Counseling & Development* 81 (3): 329–42.

Lareau, A. 2000. *Home Advantage: Social Class and Parental Intervention in Elementary Education.* Lanham, MD: Rowman and Littlefield.

Lassiter, E. 2005. *The Chicago Guide to Collaborative Ethnography*. Chicago: University of Chicago Press.

Lather, P. 2001. "Ten Years Later, Yet Again: Critical Pedagogy and Its Complicities." In *Feminist Engagements: Reading, Resisting, and Revisioning Male Theorists in Education and Cultural Studies,* edited by K. Weiler. New York: Routledge.

———. 2004a. "Scientific Research in Education: A Critical Perspective." *British Educational Research Journal* 30 (6): 759–72.

———. 2004b. "This is Your Father's Paradigm: Government Intrusion and the Case of Qualitative Research in Education." *Qualitative Inquiry* 10 (1): 15–34.

Lerner, R. 2004. *Liberty: Thriving and Civic Engagement among American Youth*. Thousand Oaks, CA: Sage.

Lerner, R., J. Lerner, J. Almerigi, C. Theokas, E. Phelps, S. Gestsdottir, S. Naudeau, H. Jelicic, A. Alberts, L. Ma, L. Smith, D. Bobek, D. Richman-Raphael, I. Simpson, E. Christiansen, and A. von Eye. 2005. "Positive Youth Development, Participation in Community Youth Development Programs, and Community Contributions of Fifth-Grade Adolescents: Findings from the First Wave of the 4-H Study of Positive Youth Development." *Journal of Early Adolescence* 25 (1): 17–71.

Lesko, N. 2001. *Act Your Age! A Cultural Construction of Adolescence*. New York: Routledge.

Lesley, M. 2012. *Invisible Girls: At Risk Adolescent Girls' Writing Within and Beyond School*. New York: Peter Lang.

Leung, R. 2009. "The Biological Clock: Women Who Want It All May Find Out It's Too Late for Children." *60 Minutes*. CBS Worldwide. Retrieved from http://www.cbsnews.com/stories/2003/08/14/60minutes/main568259.shtml.

Little, R. 1993. "What's Working for Today's Youth: The Issues, the Programs, and the Learnings." Paper presented at the Institute for Children, Youth, and Families Fellows Colloquium. Michigan State University.

Lorde, A. 1984. *Sister Outsider*. Berkeley: Crossing Press.

Lu, X., J. Shen, and S. Poppink. 2007. "Are Teachers Highly Qualified? A National Study of Secondary Public School Teachers Using SASS 1990–2000." *Leadership and Policy in Schools* 6 (2): 129–52.

Lucey, H., J. Melody, and V. Walkerdine. 2003. "Uneasy Hybrids: Psychosocial Aspects of Becoming Educationally Successful for Working-class Young Women." *Gender and Education* 15 (3): 286–99.

Luttrell, W. 2003. *Pregnant Bodies, Fertile Minds: Gender, Race, and the Schooling of Pregnant Teens*. New York: Routledge.

Lyon, G. E. 2008. *With a Hammer for My Heart*. Lexington: University Press of Kentucky.

Ma'ayan, H. D. 2012. *Reading Girls: The Lives and Literacies of Adolescents*. New York: Teachers College Press.

Macpherson, P., and M. Fine. 1995. "Hungry for an Us: Adolescent Girls and Adult Women Negotiating Territories of Race, Gender, Class and Difference." *Feminism and Psychology* 5 (2): 181–200.

Maguire, P. 1987. *Doing Participatory Research: A Feminist Approach*. Amherst, MA: Center for International Education.

Mahoney, J., R. Larson, and J. Eccles. 2005. *Organized Activities as Developmental Contexts for Children and Adolescents*. Mahwah, NJ: Lawrence Erlbaum.

Marx, K. 1852. "Der 18te Brumaire des Louis Napoleon (The Eighteenth Brumaire of Louis Napoleon)." *Die Revolution*. New York.

May, R., and M. Patillo-McCoy. 2000. "Do You See What I See? Examining a Collaborative Ethnography." *Qualitative Inquiry* 6 (1): 65–87.

Miewald, C., and E. McCann. 2004. "Gender Struggle, Scale, and the Production of Place in the Appalachian Coalfields." *Environment and Planning* (36) 6: 1045–64.

Miller, K., and T. Rowley. 2002. "Rural Poverty and Rural-Urban Income Gaps: A Troubling Snapshot of the 'Prosperous' 1990s." RUPRI Data Report P2002–5.

Mitra, D. L. 2004. "The Significance of Students: Can Increasing 'Student Voice' in Schools Lead to Gains in Youth Development?" *Teachers College Record* 106 (4): 651–88.

Morena, N. (n.d.). "Like a Mountain." Peace song featured on the musical recording *We Have a Dream: One World Peace Songs*, information about which can be accessed electronically at http://www.informatik.uni-amburg.de/ffizierke/frankie.armstrong/records/wehaveadream.html.

Morgan, D., V. Pacheco, C. Rodriguez, E. Vazquez, M. Berg, and J. Schensul. 2004. "Youth Participatory Action Research on Hustling and Its Consequences: A Report from the Field." *Children, Youth and Environments* 14 (2): 201–28.

Morino, M. 2002. "The Perfect Storm." Washington, DC: Venture Philanthropy Partners.

Mullen, C., and F. Kochan. 2000. "Creating a Collaborative Leadership Network: An Organic View of Change. *Leadership in Education* 3 (3): 183–200.

O'Brien, J. 2002. *At Home in the Heart of Appalachia*. New York: Anchor Books.

Orenstein, P. 1995. *Schoolgirls: Young Women, Self-Esteem, and the Confidence Gap*. New York: Random House.

Papa, L.. and L. E. Lassiter. 2003. "The Muncie Race Riots of 1967, Representing Community Memory through Public Performance, and Collaborative Ethnography between Faculty, Students, and the Local Community." *Journal of Contemporary Ethnography* 32 (2): 147–66.

Parrott, L., L. Spatig, P. Kusimo, C. Carter, and M. Keyes. 2000. "Troubled Waters: Where Multiple Streams of Inequality Converge in the Math and Science Experiences of Nonprivileged Girls." *Journal of Women and Minorities in Science and Engineering* 6 (1): 45–71.

Patton, M. 2003. *Qualitative Evaluation and Research Methods*. Newbury Park, CA: Sage.

Perna, L.W., H. Rowan-Kenyon, A. Bell, S. L. Thomas, and C. Li. 2008. "A Typology of Federal and State Programs Designed to Promote College Enrollment." *Journal of Higher Education* 79 (3): 243–67.

Pipher, M. 1994. *Reviving Ophelia: Saving the Selves of Adolescent Girls.* New York: Ballantine Books.

Plimpton, L., and C. J. Quint. 2007. "Good Intentions: Many Mainers Plan to Go to College, but Don't." *New England Journal of Higher Education* 22 (2): 25–26.

Porter, J. R. 2006. "Financial Strains Keep Millions Out of College, Panel Says." *Chronicle of Higher Education* 53 (5): A25.

Powell, D. R. 2007. *Critical Regionalism: Connecting Politics and Culture in the American Landscape.* Chapel Hill: University of North Carolina Press.

Ramazanoglu, C. 2002. *Feminist Methodology: Challenges and Choices.* Thousand Oaks, CA: Sage.

Resnick, M. 2000. "Protective Factors, Resiliency, and Healthy Youth Development." *Adolescent Medicine: State of the Art Reviews* 11 (1): 157–64.

Rhodes, J. 2004. "The Critical Ingredient: Caring Youth-Staff Relationships in After-School Settings." *New Directions for Youth Development,* no. 101 (Spring): 145–61.

Rhodes, J. E., and R. Spencer. 2005. "Someone to Watch Over Me: Mentoring Programs in the After-School Lives of Youth." In *Organized Activities as Contexts of Development: Extracurricular Activities, After-school and Community Programs,* edited by J. L. Mahoney, R. W. Larson, and J. S. Eccles, 419–35. Mahwah, NJ: Erlbaum.

Roffman, J., M. Pagano, and B. Hirsch. 2001. "Youth Functioning and Experiences in Inner-City After-School Programs among Age, Gender, and Race Groups." *Journal of Family Studies* 10 (1): 85–100.

Roth, J., and J. Brooks-Gunn. 2003a. "Youth Development Programs: Risk, Prevention and Policy." *Journal of Adolescent Health* 32 (3): 170–82.

———. 2003b. "What Exactly Is a Youth Development Program? Answers from Research and Practice." *Applied Developmental Science* 7 (2): 94–111.

Schilling, T. 2008. "An Examination of Resilience Processes in Context: The Case of Tasha." *Urban Review* 40 (3): 296–316.

Senge, P. 1990. *The Fifth Discipline: The Art and Practice of the Learning Organization.* New York: Currency Doubleday.

Simmons, R. 2011. *Odd Girl Out: The Hidden Culture of Aggression in Girls.* New York: Houghton Mifflin Harcourt.

Spatig, L. 2005. "Feminist Critique of Developmentalism: What's in It for Teachers?" *Theory and Research in Education* 3 (3): 299–326.

Spatig, L., and A. Amerikaner. 2005. "From Care, Challenge, and Community-Building to Classroom Competence: Lessons from Appalachian Girls' Resiliency Programs." Presentation at the annual meeting of the American Educational Studies Association, Charlottesville, VA, November 10.

Spatig, L., S. Gaines, R. Macdowell, B. Sias, L. Olson, and C. Adkins. 2009. "Like a Mountain: Performing Collaborative Research with Youth in Rural Appalachia." *Collaborative Anthropologies* 2:177–212.

Spatig, L., L. Parrott, C. Carter, M. Keyes, and P. Kusimo. 2001. "We Roll Deep: Community and Resistance in the Lives of Appalachian Girls." *Journal of Appalachian Studies* 7 (1): 64–92.

Spatig, L., K. Seelinger, A. Dillon, L. Parrott, and K. Conrad. 2005. "From an Ethnographic Team to a Feminist Learning Community: A Reflective Tale." *Human Organization* 64 (1): 103–13.

Spivak, G. C. 1990. *The Post-colonial Critic: Interviews, Strategies, Dialogues*, edited by Sarah Harasym. New York: Routledge.

Stake, R. 2004. *The Art of Case Study Research*. Thousand Oaks, CA: Sage.

Stratton, D., and A. Moore. 2002. "Older Appalachian Men and Family Life." *Arete* 26 (2): 1–13.

Swank, E. B. Fahs, and H. Haywood. 2011. "Evaluating Appalachian Distinctiveness for Gender Expectations, Sexual Violence, and Rape Myths." *Journal of Appalachian Studies* 17 (1/2): 123–43.

Taft, J. 2011. *Rebel Girls: Youth Activism and Social Change across the Americas*. New York: New York University Press.

Thomas, D. 2008. "The Digital Divide: What Schools in Low Socioeconomic Areas Must Teach." *Delta Kappa Gamma Bulletin* 7 (4): 12–17.

Thorp, L. 2006. *The Pull of the Earth: Participatory Ethnography in the School Garden*. New York: AltaMira Press.

Truscott, D. M., and S. D. Truscott. 2005. "Differing Circumstances, Shared Challenges: Finding Common Ground between Urban and Rural Schools." *Phi Delta Kappan* 87 (2): 123–230.

Trusty, J., and S. G. Niles. 2003. "High-School Math Courses and Completion of the Bachelor's Degree." *Professional School Counseling* 7 (2): 99–107.

Tyson, K., W. Darity, and D. Castellino. 2011. "It's Not 'A Black Thing': Understanding the Burden of Acting White and Other Dilemmas of High Achievement." In *The Structure of Schooling: Readings in the Sociology of Education*, 2nd ed., edited by R. Arum, I. Beattie, and K. Ford, 281–93. Thousand Oaks, CA: Pine Forge Press.

Vygotsky, L. 1987. *Mind in Society: The Development of Higher Psychological Processes*. Cambridge, MA: Harvard University Press.

Walkerdine, V., H. Lucey, and J. Melody. 2001. *Growing Up Girl: Psychosocial Explanations of Class and Gender*. Qualitative Studies in Psychology. New York: New York University Press.

Weis, L., and M. Fine. 2004. *Working Method: Research and Social Justice*. New York: Routledge.

Weller, J. 1965. *Yesterday's People: Life in Contemporary Appalachia*. Lexington: University of Kentucky Press.

West Virginia Kids Count Data Book. 2012. The Annie E. Casey Foundation.

Williams, J. 2002. *Appalachia: A History*. Chapel Hill: University of North Carolina Press.

Winn, M. 2011. *Girl Time: Literacy, Justice, and the School-to-Prison Pipeline.* New York: Teachers College Press.

Wolcott, H. 1990. "On Seeking—and Rejecting—Validity in Qualitative Research." In *Qualitative Inquiry in Education: The Continuing Debate,* edited by E. Eisner and A. Peshkin, 121–152. New York: Teachers College Press.

Woods, P., M. Boyle, B. Jeffrey, and G. Troman. 2000. "A Research Team in Ethnography." *Journal of Qualitative Studies in Education* 13 (1): 85–98.

Index

Mohanty, Chandra, 8, 168
money and college attendance, 7, 139, 146–51, 157–58, 164–65
Morino, Mario, 122
mosaic mural, creation of, 82
mother-daughter relationships, 7, 46, 74, 139, 140–46, 186–89, 195
Mountain Stage, 58
Ms. Foundation, 14, 34, 62, 118–19, 123, 124–25, 186
Mullen, Carol, 168

National Collaboration for Youth (NCY), 98, 105
Night Comes to the Cumberlands (Caudill), 29
"No Matter What," 59
"Not Every Angel," 59–60

O'Brien, John, 13, 29, 41, 46
Occupy Wall Street movement, 15–16
Olson, LeAnne: AWLP role of, 193; dissertation research of, 7, 127, 137–38, 159–60; field notes by, 195; lives of girls, knowledge about, 136; marriage and motherhood goals of girls, reaction to, 161; personality and work ethic of, 116; presentations and meetings with girls, 159–60; relationship between Ashley and, 127; relationship between girls and, 7, 126–28, 138, 139, 157–60; researcher/staff hybrid role of, 6, 115, 116–17, 125, 126–28, 157–60, 171–72, 184, 185; research project, role in, 114, 195; as role model for girls, 159; silly and playful times, 78; transition of girls from high school to college, involvement in, 138–46, 157–60
O'Reilly, Bill, 9, 19
Orenstein, Peggy, 53
Outward Bound program, 84
Owens, Chasity, 16–17

Participatory Action Research, 62
participatory research, 167
Patton, Michael, 170
photography, 4
plays, 3
poetry and song lyrics: activities of GRP, 3, 5; benefits of writing, 55–56; CDs, 3, 58–61; composite poems, 25–27, 88–92, 175, 176, 180–81; interest of girls in writing, 54–61; Lincoln County, poem about, 25–27, 180; poverty, poem about, 16–17; school consolidation, poem about, 88–92; topics for, 56, 58; transformation of girls through writing, 4
political rallies, 3
political voice and activism, 85–94

Porter, Jenny, 56
pottery, 4, 5
pottery instructor, relationship between Cassi and, 72–74
poverty: accurate and balanced stories about, 18; in Appalachia, 9, 15, 28–29; bitterness of, 4; "culture of poverty," 29; exploitation of Appalachian people and resources and, 28–29; in Lincoln County and West Virginia, 3, 8, 9, 14, 15–18; poem about, 16–17; in rural America, 15; stereotypes about, 18–20; in urban America, 15; urban/rural discrepancies, movements to address, 15–16
Powell, Douglas Reichart, 23
power relations: feminist research and, 190–92; power, voice, and language, tensions about, 8, 174–77, 186; social justice and, 190
PROMISE Scholarship, 147, 150–51, 153, 162
proximal development, zone of, 76
Pull of the Earth (Thorp), 97

qualitative research: emotional stress of and crying, 193; research methods, xii–xiii, 1, 167–70; training session for internship program, 63; writing about, 2–3
quantitative research method, xii, xiii, 63
questionnaires and surveys, xii–xiii

Rangel, Heaven, 125, 184, 185
relationships: assumptions about girls' back-stabbing relationships, 69–70; caring adults, relationships with, 3–4, 72–74, 130; emotional and social development and youth-adult relationships, 75–76; family relationships of girls, 70–71, 72; girls and GRP staff, relationships between, 74–76, 99–100, 101, 102–3, 106–8, 113, 132–33; girls and LeAnne, relationships between, 7, 126–28, 138, 139, 157–60; girls and Shelley, relationships between, 74–76, 109, 132–33; girls and their moms, relationships between, 7, 46, 74, 139, 140–46, 187, 195; healthy relationships, focus on, 5, 71–72; "hungry for an us," 71; importance of to girls, 67–68, 69; Linda and Layne, relationship between, 7–8, 186–89; modeling positive relationships, 5, 71–72; mother role of Shelley, 44–47, 72; nonfamily, adult relationships, 70; painful connections, choices about, 8–9; painful connections and meaningfulness of, 9; peer relationships, 76–78; school relationships of girls, 71; supportive relationships and capabilities of girls, 5, 69–74, 110, 111, 132–33; time for forming bonds with girls, 76; trusting relationships, development of, 6, 75–76, 132–33
research internship program, 5, 50, 62–65, 129, 169–70, 186

Virginia (*cont.*)
qualifications and competencies of, 105;
relationship between Shelley and, 108–9;
resignation of, 100, 105, 108; staff member,
transition to, 5–6, 96, 99, 101–2, 114
VISTA (Volunteers in Service to America), 12–13,
50, 187
voice: activities to promote finding of, 55–61;
concept of, 51–52; conflicting cultural messages
to girls about, 53–54; finding and using, 50–55;
finding and using as goal of GRP, 50, 58, 130;
leadership and, 52, 53; listening to and valuing
opinions, 52–53, 54, 58–59, 86, 173; opinions
about school consolidation, 88; power and
decisions about voice and language, 8, 174–77,
186; valuing voices of women, 51
Volunteers in Service to America (VISTA), 12–13,
50, 187
Vulnerable Observer, The (Behar), 179

Walkerdine, Valerie, 140
War on Poverty, 12, 16
Weis, Lois, 189
Weller, Jack, 14–15
West Virginia: economic disadvantages for women
and girls in, 19–20; education levels of people
in, 16, 19, 40, 159; exploitation of people and
resources in, 3, 8, 28–29; gender roles and biases
in, 20, 40; income of people in, 16; marriage,
motherhood, and economic security for women
and girls, 19–20; as national sacrifice area, 28–29;
poverty in, 3, 8, 9, 15–18; teacher competence,
qualifications, and out-of-field teaching
assignments, 155–56; teen pregnancy and
birthrates in, 162–64. *See also* Lincoln County
wheelchair story, 116
Williams, John, 24, 27, 29
Winn, Maisha T., 55–56, 69, 133–34, 173
Wolcott, Harry, 193
Woods, Peter, 192

Yesterday's People (Weller), 14–15
youth: after school activities for, 128–29;
capabilities of, belief of adults in, 4, 34–35, 36;
emotional and social development and youth-
adult relationships, 75–76; relationships between
caring adults and, 3–4, 72–74, 130; stereotypes
about, 35
Youth and Prevention Coalition, 159, 163
youth-development programs: after-school
programs, 128–29; changes to and growth of,
7; collaborative research and performance
as positive youth development, 172–73,
183–86; college attendance and success of,
139; commitment to programs and benefits
for individuals and communities, 7, 136;
community-based programs, ix, x–xi;
community service and contributions of youth
in, 86; Cs of, 35, 77, 84, 86, 129–32; cultural and
local context for, 3, 14; funding for, 121–22,
129; gender-segregated and gender-inclusive
programs, 43–44; home and family role of,
44–47; lessons learned and insights about, 6–7,
128–36, 193–94; long-term programs, need
for, 14; long-term relationships, need for, 110;
positive youth development, concept of, 8,
35–36, 77; problem-focused programs, 35–36;
role models and training for, 7; rural areas and
access to, 128; self-esteem of participants, 33;
societal rules and standards, promotion of, 131;
staff qualifications and competencies, 97–98,
105; staff turnover issues in, 106, 107; strengths-
based programs, xii, 34–36, 113, 131; success
and effectiveness of and quality of human
resources, 111; tensions related to research
about, 8; youth employment in and youth
ownership of, 113–14, 132–33
Youth Force program, 114
Youth Off the Streets program, 84

Zeldin, Shepherd, 70, 114, 175